THE SALT-SEA MASTODON

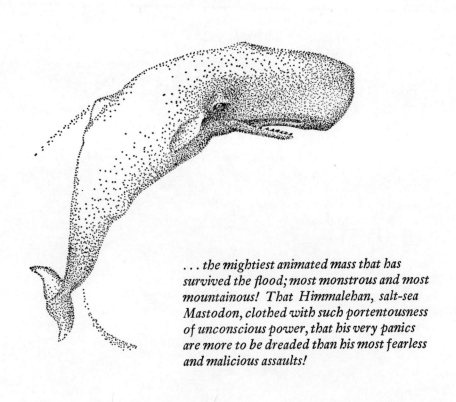

... *the mightiest animated mass that has survived the flood; most monstrous and most mountainous! That Himmalehan, salt-sea Mastodon, clothed with such portentousness of unconscious power, that his very panics are more to be dreaded than his most fearless and malicious assaults!*

THE
SALT-SEA MASTODON

A READING OF MOBY-DICK

ROBERT ZOELLNER

UNIVERSITY OF CALIFORNIA PRESS
Berkeley, Los Angeles, London

132112

University of California Press
Berkeley and Los Angeles, California

University of California Press, Ltd.
London, England

Copyright © 1973, by
The Regents of the University of California
ISBN: 0-520-02339-0
Library of Congress Catalog Card Number: 72-89793

Designed by Eleanor Mennick
Printed in the United States of America

To Anne
and Matthew, Jason, Ben, Stacey, and Evan

CONTENTS

PREFACE

This book was written in sheer self-defense. I have always found *Moby-Dick* an utterly compelling novel, like nothing else in American literature. Other novels engage me, interest me, absorb me, divert me, move me. Only *Moby-Dick* frightens me. At the same time and paradoxically, no other book in *any* literature has given me so much pleasure. Reading *Moby-Dick* is for me—the students' term is entirely appropriate—a real "trip." This is because, like Kafka, Dostoevsky, and Joyce, Melville plumbs the depths, bringing back for our scrutiny those aboriginal verities and primal truths which we would not know but which, for our own well-being, we must know. Hence the paradox: the recognition of primal truth is a fearful experience, while the satisfaction of the need for primal truth is a pleasurable one. In *Moby-Dick*, fear and pleasure are but two sides of a single coin.

Nevertheless, one must somehow defend oneself against books

such as *Moby-Dick*. Some books one simply reads, and absorbs. Others one comes to terms with—or tries to. One way to come to terms with *Moby-Dick*—probably not the best and certainly not the most courageous way, but one way—is to undertake a systematic analysis of the text in the hope of locating, delimiting, and understanding the *sources* of the incandescent emotional intensity with which Ishmael invests his story. Such an act of criticism may be fairly characterized as the fearless (more or less) examination of fear, the dispassionate examination of passion. Cognitive psychologists speak of the process called "internalization"; while the analogy does not hold at all points, this book may be regarded as an act of *externalization*.

The point is important because the conviction is abroad that an entirely new sort of criticism is needed, one free of the "sterilities" of the established critical strategies, one which deals directly and immediately with the emotive and intuitive rather than the rational and discursive realities of the work of art. Richard Poirier, for example, quotes Henry James' preface to *The Golden Bowl*: "It all comes back to that, to my and your 'fun'—if we but allow the term its full extension; to the production of which no humblest question involved, even to that of the shade of a cadence or the position of a comma, is not richly pertinent." Mr. Poirier then extends James' concept from creation to criticism: "On performance," he asserts, "on the excitement of doing, on what literature creates by the way of fun—that's where more of the emphasis should be."

The possibility of such a radically affective criticism has immense appeal, since the reading of *Moby-Dick*—or any other great work of literature—is, or should be, *fun*. But Mr. Poirier seems not to realize that the fun occurs, is experienced, precisely in proportion to the extent that one *understands* the realities, even the frightening realities, with which the artist is dealing. Unfortunately, achieving such understanding is not itself fun. Understanding, conceived of not as a state but as an activity, is usually hard, unpleasant work. It follows that since the act of criticism is nothing if not an act of understanding, a criticism which somehow illuminates, or reproduces, or conveys, the fun or joy or delight of a work of art is, sadly enough, an impossibility. Criticism can deal with the *sources* of the fun, or the joy, or the delight, but criticism cannot deal with these emotions in themselves, as Mr. Poirier's own superb essay on "Learning from the Beatles" proves unequivocally. This, then, is the purpose and province of *The Salt-Sea Mastodon*: it is written out of the conviction that the reading of *Moby-Dick* should be fun, immense, often terrifying fun, and it tries to locate the *sources* of that fun—but for the fun itself one must go to *Moby-Dick* itself.

One other matter: it is a critical truism that *Moby-Dick* is a mass of interpretive knots. Most of these will, in my opinion, capitulate to sustained analysis, but one of them is of the Gordian variety— it must be cut rather than untangled. It has to do, of course, with the problem of point of view in *Moby-Dick*. Traditional opinion proposes that the Ishmaelian, first-person point of view "breaks down," the collapse getting under way in Chapter 29, where Stubb and Ahab have a conversation which Ishmael could not possibly hear, and becoming unmistakable by Chapter 37, where Ahab, alone in his cabin, delivers a brooding monologue which Ishmael could report to us only if he were hidden under Ahab's cabin-table. From this point forward, the argument goes, Ishmael more or less disappears, and we find ourselves dealing instead with Melville. But this is taking far too mechanical and literal a view of the situation. Chapter 46, for example, is a sustained mass of *surmises* (the title of the chapter), by means of which Ishmael deals in the most explicit and detailed way with his Captain's inner thoughts, motives, and plans—and many other chapters of *Moby-Dick* have the same inferential base. Surely, then, one can argue that if Ishmael can give us conjectural material in expository form, he can also give us conjectural material in dramatic form—at least there is nothing in the Ishmaelian sensibility to preclude such a sophisticated exploitation of the imaginative and inferential faculties. Such a line of argument permits the cutting of the Gordian knot: the root assumption of *The Salt-Sea Mastodon* is that every word of *Moby-Dick*, including even the footnotes, comes from Ishmael rather than Melville. This assumption, obviously, clears a good deal of ground and simplifies the analytical task, since Ishmael is *not* Melville, any more than Huckleberry Finn is Mark Twain—a simple point which can hardly be overstressed.

Finally, there is the matter of my debts, both obvious and not-so-obvious. In prosecuting my own pursuit of the gliding great demon of the seas of life, I have (to mix some metaphors) cut the trail of nearly every Melville scholar who has gone before me. Where these identities and parallels become substantive, they are acknowledged in the footnotes, although my indebtedness to Howard P. Vincent, Newton Arvin, and M. H. Abrams is of such a special sort that it must be mentioned here. Thanks are due also to Mrs. Severn Towl of the University of California Press, who brought to the manuscript a respect for my convictions and a tolerance of my vagaries that went considerably beyond the imperatives of mere editorial obligation. On a much more general level, I wish to thank Paul Carter of the University of Colorado, Clarence A. Brown and Joseph Schwartz of Marquette University, Henry Pochmann and the late Harry Hayden Clark of the University of Wisconsin, and Court Hotchkiss of Colorado State University, all of whom, either immediately or distantly, contributed to this book in ways far too fundamental and pervasive to be specified here. I am similarly grateful to the hundreds of students here at Colorado State University, both undergraduate and graduate, who have each year opened with me the flood-gates of the wonder-world; their youth, their vitality, and the intensity of their response to *Moby-Dick* account in large part for whatever virtues this book may have.

The debt which most clearly stands beyond any possibility of repayment, however, I owe to my wife: there is scarcely a single idea in *The Salt-Sea Mastodon* which, upon first conception, I did not immediately subject to the light of her pellucid intelligence. This is to say that the Zoellners had whale for dinner for more evenings of more years than I care to remember; if my wife ever became bored with the menu, she never betrayed that fact. Finally, thanks of an especially affectionate sort are due to my children who, during the years of composition, kept my desk steadily supplied with crayon whales, construction-paper whales, origami whales, tooled-leather whales, and funny-putty whales, thus constantly reminding me that no matter how elaborate or involuted one's critical stance, one must ultimately and always approach great Leviathan, and Melville's great book about him, with the awe, the wonder, and the sheer delight which only a child can truly command.

R. Z.

Fort Collins, Colorado

THE SALT-SEA MASTODON

KANT AND LOCKE
The Protometaphorical Substrate

IT IS A MEASURE of the unity of *Moby-Dick* that despite the multi-plexity of its romantic idiom, one can always discern a core of Yankee simplicity gleaming steadily beneath the baroque surface. Newton Arvin has remarked how the voice of *Moby-Dick* reflects a series of dualities: it is "both immediate and primordial, both local and archetypal, both journalistic and mythopoeic."[1] This dualism extends outward to the whole tradition from which the novel springs, both English and American. One has constantly the sense of a sturdy Bunyan, a pedestrian Defoe, masked only partially by the verbal effulgences of a Thomas Browne. Critical attention has been directed preponderantly to the "primordial" and "mytho-poeic" in *Moby-Dick*. As a consequence, the simplicities of the novel have often been lost in the subtleties. But the simplicities are there, and since our concern in these opening chapters is not with the primordial or mythopoeic, but rather with the philosophical, it is essential that we reach them.[2]

Despite its enormous complexity, *Moby-Dick* can be reduced to one or two ultimate questions. The first question is: "Is Ahab's version of the cosmos correct?" The second is: "If Ahab is wrong concerning the meaning of the cosmos, does the novel offer an alternative version?" Restated dramatically, these questions become, first, "Is Ahab right about the White Whale?" and second, "If Ahab is wrong, then what *is* the truth about Moby Dick?" Behind these paired formulations lie two assumptions, that there is a reasonably unequivocal "statement of truth" in the novel which is susceptible to philosophical paraphrase, and that this truth is accessible to the careful reader. The place to begin testing these propositions is the "Quarter-Deck" scene in which Captain Ahab tells the assembled crew that they have shipped on the *Pequod*, not for sperm oil and profit, but rather to effect their Captain's vengeance against a great albino Sperm Whale that had, the year before, sheared off his leg in a sea-fight. "And this is what ye have shipped for, men!" shouts Ahab, "to chase that white whale on both sides of land, and over all sides of earth, till he spouts black blood and rolls fin out." But Starbuck resists the magnetically demonic power of the frantic old man. "Vengeance on a dumb brute . . . that simply smote thee from blindest instinct! Madness! To be enraged with a dumb thing, Captain Ahab, seems blasphemous."

The chief mate's objections elicit from Ahab a "little lower layer" of meaning. It is this attempt to satisfy Starbuck's pious abhorrence of Ahab's vengeful quest which gives us the philosophically pivotal passage of the entire novel:

> All visible objects, man, are but as pasteboard masks. But in each event—in the living act, the undoubted deed—there, some unknown but still reasoning thing puts forth the mouldings of its features from behind the unreasoning mask. If man will strike, strike through the mask! How can the prisoner reach outside except by thrusting through the wall? To me, the white whale is that wall, shoved near to me. Sometimes I think there's naught beyond. But 'tis enough. He tasks me; he heaps me; I see in him outrageous strength, with an inscrutable malice sinewing it. That inscrutable thing is chiefly what I

hate; and be the white whale agent, or be the white whale principal, I will wreak that hate upon him. (36: *143–44*)*

Ahab thinks he sees, in the processes and events of life, evidence of a directive intelligence, malicious and inscrutable, which Moby Dick either embodies or represents. But in the course of getting this idea across to the appalled Starbuck, Ahab manages to express a comprehensive philosophy concerning the nature of reality and his relation to it. Ahab does not trust, indeed he rejects, the evidence of his senses. The outer realm of solid stuff that we know through sensation, through the perception of shape and color and position, through taste and texture and heft—this tactile world has become for Ahab mere "pasteboard." What he does not say, but what he appears to grasp, is that color is in the eye, smell in the nose, touch in the nerve-ends in the finger-tips. He would know "visible objects" absolutely; he can only know them sensuously. The perceived world thus becomes not only a "mask" which lies, but a visible "wall," often seductively beautiful, which surrounds Ahab as he is surrounded by his skin, traps him as he is trapped by the dermal interface between himself and outer reality, making him a "prisoner."

The object-world appears to have no meaning for Ahab. He is unable to draw inferences of any kind from it; it is simply "unreasoning." But the object-world viewed relationally becomes a process-world, and in the *processes* which often define "visible objects," in the world seen as "events," as "living acts," and as "undoubted deeds"—here Ahab thinks he is able to achieve a trans-phenomenal perception of "some unknown but still reasoning thing" behind the phenomenal mask. He appears to agree with the narrator of *Pierre*, the novel written immediately after *Moby-Dick*, who, while he dismisses both "Faith and philosophy" as mere "air," nevertheless goes on to assert that "events are brass."[3] It is this brassy world of events which gives Ahab the firm epistemological toehold that mere pasteboard could never supply. Ahab realizes that no event, except superficially, can be described as "accidental." Even the most

* The number before the colon in all parenthetical references in the text indicates chapter, which will be the same for most American editions of *Moby-Dick*; the italicized numbers after the colon indicate page in the Norton Critical Edition of *Moby-Dick*, edited by Harrison Hayford and Hershel Parker (New York: W. W. Norton & Company, 1967).

spontaneous of happenings represents a concatenation of causes both immediate and remote. Brooding over the loss of his leg, Ahab finds that he cannot view it accidentally, as Starbuck suggests, but only concatenatively. Where causes concatenate, he appears to reason, there must be an intelligent concatenator.

Two metaphors structure the quarter-deck passage, the metaphor of *whiteness* and the metaphor of the *wall*, the two fusing in Ahab's statement that the White Whale is a wall "shoved near" to him. Whiteness, of course, is not simply the real color of a real albino whale. On this level we have mere pasteboard data from a pasteboard world. Rather, whiteness is metaphorical affirmation of Ahab's ability to make an inferential, trans-phenomenal thrust beyond the chromatic dungeon of phenomena to the colorless world of things-as-they-are-in-themselves. The metaphor of the wall is equally important for the entire novel because it formulates phenomenal experience as a surface or *interface*. Such a formulation establishes (given Melville's talents) a dimensional and kinesthetic vehicle for the handling of a large variety of philosophical concepts. Melville (or rather, Ishmael) will speak of that which is *above* the phenomenal interface, that which is *below* the interface, and that which appears *on* or *in* the interface. Further, one can give kinesthetic formulation to the idea of perception as the act of *rising* above the interface, or of *diving* or *thrusting* through the interface to the "other side," as when Ahab speaks of "strik[ing] through the mask."

In summary: for Ahab, phenomenal experience is a pasteboard color-world or wall; beyond the surface of the wall is the non-color world of things as they are in themselves. The wall or interface imprisons us sensibly, but inferentially it is penetrable because events or processes, the concatenative "undoubted deed," provide a trans-phenomenal *point d'appui* for one or another kind of kinesthetic movement (thrust, strike, leap, dive) from the world of appearance to the world of fact. Ahab's speech therefore gives us a three-word protometaphorical paradigm* which shapes virtually every page of *Moby-Dick*. It is *color: interface: non-color*.

---

* A *protometaphor*, for the purposes of this study, is not a metaphor in the traditional sense. Rather, it is a set of relationally and/or dynamically conceived constructs out of which a single metaphor, but more frequently

These conceptual simplicities, however, are achieved at the price of a crucially significant *over*simplification. For Ahab's quarter-deck speech makes it clear that he regards perception as unidirectional, moving from object to perceiver, never the other way. Perception is for Ahab *input* only. First, there is the phenomenal input, the seductive color-world which addresses itself to what he later calls the "low, enjoying power" (37: *147*). Ahab has, he thinks, the truth of that input: it is false, mere pasteboard. Second, the trans-phenomenal white world that he perceives as embodied in the albino whale is also, as he regards it, simply a question of input, addressed to the inferential faculty. This input he is certain is true, and he is ready to act on that truth. Nothing in what he says suggests that he has considered the possibility that perception may contain an element of *output*, moving from perceiver to object, rather than the other way around. Most revealing are the specifications which he later supplies to the *Pequod's* carpenter for a fifty-foot man with "a quarter of an acre of fine brains" and arms "three feet through the wrist." His idea of a perceptual apparatus for such a monster is hardly conventional: ". . . let me see—shall I order eyes to see *outwards*? No, but put a sky-light on top of his head to illuminate *inwards*" (108: *390*; italics mine).[4]

There are the best of dramatic reasons for this polarization of Ahab's epistemology. It is imperative that he accept both phenomenal and trans-phenomenal data as sufficient in themselves to supply a basis not only for judgment, but for action. To doubt the autonomy or the judgmental viability of either the phenomenal data which he rejects or the trans-phenomenal data which he accepts would be to throw into doubt his whole quest, and to destroy the certainty of what Moby Dick represents. Ahab's monomania will live and thrive only so long as he keeps intact his simplistically sensational, unidirectional epistemology.

From a characterological point of view, too, it is appropriate that

---

a series of inter-connected metaphors, may develop. Thus *thesis-antithesis-synthesis, challenge-and-response, action-and-reaction, death-and-rebirth, systole-and-diastole, point-and-counterpoint*, all normally used conceptually or schematically by the philosopher, historian, physicist, biologist, and musician, would become protometaphors if used as the basis of aesthetic statement by the literary artist.

Ahab should hew undeviatingly to the idea of perception as input. He is not a philosopher; he is a shaggy Nantucket sea-captain. Although, as Peleg tells Ishmael, "Ahab's been in colleges, as well as 'mong the cannibals" (16: 76), his fundamental patterns of thought have been formed, not in the academy, but rather in "the stillness and seclusion of many long night-watches in the remotest waters, and beneath constellations never seen here at the north." His whole life's experience on the primordial sea has suggested to him that the vast realm of nature, phenomenally or trans-phenomenally regarded, impresses itself upon us, never the other way around. As Ishmael puts it, in the long night-watches, Ahab's "globular brain and . . . ponderous heart" have received (the passive tonalities of the passage are important) "all nature's sweet or savage impressions fresh from her own virgin, voluntary, and confiding breast" (16: 71). Ahab's greatness—and his weakness—lie in the tragic simplicity and terrible necessity with which he accepts, child of the waters that he is, the input from the natural world and, having accepted, judges and acts upon it.

But if Ahab is philosophically unsubtle, if his ontological divinations are as rough-and-ready as the peg-leg with which he stumps about the *Pequod*, he is quietly and constantly observed by a mind of bookish, even pedantic, subtlety—by Ishmael, who, as he tells us his story, assures us that he has "swam through libraries" (32: *118*). Ahab is philosophically significant, but he cannot be philosophically informative. The rigidities of his monomania, the committed intensity of his hatred for Moby Dick, make him dogmatically affirmative rather than speculatively tentative. He dominates the crew and drives the *Pequod* forward by force rather than philosophy. It is Ishmael, obsessed by hypos, hounded by unbidden infidelities, skeptical of all things (and most especially of philosophy!) [5] who is the book's true philosopher, the steadily on-going voice that supplies the meditative, introspective counterpoint to Ahab's dogmatism.

The passage which best typifies both Ishmael's philosophical cast of mind and his sailor's suspicion of formal philosophy occurs near the end of Chapter 73. With the gigantic head of a Sperm Whale hoisted up on one side, the *Pequod* is canted over perilously. So Stubb and Flask kill a right whale and hoist its head on the other side:

As before, the Pequod steeply leaned over towards the sperm whale's head, now, by the counterpoise of both heads, she regained her even keel; though sorely strained, you may well believe. So, when on one side you hoist in Locke's head, you go over that way; but now, on the other side, hoist in Kant's and you come back again; but in very poor plight. Thus, some minds for ever keep trimming boat. Oh, ye foolish! throw all these thunderheads overboard, and then you will float light and right. (73: *277*).[6]

A hasty reading might suggest a flat rejection of philosophy, but Ishmael's own constant philosophizing makes it more likely that he is expressing a sailor's impatience with schools and creeds, with the divisions and discriminations of formal philosophical inquiry. Ishmael is speculatively inclined, but the intensity of his personal quest would make him wildly impatient with, for example, Locke's division of ideas into simple and complex, or his discussion of complex ideas as modal, substantial, or relational. All such hair-splitting would strike the bedeviled Ishmael as so much thunder.

Nevertheless, certain saliences of the over-all Lockean topography would appeal deeply to Ishmael's imaginative apprehension. Locke's stress on intuitive knowledge, characterized by a Cartesian clarity and vividness, would have struck a responsive chord in the Ishmaelian sensibility, itself so habitually intuitive. Locke's affirmation of the reality of some sort of external and substantial world as something more than bare possibility would appeal deeply to the radically tactile sensibility of a schoolmaster turned sailor, the bookish man in an action-world. More narrowly, Locke's division of the qualities of the external world into *primary* ones such as solidity, extension, figure, motion, and number; and *secondary* ones such as color, sound, and taste—the perceptual dualism implicit in this formulation would at least distantly account for Ishmael's sensuous apprehension of a colored or "secondary" cosmos beneath which is hidden a "primary" cosmos of "palsied" whiteness (42: *170*).

Before Ishmael followed his own advice (if indeed he did) and threw the Lockean thunderhead overboard, he would almost certainly retrieve Locke's stress on sensation, the immediate impact of the substance-out-there as the source of simple, true, and ineluctable ideas which are the raw matter of knowledge. One of the most most striking things about the world of the *Pequod* as Ishmael reconstructs it for us is that it is in no real sense reflective or ratiocinative. Ishmael may be a meditative, thoughtful fellow, but nevertheless all of the problems posed to him, the insights he achieves, and the resolutions he experiences, occur consistently in the sensuous world rather than the reflective. Ishmael is overwhelmed by things rather than ideas. Indeed, ideas themselves tend to become things: when Ishmael speaks of the "overwhelming idea of the great whale himself" (1: *16*) as finally driving him to sea, he is speaking of the tactile thing-as-idea rather than of an idea as such. At least some of this tactility would seem to have its source in Lockean sensationalism. In *Moby-Dick* ideas carry an unmistakable empirical coloration, have almost literally, like the two philosophical whale heads, sheer mass and tonnage.[7]

If we cross the *Pequod's* deck to contemplate the Kantian thunderhead, we will find it easy to imagine Ishmael's impatience with the German philosopher's meticulous distinctions between, say, sensibility and understanding, or his schematization of the categories of quantity, quality, relation, and modality—again, so much sheer thunder, of little help to a man pursuing the "gliding great demon of the seas of life" (41: *162*). But surely, before he consigned the Kantian head to the abyss, he would have noticed that Kant confirms the sensationalist basis of experience, while insisting upon *a priori* conditions which make the experience possible. Kant's stress on the way the mind is not only able to *perceive* data, but also to *think* such data —in effect, the mind's ability to *think objects* (not to be confused with knowing them)—would have found a deep response in the habitual analogism of Ishmael's own perceptual apparatus. It seems fairly clear that the dynamic interpenetration of percept and concept in the Kantian critique lies behind the "linked analogies" and "cunning duplicate[s]" (70: *264*) of the inner and outer worlds of *Moby-Dick*.

Kant's conviction that, while we do not make the world as it is in itself, nevertheless we create what we call the "objective" world by the imposition of space, time, and the categories upon the raw sensational input—this shaping and ordering power would find resonant affirmation at every level of Ishmael's creative sensibility, a sensibility for which the only world which is real is in large part the world as individually perceived, and thereby made. Ishmael will discover that Ahab's cosmos is not *his* cosmos, nor Ahab's whale *his* whale. Behind this discovery at some undefined remove there lies the Kantian conviction that we do indeed, in some limited sense, make our own world out of the raw stuff of the noumenal substrate. In making this extrapolation from philosophy to literature, Ishmael will convert the impersonal Kantian universals into the personal and private imperatives of his own creative faculty, but the connection is discernible despite this shift. The Kantian thunderhead may go overboard with the Lockean, so that Ishmael may ride light and right as befits a sailor, but a conceptual residue remains to shape the great metaphors in which he tells his story.

I do not suggest that this residue represents a Kantian-Lockean synthesis which is internally consistent in any formal sense. It is sometimes possible to achieve aesthetic coherence only at the price of philosophical inconsistency. No doubt *Kant* and *Locke* are merely counter-words for the broad philosophical polarities represented by "empiricism" versus "idealism," or that which is "imaginative" contrasted to that which is "real." Taken in this way, evidences of an *aesthetic* synthesis are unmistakable in much that Ishmael says. In Chapter 114, "The Gilder," afloat on a sea of "dreamy quietude," Ishmael discovers a "land-like feeling towards the sea," with its "long-drawn virgin vales" and "mild blue hill-sides." "You almost swear that play-wearied children lie sleeping in these solitudes, in some glad May-time, when the flowers of the woods are plucked." In the contemplative stillness, external empirical fact and internal imaginative construct synthesize, becoming indistinguishable: "And all this mixes," Ishmael continues, "with your most mystic mood: *so that fact and fancy, half-way meeting, interpenetrate, and form one seamless whole*" (114: *405–06*; italics mine).

This seamless unity of perceiver and perceived, of the outer world and the inner, sets Ishmael apart from Ahab. This is what will save Ishmael while Ahab goes down to destruction: his sense of oneness, increasing radically as *Moby-Dick* progresses, with the external world. These differences are illuminated by Chapter 99, "The Doubloon," where seven members of the crew comment on the gold coin from the Republic of Equador nailed to the mast as a reward to the sailor who first sights Moby Dick. The gold piece is elaborately inscribed: ". . . you saw the likeness of three Andes' summits;

from one a flame; a tower on another; on the third a crowing cock; while arching over all was a segment of the partitioned zodiac." Such coins are glowing Quito symbols for the sensuously apprehended phenomenal world: "Here palms, alpacas, and volcanoes; sun's disks and stars; ecliptics, horns-of-plenty, and rich banners waving, are in luxuriant profusion stamped" (99: *359*). Each perceiver sees something different in the doubloon. "Egotistical" Ahab sees "three peaks as proud as Lucifer. The firm tower, that is Ahab; the volcano, that is Ahab; the courageous, the undaunted, and victorious fowl, that, too, is Ahab; all are Ahab." Pious Starbuck sees "three mighty, heaven-abiding peaks, that almost seem the Trinity." Stubb, attracted to the zodiacal symbols, fetches his almanac to help him give a rollicking rendering of life's stages, while little Flask reduces this golden microcosm to sixteen dollars: ". . . and at two cents the cigar, that's nine hundred and sixty cigars." After the Manxman, Queequeg, and Fedallah provide equally individualized readings, little mad Pip sums up for all, emphasizing the apparently subjective nature of the act of perception by quoting from Murray's *Grammar*: "I look, you look, he looks; we look, ye look, they look" (99: *359–62*).

The *Pequod's* Captain asserts that "this round gold is but the image of the rounder globe"—and this is obvious enough. What deserves careful scrutiny is the inference he derives from this analogy. He goes on to say that the doubloon is "like a magician's glass" which "to each and every man in turn but mirrors back his own mysterious self." This is in consonance with the epistemological version of reality which Ahab gave to Starbuck in the quarter-deck scene. There he asserted that the phenomenal world was a "wall" or "pasteboard mask" which cozened the perceiver, and prevented him from knowing reality absolutely. Here, the wall-mask becomes reflective, opaque in the sense that a mirror is opaque, bouncing back man's interior image *of* himself *at* himself, in a deceptive process of hopeless circularity. This opacity exasperates Ahab: "Great pains, small gains for those who ask the world to solve them; it cannot solve itself."[8] Two points distinguish this epistemological view from Ishmael's. First, in contrast to Ishmael's meditation amid the "dreamy quietude" of the sea, Ahab's scrutiny of the doubloon suggests no interpenetration of "fact" and "fancy," of external empirical datum and internal imaginative construct to form "one seamless whole." Imagination figures not at all in this mechanical version of perception. Instead, Ahab and the world he perceives remain dichotomized: the mirror is *only* a mirror, standing outside of and apart from Ahab. The fact that it shows him himself does not mean that there is any sort of substantive identity between within and without, but only a mechanical, abortive sort of reflecting. Second, the failure of Ahab to account for imagination or creative intuition in his mirror-paradigm eliminates the possibility, which Ishmael's "seamless whole" keeps open, *that the perceiver himself may possibly contribute something to the data of perception.* Shortly after Ahab abandons the doubloon, Stubb, leafing through his almanac in search of zodiacal information, makes a remark about books which applies as well to the doubloon-mirror: ". . . the fact is, you books must know your places," mutters Stubb to his almanac. "You'll do to give us the bare words and facts, *but we come in to supply the thoughts*" (99: *360–61*; italics mine). Data from the outer world must be accompanied by data from the inner world, the two inter-blending. It is Ahab's failure to take into account the possibility that *he* makes a contribution to the act of perception that sustains his tragic dissociation from the object-world of phenomena. Thus, the difference between Ahab, the dramatic expositor of *Moby-Dick*, and Ishmael, the narrative expositor, is epistemological. They do not agree on the relationship between perceiver and perceived. This disagreement lies at the root of any attempt to establish a definitive interpretation of *Moby-Dick*. If Ahab is right, then Ishmael is wrong; if Ishmael is right, then Ahab is wrong. These alternatives articulate a precise investigative trajectory: if we are ever to make sense of the novel, we must first try to discover whether the text and the extracetological data, taken together, offer bases sufficient to justify a choice between the Ahabian and Ishmaelian epistemologies.

In *The Mirror and the Lamp*, M. H. Abrams' study of the romantic sensibility, he discriminates between "illustrative" and "constitutive" metaphor, the latter being made up of "more or less submerged conceptual models" which help one "to select, interpret, systematize, and evaluate the facts of art." "While many expository analogues, as conventional opinion proposes, are casual and illustrative, some few seem recurrent and, not illustrative, but *constitutive*: they yield the ground plan and essential structural elements of a literary theory, or of any theory."[9] Abrams demonstrates that such constitutive metaphors define not only literary theory, but often the internal structuring of the work of art itself. Following his suggestion, I propose to isolate what seem to me to be the constitutive metaphors which undergird *Moby-Dick*, to suggest how these metaphors grow out of the protometaphor of *color: interface: non-color*, and finally to ascertain whether these structuring metaphors are in consonance with the Ahabian epistemology or the Ishmaelian. These determinations should furnish a normative epistemology against which the multiplex data of *Moby-Dick* can be measured.

THE CREATIVE LAMP-MIND
The Metaphor of Illumination

THE MOST IMPORTANT constitutive analogue of *Moby-Dick* is the *metaphor of illumination*, which sometimes takes a variant or combined form as the *metaphor of seeing*. F. O. Matthiessen lists as one of the "recurrent themes" of the *American Renaissance* "the effect of the nineteenth century's stress on seeing, of its identification of the poet with the prophet or seer," and "the connection . . . between this emphasis on vision and that put on light by the advancing arts of photography and open-air-painting."[1] How this light-sight formulation functions for Melville can best be seen in a broad range of extracetological sources such as the letter of 8 January, 1852, to Sophia Hawthorne in response to her laudatory—and no longer extant—letter concerning the recently-published *Moby-Dick*:

> It really amazed me that you should find any satisfaction in that book [Melville writes]. It is true that some *men* have said they were pleased with it, but you are the only *woman*—for as a general thing, women have small taste for the sea. But, then, since you, with your spiritualizing nature, see more things than other people, and by the same process, refine all you see, so that they are not the same things that other people see, but things which while you think you but humbly discover them, *you do in fact create them for yourself*— Therefore, upon the whole, I do not so much marvel at your expressions concerning Moby Dick.[2] (italics mine)

To see is to create, or at the very least, to refine. Implicit is the metaphor of the perceiver as illuminator, irradiating, by the act of perception, a surrounding world in some degree created by that act. The translation from seeing to lighting is an easy and obvious one which occurs, for example, in Chapter XLIV of *The Confidence-Man*, a "discourse" contrasting the "novel," "singular," "striking," "captivating," and "odd" characters of fiction with the truly "original" character. The former sort "sheds not its characteristics upon its surroundings," but the genuinely "original" one does:

> ... the original character, essentially such, is like a revolving Drummond light, raying away from itself all round it—everything is lit by it, everything starts up to it (mark how it is with Hamlet), so that, in certain minds, there follows upon the adequate conception of such a character, an effect, in its way, akin to that which in Genesis attends upon the beginning of things.

The correlation with seeing is immediately made: to bring into being just one such creative, Drummond-light character, the narrator asserts, an author must not only be lucky, he "must have seen much, and seen through much."[3]

Similar metaphors, which associate the *head* or *mind* with projective and creative light are fairly common in Melville, as in "The Conflict of Convictions," a poem concerned with the problem of keeping religious faith fresh for "age after age" when engulfed in the darkness of doubt:

> Ay, in caves the miner see:
> His forehead bears a taper dim;

> Darkness so he feebly braves
> Which foldeth him![4]

Occasionally the quality of light is analogized with the quality of perception, and this in turn with the degree of philosophical certainty with which one confronts reality. Chapter IX of *Pierre* begins: "In those Hyperborean regions, to which enthusiastic Truth, and Earnestness, and Independence, will invariably lead a mind fitted by nature for profound and fearless thought, all objects are seen in a dubious, uncertain, and refracting light."[5] Such fundamental light-illumination metaphors are recast in optical terms in *Mardi*. Donjalolo sends two emissaries, Zuma and Varnopi, to report to him concerning the island of Rafona. Although they saw the same things there, their accounts do not agree. This perceptual disparity upsets Donjalolo: ". . . here, these two varlets, sent expressly to behold and report, these two lying knaves, speak crookedly both. How is it? Are the lenses of their eyes diverse-hued, that objects seem different to both[?]"[6] Zuma and Varnopi, being two different projective Drummond lights, have seen two different worlds, and it is upon these that they have each reported.

The major extracetological statement of the power of the mind as a creative perceptor, however, is the short story, "Cock-a-Doodle-Doo!," the narrator of which undergoes an extraordinary change of mood and therefore of projective and creative perception. "Being too full of hypos to sleep," he explains, "I sallied out to walk on my hill-side pasture." His malaise creates a horrible world: "The country looked underdone, its raw juices squirting out all round":

> I sat down for a moment on a great rotting log nigh the top of the hill. . . . Along the base of one long range of heights ran a lagging, fever-and-agueish river, over which was a duplicate stream of dripping mist, exactly corresponding in every meander with its parent water below. Low down, here and there, shreds of vapour listlessly wandered in the air, like abandoned or helmless nations or ships—or very soaky towels hung on criss-cross clothes-lines to dry. Afar, over a distant village lying in a bay of the plain formed by the mountains, there rested a great flat canopy of haze, like a pall . . . doubtless hiding many a man with the mumps, and many a queasy child.

A train appears in the valley, reminding the hypo-ridden narrator of a friend recently killed in a railroad accident. "Hark! here comes that old dragon again—that gigantic gad-fly of a Moloch . . . the chartered murderer! the death monopoliser! . . . [the] iron fiend!"

Suddenly these vernal dumps are irradiated by the crowing of a barnyard rooster, the "noble cock Benevantano." The bird acts as a perceptual catalyst: the narrator is revitalized by his regal crowing. In an instant he projects a completely different world, using the same details of landscape and view which had but a moment before only exacerbated his depression:

> Ah, here comes the down-train: white cars, flashing through the trees like a vein of silver. How cheerfully the steam-pipe chirps! Gay are the passengers. . . . Look at the mist yonder; what soft curls and undulations round the hills, and the sun weaving his rays among them. See the azure smoke of the village, like the azure tester over a bridal-bed. How bright the country looks there where the river overflowed the meadows. The old grass has to knock under to the new. Well, I feel the better for this walk.

The passage is cast only obliquely in terms of the constitutive metaphor of illumination, in references to the sun, to flashing light, to bright country. But the conceptual model based on illumination comes through unmistakably when the narrator discovers the miraculous rooster in the abject squalor of Merrymusk's shack:

> I looked at the cock. There he stood majestically in the middle of the room. He looked like a Spanish grandee caught in a shower, and standing under some peasant's shed. There was a strange supernatural look of contrast about him. He irradiated the shanty; he glorified its meanness. He glorified the battered chest, and tattered gray coat, and the bunged hat.[7]

All such analogues deal entirely with the first term of the protometaphor of *color: interface: non-color*. The metaphor of illumination conceptualizes the relation of perceiver to the object perceived. Under this paradigm, the Drummond light of the mind supplies the phenomenal "color" which appears on the "interface," giving reality its emotive, moral, aesthetic, and personal significance.

Taken together, these various extracetological light-metaphors simply measure the depth of Melville's identification with English and Continental romantic theory which, as M. H. Abrams points out, is based on "two common and antithetic metaphors of mind." The first "compares the mind to a reflector of external objects." The second makes the mind a "radiant projector which makes a contribution to the objects it perceives":

> In eighteenth-century theory, the minor topic of the way feelings may enter into and alter objects of sense had been discussed under the heading of "style," as one of various justifying causes of certain figures of speech. In the nineteenth century, this problem moves into a position at the very center of poetic theory. Often the matter is left in terms of analogy. Feelings project a light—especially a colored light—on objects of sense, so that things, as Mill said, are "arranged in the colours and seen through the medium of the imagination set in action by the feelings."

This shift is, Abrams suggests, essentially Kantian: "The Copernican revolution in epistemology—if we do not restrict this to Kant's specific doctrine that the mind imposes the forms of time, space, and the categories on the 'sensuous manifold,' but apply it to the general concept that the perceiving mind discovers what it has itself partly made—was effected in England by poets and critics before it manifested itself in academic philosophy." The result is a "radiant give-and-take with the external world," illustrated by Hazlitt, who "complicates the analogy by combining the mirror with a lamp, in order to demonstrate that a poet reflects a world already bathed in an emotional light he has himself projected":

> Neither a mere description of natural objects [Hazlitt asserts], nor a mere delineation of natural feelings, however distinct or forcible, constitutes the ultimate end and aim of poetry. . . . The light of poetry is not only a direct light but also a reflected light, that while it shews us the object, throws a sparkling radiance on all around it.[8]

Hazlitt's attempt to combine the Kantian analogue of the illuminating lamp with the Lockean analogue of the reflective mirror is pertinent because Melville essays an even more complex formulation. In "The Doubloon" chapter, the projective minds of seven different percipients throw light on a single reflector, the microcosmic doubloon. But Melville departs from the basic analogues in one essential particular. While both the mirror and the lamp are, in

English and Continental versions, analogues of mind, in *Moby-Dick*
the *lamp remains an analogue of mind, but the mirror becomes an
analogue of external reality.*

But even this is an oversimplification. First, subtle epistemological
discriminations in *Moby-Dick* derive from the fact that the mirror-
reality analogue takes two forms. Some reality-mirrors are both
totally reflective and entirely opaque: the doubloon is an instance
of this kind of solipsistic reflector. On the other hand, some ana-
logistic mirror-surfaces achieve a more comprehensive, less solipsistic articulation of the *color: interface: non-color* protometaphor
by being not only reflective but also transparent: the fountain-
mirror of Narcissus and more especially the macro-mirror of the
ocean surface are instances of this subtilized analogue.

Second, the lamp-mind analogue is complicated by the fact that
the perception of reality provided by the illuminating mind is frequently supplemented by a simultaneous illumination thrown on the
external object by certain physical, extra-mental sources of irradi-
ation which can themselves become externalized analogues of mind.
These externalized analogues are in turn divided into "natural" and
"unnatural," "true" and "false." The most important extra-mental,
natural source of light, supplementing and/or confirming the perceptive illumination of the mind, is the tropical sun of *Moby-Dick*,
showering Quito effulgences upon the circumnavigative *Pequod*,
or creating a rainbow in the whale's misty spout. When the sun is
obscured by night or storm, certain "unnatural" (contrived or
extraordinary) sources of illumination come into play. These may
be man-made, such as light from a whale-oil lamp, or from the open
door of the try-works. They may be atypical natural manifestations,
such as the corpusants which pallidly illumine the *Pequod's* tossing
decks during the typhoon, or the silvered moonlight which irradiates
the spirit-spout. Finally, the complexity of these epistemological
elaborations reaches baroque proportions when one realizes that the
illuminating perceptions of one irradiating mind, enhanced or distorted by these natural and unnatural extra-mental sources, may
blend with the perceptions of *another* mind, itself illuminative. The
massively important instance of this mental interpenetration is that
large block of *Moby-Dick*, inadequately delimited in the majority of
critical interpretations, when Ishmael, having asserted that "Ahab's

quenchless feud seemed mine" (41: *155*),* sees the world—temporarily—*as Ahab illuminates it.*

Leviathan himself, in all his portly bulk, stands at the center of the metaphor of illumination, becomes himself epistemologically expressive. The great Sperm Whale, reduced to unguent quintessentials in the try-works fire, lights the world. "Illumination," asserts Newton Arvin in one of those sharp, quick probings to the axis of the novel which distinguish his analysis, "not darkness and terror, is Moby Dick's great boon to humanity."[9] The microcosm of the *Pequod* is filled with light. In Chapter 97, "The Lamp," Ishmael meditates on how the whaler "seeks the food of light," and "lives in light," making "his berth an Aladdin's lamp" from the casked plethora of whale oil around him. Just as ultraviolet light, thrown on certain mundane-looking minerals, excites them to a transfiguring fluorescence, so does whale oil, this "unvitiated" essence-of-Leviathan, illuminate the tar-bucket-and-blubber realities of the *Pequod* so that the inner truth of ordinary things becomes epistemologically accessible, ontologically fluorescent:

> Had you descended from the Pequod's try-works to the Pequod's forecastle, where the off duty watch were sleeping, for one single moment you would have almost thought you were standing in some illuminated shrine of canonized kings and counsellors. There they lay in their triangular oaken vaults, each mariner a chiselled muteness; a score of lamps flashing upon his hooded eyes. (97: *355*)

Much more complex, however, is Captain Ahab's soliloquy before the cabin-window at sunset. The setting sun, a natural illuminator, irradiates a watery world of intensely sensuous *color*: "Yonder, by the ever-brimming goblet's rim, the warm waves blush like wine. The gold brow plumbs the blue. The diver sun—slow dived from noon,—goes down." From the stern windows of the *Pequod's* cabin, Ahab sees that the ship's keel, cutting like an epistemological knife through the phenomenal wine and gold and blue painted by the sun on the watery *interface*, reveals the substrative *non-color* of the

---

* The number before the colon in all parenthetical references in the text indicates chapter, which will be the same for most American editions of *Moby-Dick*; the italicized numbers after the colon indicate page in the Norton Critical Edition of *Moby-Dick*, edited by Harrison Hayford and Hershel Parker (New York: W. W. Norton & Company, 1967).

transphenomenal world which is Ahab's central preoccupation. "I leave a white and turbid wake; pale waters, paler cheeks." This insight into the white noumenal realm is what Ahab calls his "high perception," his despair-engendering "gift." It causes him to reject the pasteboard surface-data of the natural sun-world. "This lovely light, it lights not me; all loveliness is anguish to me, since I can ne'er enjoy.... damned, most subtly and most malignantly! damned in the midst of Paradise!" (37: *146–47*).

The sun is not the only illuminator at work in this scene. Peleg has reminded Ishmael that "Ahab of old, thou knowest, was a crowned king!" (16: 77). The *Pequod's* Ahab also wears an intellective crown, the consequence of his tragic "high perception." It is not made of gold, which would relate it to the phenomenal color-world. Rather, it is a noumenally pale crown of iron: "... this Iron Crown of Lombardy," which Ahab feels is "too heavy" for him to bear. The crown is split in a way that suggests Ahab's dissociation from the sensuous-phenomenal realm: " 'Tis split, too—that I feel; the jagged edge galls me so, my brain seems to beat against the solid metal." This crown of high perception becomes a clear analogue of mind. Like the doubt-enshrouded "miner" from "The Conflict of Convictions," whose "forehead bears a taper dim," Ahab's "crown" throws its own light on reality: it is "bright with many a gem; I, the wearer, see not its far flashings; but darkly feel that I wear that, that dazzlingly confounds." Ahab cannot perceive the illuminative power of his own perceptions—this he can only "darkly feel" (37: *147*).

This Ahabian illuminative power is pervasive in *Moby-Dick*, a sort of enshrouded and baleful "dark light" which, unlike the natural light of the sun, suppresses growth instead of encouraging it:

> As the unsetting polar star, which through the livelong, arctic, six months' night sustains its piercing, steady, central gaze; so Ahab's purpose now fixedly gleamed down upon the constant midnight of the gloomy crew. It domineered above them so, that all their bodings, doubts, misgivings, fears, were fain to hide beneath their souls, and not sprout forth a single spear or leaf. (130: *437–38*)

The darkness of Ahab's intellectual light is further associated with dark-skinned Pip who, as Ishmael remarks, "was at bottom very bright." He was, indeed, "brilliant, for even blackness has its brilliancy; behold yon lustrous ebony, panelled in kings' cabinets." But Pip's natural brightness "in the end was destined to be luridly illumined by strange wild fires" which give him "ten times the natural lustre" he originally possessed. The metaphor is complex—dark illumination itself darkly illuminated. In an attempt to clarify it Ishmael undertakes an explication of the fundamental constitutive metaphor of *Moby-Dick*:

> So, though in the clear air of day, suspended against a blue-veined neck, the pure-watered diamond drop will healthful glow; yet, when the cunning jeweller would show you the diamond in its most impressive lustre, he lays it against a gloomy ground, and then lights it up, not by the sun, but by some unnatural gases. Then come out those fiery effulgences, infernally superb; then the evil-blazing diamond, once the divinest symbol of the crystal skies, looks like some crown-jewel stolen from the King of Hell. (93: *345*)

The passage assigns a *moral*—rather than simply epistemological—significance to the faculty of cognizing illumination. External reality —the diamond drop—is not itself intrinsically moral. Rather, the moral meaning—whether as symbol of the "healthful," the "clear air of day," or as an "evil-blazing" symbol of the "King of Hell"— is infused into reality from without, by the particular mind that does the illuminating. Ishmael appears to be suggesting that the projective mind *actualizes reality* by endowing the ontologically rough-hewn elements of the noumenal, extra-mental world, the world of the amoral not-me, with final moral finish and shaped moral significance. Man does not make his world—Melville, unlike Emerson, was unable to view the not-me as transcendentally plastic—but he may nevertheless make the *moral world*, or more precisely, *make his world moral*. Such an analysis assigns the moral dimension of man's world to the *color* term of the protometaphor. Color in *Moby-Dick* carries an inherent moral significance.

Ahab's "dark" light is contrasted dramatically to the "pallid" light, the "white flame" of the corpusants which burn at the yard-arm tips during the typhoon. Ahab himself makes this comparison: "Light though thou be, thou leapest out of darkness; but I am darkness leaping out of light, leaping out of thee!" (119: *417*). As this corpusant-light falls upon the terrified crew, it endows them, like the "unnatural gases" endowed the diamond drop, with a hellish moral coloration:

> While this pallidness was burning aloft, few words were heard from the enchanted crew; who in one thick cluster stood on the forecastle, all their eyes gleaming in that pale phosphorescence, like a far away constellation of stars. Relieved against the ghostly light, the gigantic jet negro, Daggoo, loomed up to thrice his real stature, and seemed the black cloud from which the thunder had come. The parted mouth of Tashtego revealed his shark-white teeth, which strangely gleamed as if they too had been tipped by corpusants; while lit up by the preternatural light, Queequeg's tattooing burned like Satanic blue flames on his body. (119: *415–16*)

The unnatural light of the try-works, irradiating the dark of night, gives an equally distorted vision of the *Pequod's* reality. The crew's "tawny features, now all begrimed with smoke and sweat, their matted beards, and the contrasting barbaric brilliancy of their teeth, all these were strangely revealed in the capricious emblazonings of the works":

> ... as their uncivilized laughter forked upwards out of them, like the flames from the furnace; as to and fro, in their front, the harpooneers wildly gesticulated with their huge pronged forks and dippers; as the wind howled on, and the sea leaped, and the ship groaned and dived, ... then the rushing Pequod, freighted with savages, and laden with fire, and burning a corpse, and plunging into that blackness of darkness, seemed the material counterpart of her monomaniac commander's soul. (96: *353–54*)

This is reality as Ahab's illuminating mind creates it, a nightmare world which is the projection of his own moral constitution. It is this reality that Ishmael sees until he escapes from Ahab's hypnotic spell. At the ship's tiller during the try-works scene, Ishmael dozes off only to waken to a reversed world. "Lo! in my brief sleep I had turned myself about, and was fronting the ship's stern, with my back to her prow and the compass. In an instant I faced back, just in time to prevent the vessel from flying up into the wind, and very probably capsizing her." Relieved of this "unnatural hallucination of the night," Ishmael contrasts the mind-analogue of fire and the mind-analogue of the sun:

> Look not too long in the face of the fire, O man! Never dream with thy hand on the helm! Turn not thy back to the compass; accept the first hint of the hitching tiller; believe not the artificial fire, when its redness makes all things look ghastly. To-morrow, in the natural sun, the skies will be bright; those who glared like devils in the forking flames, the morn will show in far other, at least gentler, relief; the glorious, golden, glad sun, the only true lamp—all others but liars! (96: *354*)

This affirmation of the truth of the sun-analogue contrasts sharply with Ishmael's analysis of sunlight at the end of "The Whiteness of the Whale" chapter. If Ishmael in the try-works scene affirms, abruptly and without preamble, that the natural sun, the chromatic apprehension, is the "only true lamp," in the earlier passage he appears to think quite otherwise:

> And when we consider that other theory of the natural philosophers, that all other earthly hues—every stately or lovely emblazoning—the sweet tinges of sunset skies and woods; yea, and the gilded velvets of butterflies, and the butterfly cheeks of young girls; all these are but subtle deceits, not actually inherent in substances, but only laid on from without; so that all deified Nature absolutely paints like the harlot, whose allurements cover nothing but the charnel-house within; and when we proceed further, and consider that the mystical cosmetic which produces every one of her hues, the great principle of light, for ever remains white or colorless in itself, and if operating without medium upon matter, would touch all objects, even tulips and roses, with its own blank tinge—pondering all this, the palsied universe lies before us a leper; and like wilful travellers in Lapland, who refuse to wear colored and coloring glasses upon their eyes, so the wretched infidel gazes himself blind at the monumental white shroud that wraps all the prospect around him. (42: *169–70*)

The key word in the passage is "medium." Light must operate through and/or with a medium upon matter; were the medium not present, there would be no color in tulips and roses, but only a "blank tinge" correlative to the whiteness of natural sunlight. What Ishmael means by "medium" is not entirely clear, but appears to be the apprehending consciousness, the perceptual apparatus in man, which is an essential element in the mechanism of color-illumination. It is the mind of man, working in conjunction with the white, non-color light falling on the natural world, which produces the color-world, the Kantian "sensuous manifold." More precisely, and rendered epistemologically, Ishmael appears to be suggesting that natural light makes the noumenal substrate, the object as it is in itself, available in some limited way to the mechanism of perception, and it is the lamp-mind, as part of the very act of perception, which supplies the color, "laid on from without," which results in the phenomenal world we know. It is in this passage that the fusion of the *light of nature* and the *light of the mind* is most precisely set forth, clarifying in a decisive way what Ishmael means when he speaks of the interpenetration and integration of external sense-data with the internal imaginative construct to form one monolithic "seamless whole" (114: *406*). The apprehension of reality involves *two* kinds of light, rather than just one: this development of the usual nineteenth-century mind-light analogue saves *Moby-Dick* from that radical solipsism frequently implicit in both English and Continental versions.

It is crucially important to notice that Ishmael's contemplation of reality in "The Whiteness of the Whale" chapter, full of brooding despair though it is, nevertheless differs from Ahab's contemplation of reality in two essential respects. In the first place, while Ahab describes the phenomenal world in terms of "pasteboard," a *mask-metaphor*, Ishmael talks in terms of "hues" and "tinges," a *color-metaphor*. This difference is of enormous significance. A pasteboard mask makes any apprehension of the noumenal substrate impossible: there is no way of knowing what, if anything, lies behind a mask. Ahab is therefore reduced to the event-centered, trans-phenomenal inferences I have described, one consequence of which is his perceptual dissociation from phenomena. The "tinges," "hues," and "emblazonings" that Ishmael speaks of may partially hide or obscure noumenal reality, but they do not *mask* it absolutely. The butterfly-as-it-is-in-itself is somehow apparent *through* the "gilded velvets" with which the lamp-mind invests it. This epistemological *translucency* (as distinguished from *transparency*) of color makes possible a limited but nevertheless direct intuition of the absolute world. Indeed the whole burden of "The Whiteness of the Whale" chapter is that man can achieve such intuitions, however minimal, however confused (as Locke would say), however marginally subliminal. The phenomenal world is *not quite* a dungeon. That which is *colored* is considerably more accessible than that which is *masked*.

In the second place, Ishmael never, even in the "Whiteness" chapter, employs the metaphor of the mirror in the absolute sense that Ahab uses it in the "Doubloon" scene. Ahab sees a hopelessly circular solipsism in the total reflectivity of the doubloon-microcosm, and the varying interpretations of the coin given by the six percipients who follow him appear to reinforce this view. But Ishmael, while he faithfully reports all that is said in this scene, including what Stubb-as-observer reports, does not himself comment upon the doubloon in any but the most objective terms. The "Doubloon" chapter belongs to Ahab, not Ishmael. The solipsism implicit in it is therefore Ahab's, not Ishmael's.

The most effective statement of this conviction, that the phenomenal manifold is *not quite* a dungeon, is Melville's short story, "The Two Temples." The narrator, after being turned away from a church by a "great, fat-paunched beadle-faced man," discovers a "small door" into the bell-tower. "Ascending some fifty stone steps along a very narrow curving stairway, I found myself on a blank platform forming the second story of the huge square tower." He is "inside some magic-lantern," a translucent glass version of the phenomenal cosmos: "On three sides, three gigantic Gothic windows of richly dyed glass, filled the otherwise meagre place with all sorts of sunrises and sunsets, lunar and solar rainbows, falling stars, and other flaming fireworks and pyrotechnics." But this ambience of harlot color is an epistemological trap: ". . . after all, it was but a gorgeous dungeon; for I couldn't *look out* [italics mine] any more than if I had been the occupant of a basement cell in 'the Tombs.'" The narrator, however, is able to meliorate his entrapment. "With some pains, and care not to do any serious harm, I contrived to scratch a *minute opening* [italics mine] in a great purple star forming the center of the chief compartment of the middle window." This minute breach in the phenomenal continuum does not give the narrator any absolute grasp of what lies beyond, but only a *glimpse*. What he sees is "The beadle-faced man . . . just in the act of driving three ragged little boys into the middle of the street." The "minute opening" he has scratched in the great church window represents a limited but nevertheless very real break-out from the phenomenal and chromatic dungeon.[10]

The qualified epistemological affirmation which underlies "The Two Temples" also underlies the closing paragraphs of "The Whiteness of the Whale" chapter. Ishmael's despairing rhetoric should not obscure this fact. There *is* a germ of hope in the chapter: Ishmael does achieve a minimal, perhaps only subliminal, apprehension of the noumenal world, although he himself cannot *as yet* see the philosophically hopeful implications of this fact. Ishmael despairs here, becomes himself a "wretched infidel," because he is still, like Ahab, an epistemological absolutist, seeking a total rather than a partial comprehension of reality. He will not, *at this point* in *Moby-Dick*, be satisfied with any mere "minute opening" in the prison of the senses. This absolutist stance makes him see both nature and the natural processes of perception as corrupt. Nature is a painted harlot using "subtle deceits" to mask the "charnel-house" of a "palsied universe." The emotive vocabulary springs, one suspects, out of Ishmael's residual Presbyterianism. He has perceived, through the "minute opening" which imaginative intuition affords, a terrifying noumenal world which cannot be articulated in the chromatic idiom of normal perception. It is therefore, to his still-orthodox eyes, totally dehumanized, absolutely amoral, unutterably alien. Ishmael's Christian shock as he intuits this metaperceptual region bathed in leprous light is akin to the Christian shock of Henry Adams who, fifty years later, lay in the great hall of the dynamos at the Paris Exposition with his historical back broken, surrounded by blind forces, X-rays and electricity, which were, like Ishmael's white world, "occult," "irrational," "supersensual." Radium, Adams asserted, denied its God—and so do Ishmael's noumenal intuitions.

Ishmael also is wretched because his scientifically correct analysis of perception brings him to the despairing realization that he will never know an autonomous reality independent of his lamp-mind. The aesthetically coherent world, the sun-filled, light-irradiated realm of "lovely emblazonings" and "sweet tinges," which is the source of his greatest hope is, after all, only a world that he himself helps to make. Because he participates in the making of it, he concludes that it is deceitful, nothing but harlot-colors "laid on from without." But the day comes, many pages later, when he insists that the sun is, after all, "the only true lamp—all others but liars!" How is this reversal effected? The answer is that Ishmael will gradually come to see that the lamplight of perception, working upon an object-world made available by the sunlight of nature, is not a tendentious faculty devoted to lovely falsehoods, but quite the opposite. In lowering after lowering, as Ishmael encounters the actual flesh-and-blood whale, he will gradually develop a set of perceptions of Leviathan, and what Leviathan represents, radically different from those furnished to him ready-formed by Ahab. Ishmael will realize that perception, far from being a faculty of deceit, is instead *a moral faculty of almost unlimited power*. But this is the business of a later chapter. Right now we must turn from the perceiver to the perceived, from the chromatic world of sensible apprehension to the achromatic world of primal forms.

Before addressing ourselves to these matters, however, it may be useful to summarize these first two chapters, differentiating Ahab from Ishmael in categorical terms. Ahab is event-oriented; Ishmael is object-oriented. Ahab rejects the phenomenal world as pasteboard; Ishmael does not. Ahab makes inferential derivations from the abstractive event-world; Ishmael makes intuitional derivations from the concrete object-world. Ahab sees the mind as a *camera-obscura*, passively receiving impressions from without; Ishmael sees the mind as a lamp, contributing actively to the creation of the final percept. Ahab sees perception as unidirectional input; Ishmael sees perception as bi-directional, both input and output. Ahab sees absolute reality as masked, perceptually inaccessible; Ishmael sees absolute reality as colored, intuitionally accessible. Ahab conceives of a total dissociation between his perception and the outer world; Ishmael suggests that the mind illuminates reality so that an organic relationship between inner imaginative construct and outer empirical datum occurs, forming "one seamless whole." Most important (I glance ahead here), not only the lamp-mind metaphor, but also the other constitutive metaphors which exfoliate from the protometaphor, correlate remarkably well with both Ishmael's epistemology *and* the extracetological epistemology of the Melville canon. The correlation with Ahab's epistemology, on the other hand, is much less apparent. It is Ishmael who truly shadows forth Melville, not Ahab. We will therefore, in succeeding chapters, take Ishmael, not Ahab, as our "only true lamp."

PRIMAL FORMS AND MACRO-MIRRORS
Other Constitutive Metaphors

WE TURN NOW to the *thing perceived*, the object "out there" on which the illumination of the lamp-mind falls. Such a shift means that we enter the Laplandish non-color world of trans-phenomenal intuition, in the midmost of which there floats the ultimate object of our quest, "one grand hooded phantom, like a snow hill in the air" (1: *16*).* The transition itself, however, raises a crucial prob-

---

* The number before the colon in all parenthetical references in the text indicates chapter, which will be the same for most American editions of *Moby-Dick*; the italicized numbers after the colon indicate page in the Norton Critical Edition of *Moby-Dick*, edited by Harrison Hayford and Hershel Parker (New York: W. W. Norton & Company, 1967).

lem. We have seen that the lamp-mind is creative, that in some sense it "makes" the outer world. Melville tells Sophia Hawthorne that her "spiritualizing nature" refines everything she sees, so that "things which while you think you but humbly discover them, you do in fact create them for yourself." The question is: what is the extent and nature of this creating or making? Is it total or partial? Such questions are important because the ultimate meaning of *Moby-Dick* depends in the most crucial way upon the ontological status of the trans-phenomenal not-me. We are launched upon a whale-hunt, and it makes a great deal of difference whether we are pursuing a real, substantial whale or a magnificent but tenuous projection of the romantic mind. Emerson, who pushes the projective power of the mind about as far as it can go, optimistically tells us to "make, therefore, your own world." Under the paradigm of his radical transcendentalism the outer world becomes entirely plastic and increasingly impalpable, until he arrives at the "noble doubt" as to whether nature "outwardly exists." Nature becomes little more than a spiritualized idea, the projective product of the lamp-mind.

Is this the case with *Moby-Dick*? Does the lamp-mind create the *Pequod's* watery world? Certain passages seem to suggest this. It is paradoxical that it is Ahab himself, despite his infantile faith in the efficacy of welded metal and Titan power, who suggests that the not-me may be utterly plastic, the whole world but an idea. When Queequeg's coffin is converted into a life-buoy, Ahab's corrosive doubts about reality find specific expression:

> Oh! how immaterial are all materials! What things real are there, but imponderable thoughts? Here now's the very dreaded symbol of grim death, by a mere hap, made the expressive sign of the help and hope of most endangered life. A life-buoy of a coffin! (127: *432–33*)

Occasionally Ahab does seem able to make the outer world anything he wishes it to be. At the beginning of the third day of the chase of Moby Dick, Ahab broodingly delivers a monologue upon the wind. First he remarks that it is a "vile wind that has no doubt blown ere this through prison corridors and cells, and wards of hospitals, and ventilated them. . . . Out upon it!—it's tainted." But no sooner does he decide that the wind is "vile" than his thoughts tack, and the wind becomes a "noble and heroic thing" which no man ever conquered: "Run tilting at it, and you but run through it"—a consideration which causes yet a third tack. "Ha! a coward wind that strikes stark naked men, but will not stand to receive a single blow." And then he concludes by deciding that in spite of all "... there's something all glorious and gracious in the wind" (135: *460–61*). Reality here is of a wind-like impalpability, unequivocally plastic. But can the passage be taken in any sense as normative?

The weight of the extracetological evidence suggests unequivocally that Melville would reject such an Emersonian idea. Melville's books are characterized, with the possible exception of *Mardi*, by a tactile sense of the heft and weight of the outer world, a sense which prevented him from ever taking idealists and compensationists very seriously. In 1849 Emerson's reputation suggested to Melville that the leader of the transcendentalist movement was a "denizen of the land of gingerbread," "full of transcendentalisms, myths & oracular gibberish." Over a decade later, in 1862, Melville concedes that there is much that is "admirable" in Emerson, but he nevertheless returns to the Concord savant's "gross and astonishing errors and illusions." Typical of such gibberish and illusions would be, one suspects, Emerson's assertion in *Nature* that "The ruin or blank that we see when we look at nature, is in our own eye," or his dictum in "Spiritual Laws" that "The good, compared to the evil which [a man] sees, is as his own good to his own evil." Melville's exasperated scrawl in the margin—"A perfectly good being, therefore, would see no evil.—But what did Christ see?—He saw what made him weep"—suggests his conviction that there is a substantive realm beyond phenomena which cannot be reduced to that which exists in the eye of the beholder or in the illuminating mind alone.[1]

The fact that Melville uses whiteness to symbolize this noumenal realm has led many critics to suppose that it is an ontologically evacuated region. Ronald Mason, remarking how Melville's "beguiling surfaces dislimn into a common colourless whiteness," concludes that this is a whiteness "signifying Nothing"—and he is not the only critic to suggest that the white shapes of the squid, the albatross, and the albino whale merely express a metaphysical void.[2] But there is evidence to suggest that Melville regarded the noumenal realm, regardless of its perceptual inaccessibility, to the most substantive of worlds. The most important statement of this noumenal substanti-

ality is the white form that looms up with such massiveness in the
oneiric vision of "The Berg: (A Dream)," published in *John Marr
and Other Sailors* (1888). The poet sees a "ship of martial build,"
directed by "madness mere," ram full sail "Against a stolid iceberg."
Melville then devotes over thirty lines to the fact that the juggernaut
man-of-war makes not the slightest impression, sends not the most
minuscule shiver along the berg's "dead indifference of walls":

> Along the spurs of ridges pale,
> Not any slenderest shaft and frail,
> A prism over glass-green gorges lone,
> Toppled; or lace of traceries fine,
> Nor pendent drops in grot or mine
> Were jarred, when the stunned ship went down.
>
> . . . .
>
> No thrill transmitted stirred the lock
> Of jack-straw needle-ice at base;
> Towers undermined by waves—the block
> Atilt impending—kept their place.

The berg is simply "lumpish," a "lumbering lubbard,"[3] reminding
one of Ishmael's description of the "half-horrible stolidity" and "all-
ramifying heartlessness" of the *Pequod's* carpenter, an utterly "impersonal" person:

> ...impersonal, I say; for [his stolidity] so shaded off into the sur-
> rounding infinite of things, that it seemed one with the general
> stolidity discernible in the whole visible world; which while pause-
> lessly active in uncounted modes, still eternally holds its peace, and
> ignores you, though you dig foundations for cathedrals. (107: *388*)

During Ishmael's visit to "A Bower in the Arsacides" (Chapter
102) it is this berg-like underworld, embodied in the hard pale bones
of King Tranquo's whale skeleton, which supports the "weaver-
god's" phenomenally "gorgeous carpet" of "ground-vine tendrils"
and "living flowers" (102: *374*). Indeed, Melville returns to similar
imagery in *Pierre* to suggest the tapestried phenomenal derma which
conceals the berg-like realities of life: Chapter 22 is entitled "The
Flower-Curtain Lifted From Before a Tropical Author...."[4] Behind Melville's "flower-curtain" looms what Lewis Mumford calls
the "colourless, unintegrated, primal world that underlies and ante-
dates that which we know through our senses."[5] The catalyst which

gives the questing intelligence its first glimpse of this anteperceptual world is philosophical or religious doubt, impinging corrosively upon man's Adamic acceptance of the phenomenal datum. In *Clarel,* while recounting Nathan's spiritual saga, Melville describes how this searcher. "Alone, and at Doubt's freezing pole / ... wrestled with the pristine forms / Like the first man" (I, xvii, 194–96); Nathan has "the heart to brave / All questions on that primal ground / Laid bare by faith's receding wave" (I, xix, 28–30).[6]

The consequence of faith's receding wave is the dissolution of those hard, sharp lines, those incisive shapes, which characterize a thoughtless acceptance of appearances. Presbyterian Ishmael, assailed by unbidden infidelities, encounters this epistemological effect when he tries to make sense of the picture hanging in the entry-way of the Spouter-Inn. The picture is so "be-smoked" and "defaced" that Ishmael can make nothing of it. "Such unaccountable masses of shades and shadows" can only represent, he thinks, "chaos bewitched." "A boggy, soggy, squitchy picture truly, enough to drive a nervous man distracted." But, his intuitional capacities sharpening as his faith dissolves, he senses "a sort of indefinite, half-attained, unimaginable sublimity about it that fairly froze you to it." What particularly attracts him is a "long, limber, portentous, black mass of something hovering in the centre of the picture over three blue, dim, perpendicular lines floating in a nameless yeast." This inchoate vision is his first blurred anteperceptual glimpse of the noumenal Leviathan (3: *20*).

The same epistemological effect is apparent next morning when Ishmael awakens to discover Queequeg's arm thrown over him "in the most loving and affectionate manner." He finds that he cannot distinguish the cannibal's arm, "tattooed all over with an interminable Cretan labyrinth of a figure," from the counterpane itself:

> ... this same arm of his, I say, looked for all the world like a strip of that same patchwork quilt. Indeed, partly lying on it as the arm did when I first awoke, I could hardly tell it from the quilt, they so blended their hues together; and it was only by the sense of weight and pressure that I could tell that Queequeg was hugging me. (4: *32*)

Such epistemological blurring is accompanied by the gradual emergence of what Melville, writing to Hawthorne in 1861, called "visible truth," which he defined as an "apprehension of the absolute condition of present things as they strike the eye of the man who fears them not, though they do their worst to him."[7] "Visible truth" forms the basis of what Melville, in an 1860 journal entry discussing death as the "King of Terrors," called the "Primal Philosophy."[8] It is also what he had in mind when, in 1890, he rated James Thomson's "City of the Dreadful Night" as a "modern Book of Job," like the Biblical original "duskily looming with the same aboriginal verities."[9] It is such primordial verities which little Pip sees when, having jumped out of Stubb's boat, he is left in the middle of the vast ocean, his soul in terror

> ... carried down alive to wondrous depths, where strange shapes of the unwarped primal world glided to and fro before his passive eyes; and the miser-merman, Wisdom, revealed his hoarded heaps; and among the joyous, heartless, ever-juvenile eternities, Pip saw the multitudinous, God-omnipresent, coral insects, that out of the firmament of waters heaved the colossal orbs. He saw God's foot upon the treadle of the loom, and spoke it. (93: *347*)

Ishmael's reference to the "strange shapes of the unwarped primal world" gives us the second constitutive metaphor of *Moby-Dick*, the metaphor of the *primal form*. It is, like the figure of illumination, epistemological, an analogical rendering of the object as seen intuitively and trans-phenomenally. The "unwarped primal world" which Pip sees is the world as it is in itself, before it is "warped" or distorted or added to by the creative light of the illuminative mind. What distinguishes the metaphor of the primal form from the metaphor of illumination is that while the latter is addressed to the perceptual *process*, the former is directed to the perceptual *object*, as it would be if viewed anteperceptually. The metaphor of the primal form makes possible that logical and phenomenological contradiction, anteperceptual perception. The "matter" or "object" of such anteperception is the visual rendering of an essentially *con*ceptual formulation. The broad ocean, for example, is the most pervasive primal form in *Moby-Dick*; it is the anteperceptual expression of that which may perhaps be expressed verbally as "the inchoateness of the primal liquidity."

Such a primal form, too, although less susceptible to verbalization, is Ishmael's description of the "wide field of leaning spires, wrenched cope-stones, and crosses all adroop" which is "tearless Lima, the strangest, saddest city thou can'st see":

> For Lima has taken the white veil; and there is a higher horror in this whiteness of her woe. Old as Pizarro, this whiteness keeps her ruins for ever new; admits not the cheerful greenness of complete decay; spreads over her broken ramparts the rigid pallor of an apoplexy that fixes its own distortions. (42: *167–68*)

This is again the visual rendering of a conceptual formulation. It may be articulated, very approximately, as the City of Man before man existed, the City before men ever built one, the City as ante-perceptual and antechronical archetype, a pallid metropolis awaiting through countless eons of time the softening and coloring of man's perception, the humanizing of the illuminating mind. It is the desolation of the cosmos outside of man's ambient and creative awareness, rendered in an image of deserted houses and empty streets locked in the eternal stillness of an apoplectic, preconscious trance.

My far-from-successful attempt here to verbalize what Ishmael means by his pallid image of Lima highlights the fact that the metaphor of the primal form analogizes not only the anteperceptual and the antechronical, but the anteverbal as well. What the primal forms of *Moby-Dick* say cannot really be said. They are, like the images of Coleridge's *Ancient Mariner*, loomingly eloquent nevertheless. Thus the long-from-home *Goney*, one of the whalers which gams with the *Pequod*, is no real ship, but rather the albescent image of the questing craft voyaging out of space and beyond time, stripped of both color and that sharpness of outline which would place her in the real world of sensible apprehension: "As if the waves had been fullers, this craft was bleached like the skeleton of a stranded walrus. All down her sides, this spectral appearance was traced with long channels of reddened rust, while all her spars and her rigging were like the thick branches of trees furred over with hoar-frost" (52: *203*).

It is, however, the *animal* as primal form which most engages Melville's attention. Not infrequently the analogue approaches allegory, as when he speaks, in "Hawthorne and His Mosses," of Truth which is sometimes "forced to fly like a scared white doe in the woodlands." Ishmael too articulates some of his most subtle analogues through the animalistic primal form. One thinks immediately of his evocation of the Jovian snow-white bull, the White Dog of the Iroquois, the white bear of the polar regions, the White Steed of the Prairies, and St. John's apocalyptic pale horse, bearing a pale rider. But it is the sea-animals of *Moby-Dick*, those "native inhabitants" of an "everlasting terra incognita," outlandish forms which man has always regarded "with emotions unspeakably unsocial and repelling," which give the metaphor of the primal form a sentient dimension expressing Ishmael's awareness of the alien quality of the noumenal world: ". . . you can hardly regard any creatures of the deep," he tells us, "with the same feelings that you do those of the shore" (58: *234-35*). These abyssal creatures, flitting like pale shadows through the watery depths, are analogues for that region of the human mind which is so primitive, so primordially oneiric, that it defies articulation. Thus, the mast-head stander, lulled into a trance by the "cadence of waves with thoughts," analogizes outer sea with inner mind, so that every "strange, half-seen, gliding, beautiful thing that eludes him; every dimly-discovered, uprising fin of some undiscernible form, seems to him the embodiment of those elusive thoughts that only people the soul by continually flitting through it" (35: *140*).

Next to the whale himself, the clearest example in *Moby-Dick* of the anteperceptual articulation of an abstract concept is the *squid*, Melville's attempt to render that which is not only antechronical, but anteformal as well. In a late poem, "The New Ancient of Days," which comments satirically on the Darwinian thesis, Melville characterizes the "man of bone" as a "wizard one" producing a "horrible show" of antechronical monsters: "His totals of time make an awful schism, / And old Chronos he pitches adown the abysm / Like a pebble down Carisbrook well." The result is a "Barnum-show" vision of the life-urge,

> The vomit of slimy and sludgey sea:
> Purposeless creatures, odd inchoate things
> Which splashed thro' morasses on fleshly wings;
> The cubs of Chaos, with eyes askance,
> Preposterous griffins that squint at Chance
> And Anarch's cracked decree!

Nevertheless, the "Megalosaurus, iguanodon, / Palaeotherium Glypthaecon" which lumber and slither through the poem are real creatures defined by real form, however preposterous.[10] The squid, in contrast, is monstrous because of its *lack* of form. It reveals itself "one transparent blue morning, when a stillness almost preternatural spread over the sea." "In the distance, a great white mass lazily rose, and rising higher and higher, and disentangling itself from the azure, at last gleamed before our prow like a snow-slide, new slid from the hills. Thus glistening for a moment, as slowly it subsided, and sank. Then once more arose, and silently gleamed" (59: *236*). Ishmael gives but a single detail which suggests recognizable form: the squid has "innumerable long arms radiating from its centre, and curling and twisting like a nest of anacondas." But he stresses that it is little more than "A vast pulpy mass, furlongs in length and breadth," devoid of the formal characteristics which make the phenomenal world comprehensible. "No perceptible face or front did it have; no conceivable token of either sensation or instinct; but undulated there on the billows, an unearthly, formless, chance-like apparition of life" (59: *237*).

The squid is not a real animal at all, but rather a visual articulation in anteperceptual terms of a philosophical idea. Endowed with minimal formality, it is, to use a phrase which Ishmael later applies to the *Pequod's* carpenter, "a stript abstract; an unfractioned integral" (107: *388*). The nature of the abstractive concept of which the squid is a metaphorically noumenal rendering is not far to seek: in a passage concerning the sharks which swarm about the *Pequod*, Ishmael makes a precise distinction between two sorts of vitality:

> A sort of generic or Pantheistic vitality seemed to lurk in their very joints and bones, after what might be called the individual life had departed. Killed and hoisted on deck for the sake of his skin, one of these sharks almost took poor Queequeg's hand off, when he tried to shut down the dead lid of his murderous jaw. (66: *257*)

Behind "individual life," and far more pervasive and fundamental, is what might be termed the biological dynamism of the cosmos, a "generic or Pantheistic vitality." The Scholastic philosophers, one recalls, spoke of "Prime Matter," by which they meant matter as it would exist anterior to the imposition of form. The concept is useful here: the squid is not so much living matter as "Prime Life," the importunate quintessential protoplasm, the inexorable Life Force which is a constitutive *quality* of the anteperceptual cosmos. It is, moreover, specifically related to the White Whale: Ishmael's comparison of the squid to a "snow-slide, new slid from the hills" parallels his image of "one grand hooded phantom, like a snow hill in the air" (1: *16*). The squid is Moby Dick viewed anteformally, noumenal essence anterior to noumenal object. The squid is not Leviathan, but it is dynamistic Leviathan*ism*, part of the ultimate substrate of the "unwarped primal world."

This philosophically eloquent use of the primal form to achieve a visual rendering of the immanently qualitative and conceptual aspects of the cosmos reaches its highest development in the densely exfoliative metaphor of the whale himself. Leviathan must have his separate chapters, but the primal form used to express *cachalotisme* is worthy of attention here. Ishmael stresses the antechronical nature of the whale: "Leviathan comes floundering down upon us from the head-waters of the Eternities" (105: *381*). "I am horror-struck at this antemosaic, unsourced existence of the unspeakable terrors of the whale, which, having been before all time, must needs exist after all humane ages are over" (104: *380*). The primogeniture of the whale extends back to that epistemologically blurred epoch when the world was still submerged in the chaotic liquidity and the universe itself had only partially emerged from formlessness:

> When I stand among these mighty Leviathan skeletons, ... I am ... borne back to that wondrous period, ere time itself can be said to have begun.... Here Saturn's grey chaos rolls over me, and I obtain dim, shuddering glimpses into those Polar eternities; when wedged bastions of ice pressed hard upon what are now the Tropics; and in all the 25,000 miles of this world's circumference, not an inhabitable hand's breadth of land was visible. Then the whole world was the whale's. (104: *380*)

In this endless antechronical vista Leviathan loses definition as an animal or even a thing, and becomes instead a dynamistically conceived *quality* immanent in the chaos of a world half-made, older than mountains, more primordial than suns. Reduced thus to abstractive essence, the whale glimmers tantalizingly on the subliminal periphery of both conception and perception, intuited rather than apprehended, floating at the secret ontological heart of cosmic reality. As such, he represents the furthest limits of epistemological possibility: "Dissect him how I may, then, I but go skin deep; I know him not, and never will" (86: *318*), Ishmael confesses. This is the meaning of the "Etymology" which prefaces *Moby-Dick*. Having many names, from the Danish *Hvalt* to the Erromangoan *Pehee-Nuee-Nuee*, Leviathan has no name and, like Yahweh, is unnamed and unnameable. This is the meaning, too, of the "Extracts" accumulated by a "mere painstaking burrower and grub-worm of a poor devil of a Sub-Sub[-Librarian]": centuries of speculation, of that which is "said, thought, fancied, and sung of Leviathan" have resulted in a morass of "higgledy-piggledy whale statements" which brings one only minutely closer to the basaltic verities of the primal world.

The epistemological nature of the primal form is brought to full definition in Chapter 55, "Of the Monstrous Pictures of Whales." Ishmael remarks that "though elephants have stood for their full-lengths, the living Leviathan has never yet fairly floated himself for his portrait." The reason is that at sea his "full majesty and significance" is buried in "unfathomable waters." There is no way that one can get a solid glimpse of all the "mighty swells and undulations" of "Platonian Leviathan." Just as the "boggy, soggy, squitchy" picture at the Spouter-Inn is philosophically expressive, so is Leviathan: even the suckling whale hoisted on deck refuses to take on that distinctness of shape and sharpness of outline which characterize phenomenal apprehension: "... such is then the outlandish, eel-like, limbered, varying shape of him, that his precise expression the devil himself could not catch":

> So there is no earthly way of finding out precisely what the whale really looks like. And the only mode in which you can derive even a tolerable idea of his living contour, is by going a whaling yourself; but by so doing, you run no small risk of being eternally stove and sunk by him. Wherefore, it seems to me you had best not be too fastidious in your curiosity touching this Leviathan. (55: *227–28*)

Such are the dangers of the philosophical exploration of the noumenal realm.

That the primal form is trans-phenomenally qualitative, Leviathan often merging into Leviathanism, comes clear in Chapter 57, where

Ishmael discovers the whale-shape in non-oceanic realms, in "paint; in teeth; in wood; in sheet-iron; in stone; in mountains; in stars" (57: *231*). He reminds us that "In bony, ribby regions of the earth, where . . . masses of rock lie strewn in fantastic groupings upon the plain, you will often discover images . . . of the Leviathan partly merged in grass." Moreover, "in mountainous countries . . . you will catch passing glimpses of the profiles of whales defined along the undulating ridges." "Nor . . . can you fail to trace out great whales in the starry heavens." Leviathanism thus manifests itself in every aspect of the cosmos. But Ishmael cautions that one must be a "thorough whaleman, to see these sights"—one must have the meta-physical agility to return when necessary to the same epistemological vantage-point: ". . . you must be sure and take the exact intersecting latitude and longitude of your first stand-point, else—so chance-like are such observations of the hills—your precise, previous stand-point would require a laborious re-discovery" (57: *233*).

Ishmael's perception here, half-imaginative and half-factual, of an immanent Leviathanism in nature, brings us back to his assertion that the Lockean empirical datum and the Kantian imaginative con-struct interpenetrate, forming "one seamless whole" (114: *406*). And having established the intractable substantiality of the trans-phenomenal realm in *Moby-Dick*, we can now describe with some precision the relationship obtaining between the creative lamp-mind and the berg-stolid noumenal entities which are the object of its illumination. Again, the extracetological canon throws important light on *Moby-Dick*. The philosopher-sage Babbalanja of *Mardi* supplies an invaluable key. Addressing King Media he says: "The essence of all good and all evil is in us, not out of us. Neither poison nor honey lodgeth in the flowers on which, side by side, bees and wasps oft alight. My lord, nature is an immaculate virgin, forever standing unrobed before us."[11] Babbalanja's "immaculate virgin" is unmistakably a primal form, whiteness being implicit in both "im-maculate" and "virgin." The flowers, containing neither poison nor honey, affirm the moral neutrality of the natural world. Conse-quently, the moral actualization of the flower depends absolutely on an agent external to itself: the bee will extract that which be-becomes honey; the wasp, availing himself of the same neutral sustenance, produces poison. Babbalanja's figure proposes *an inde-pendent reality, the moral significance of which inheres in the agent apprehending that reality*. Implicit in the multiplex virgin-flower metaphor is the suggestion that "unrobed" nature is somehow "robed" by the act of perception. Such a "robing" analogue is a suggestive variation of the general metaphor of illumination: the light of the mind, in the act of perception, endows nature with a moral investiture commensurate with the mind's own moral im-peratives. To repeat: we cannot make the world, but we can make the world *moral*. The same idea appears in *Pierre*: "Say what some poets will, Nature is not so much her own ever-sweet interpreter, as the mere supplier of that cunning alphabet, whereby selecting and combining as he pleases, each man reads his own peculiar lesson according to his own peculiar mind and mood."[12] Like Babbalanja, the narrator of *Pierre* proposes a reality—the "cunning alphabet"—anterior to and independent of the perceiver. This "alphabet" is the same sort of noumenal analogue as Babbalanja's "immaculate vir-gin." In this instance the illumination of the mind is re-analogized as the process of "selecting and combining" the elements of the noumenal alphabet to produce an implicitly moral "lesson." Finally, the narrator of *White Jacket* amplifies these ideas by recasting the moral neutrality of Babbalanja's flower-analogue as the "armed neutrality" of Fate with regard to the affairs of men:

> ... in our own hearts, we mold the whole world's hereafters; and in our own hearts we fashion our own gods. Each mortal casts his vote for whom he will to rule the worlds; I have a voice that helps to shape eternity; and my volitions stir the orbits of the furthest suns. In two senses, we are precisely what we worship. Ourselves are Fate.[13]

In *Moby-Dick* itself the nature and limits of this shaping and fashioning power of the perceiving mind are expressed through a specialized metaphor dealing with the relationship between Quee-queg and his coffin: it is the *metaphor of the sculptured noumenon*. The cannibal's coffin is "sculptured" in two distinct but interrelated senses. First, the "box" (110: *398*) fashioned from some "heathenish, coffin-colored old lumber" (110: *396*) for the dying Queequeg by the carpenter is really no more than a neutral geometric, an on-tologically rough-hewn entity, an indeterminate bit of the noumenal "alphabet" which can be shaped to different ends and purposes depending on the moral intentions of the various percipients who variously illuminate it. To shift the figure, the carpenter's "box" can be "robed," like Babbalanja's "immaculate virgin," with an investiture of significations dependent entirely upon Queequeg, or Starbuck, or any percipient who happens by. This is precisely what happens. Queequeg, remembering a "little duty" ashore he had left undone, decides he cannot die, and suddenly recovers, whereupon the carpenter's "box" becomes, with a "wild whimsiness" on Queequeg's part, his sea-chest (110: *398–99*). Finally, when a sailor falls overboard and the ship's regular life-buoy, having shrunk from long exposure, itself sinks, then Starbuck, following "certain strange signs and innuendoes" from Queequeg, orders the coffin-cum-sea-chest sealed and calked to make a new life-buoy (126: *430*). The significance of this sequence is clear. The "box" the carpenter builds expresses the essential stolidity of form and substance which characterizes the not-me. It exhibits none of that radical plasticity which distinguishes the transcendental version of reality. It is a box, it will always be a box, it can be nothing other than a box. On the other hand, it is, as substantive entity, sufficiently generalized—ontologically rough-hewn—so that the illuminating mind, *within sharp limits*, can endow it with final, constitutive signification. The mind cannot make the box—but it can *make the box's meaning*.

The carpenter's box is "sculptured" not only metaphorically, but literally. After the coffin becomes a sea-chest, and before it becomes a life-buoy, Queequeg spends "Many spare hours . . . in carving the lid with all manner of grotesque figures and drawings." The cannibal actually sculptures the primal box into an image of his own person: ". . . and it seemed that hereby he was striving, in his rude way, to copy parts of the twisted tattooing on his body":

> And this tattooing, had been the work of a departed prophet and seer of his island, who, by those hieroglyphic marks, had written out on [Queequeg's] body a complete theory of the heavens and the earth, and a mystical treatise on the art of attaining truth; so that Queequeg in his own proper person was a riddle to unfold; a wondrous work in one volume. (110: *399*)

Queequeg, in this vividly Kantian analogue, imposes his own self-image upon the noumenal substrate—the unrealized Lockean empirical datum—and in so doing endows it with both intellective and moral meaning. Queequeg's relationship to the carpenter's box is any man's relation to reality. Just as Queequeg by his carving orders and gives meaning to the box, so does the illuminating mind order and give meaning to the intractable reality of the trans-phenomenal not-me. But the limits of that creativity are established decisively by the ontological geometrics of that which the mind illuminates. Ahab is wrong when, contemplating the coffin-become-life-buoy, he speaks of "how immaterial are all materials!" (127: *432*). The noumenal world is not "immaterial": it is only *rough-hewn*, lacking final moral finish and final definition.

Such a reading of the philosophical bases of *Moby-Dick* demands certain subtle refinements of established critical interpretations. Alfred Kazin speaks of Melville's ability "to make us see that man is not a blank slate passively open to events, but a mind that constantly seeks meaning in everything that it encounters."[14] Such a reading misses the mark by a minute but crucial distance. One ought to say, rather, that the mind *imposes* meaning—moral meaning—on everything that it encounters. Similarly, Richard Chase suggests that "One may, like Ahab, look into the water, or into the profound and ultimately unknowable abyss of nature, and see only one's own image of an ungraspable phantom, a white whale which is only a projection of self."[15] Here, too, the noumenal substrate is insufficiently attended to. One ought rather to speak of a reality which is *partially* one's own image, and of a White Whale which is *in part* a projection of self. Lacking such qualification, *Moby-Dick* becomes hopelessly solipsistic, inaccessible to anything even distantly approximating a definitive—or defensible—interpretation.

The reflective element in the epistemology of *Moby-Dick* which Richard Chase stresses must not, however, be minimized; it is unmistakably there. When it is Queequeg's turn to examine the doubloon, Stubb delivers this report: "Dodge again! here comes Queequeg—all tattooing—looks like the signs of the Zodiac himself. . . . As I live he's comparing notes; looking at his thigh bone; thinks the sun is in the thigh, or in the calf, or in the bowels, I suppose" (99: *362*). Just as Queequeg *imposes* the "Cretan labyrinth" of self

on the noumenal coffin, so also does he *discover* self in the phenomenal doubloon. The outer world, noumenally regarded, is illuminated, and phenomenally regarded, is reflective. But this connection
should not obscure the crucially important point that the doubloon-
as-reflector stands well outside the epistemological mainstream of
Moby-Dick for the simple reason that it is *totally opaque*, an instance of what Ahab later calls "The dead, blind wall [which] butts
all inquiring heads at last" (125: *427*).

The epistemological mainstream of *Moby-Dick*, however, does
not establish such a blind wall of solipsistic opacity between the illuminating mind and its object. The wall—the interface—is there,
but it is often partially transparent. In *Moby-Dick* the mirror-
metaphor is embodied *preponderantly* in water-images, and most
especially in the ocean as macro-mirror. Melville subtilizes the
mirror-analogue by the simple expedient of moving from glass to
water. The result is an epistemology, centered in Ishmael, which is
infinitely more sophisticated than Ahab's. The water-surface, standing as interface between the phenomenal color-world and the
noumenal non-color world, is never flatly opaque, but rather simultaneously *partially opaque, partially reflective, and partially
transparent*. It is this protean analogical capacity of the water-
mirror which makes it the central figure of intuition in *Moby-Dick*.
By means of it Ishmael is able to express those elements in life and
awareness which are only dimly sensed or briefly glimpsed, which
lurk tantalizingly on the subliminal threshold of perception, which
take the form of what Ishmael calls "morbid hints, and half-formed
foetal suggestions" (41: *156*). The blending of opacity, reflectivity,
and transparency gives embodiment to those inchoate psychic realities which are often "too analytic to be verbally developed"
(46: *184*), composing the intuitional level of consciousness, the
"half known life" (58: *236*). It is out of the primal liquidity that
Melville fashions the third constitutive metaphor of *Moby-Dick*,
the metaphor of *reflective transparency*.

The weather of the *Pequod's* world, which determines the appearance of the watery interface, is frequently handled in terms of
an opacity not quite complete: there is always the hint of something
lurking, half-seen, beneath. About the time that the spirit-spout
appears, Ishmael remarks on the "serenity of the weather, in which,

beneath all its blue blandness, some thought there lurked a devilish charm." A few lines later he speaks of the "perfidious silences" of the tropical calm (51: *201*). The water-mirror in such placid intervals functions as a kind of alluring derma to inner reality, more predictive than deceptive: "Again: ... the profound calm which only apparently precedes and prophesies of the storm, is perhaps more awful than the storm itself; for, indeed, the calm is but the wrapper and envelope of the storm; and contains it in itself, as the seemingly harmless rifle holds the fatal powder, and the ball, and the explosion" (60: *241*). Again, Ishmael analogizes the watery interface between the color and non-color worlds as a "skin," speaking of the "times of dreamy quietude" upon the ocean, the boats surrounded by "smooth, slow heaving swells" that "like hearthstone cats ... purr against the gunwale." At such entranced moments, "when beholding the tranquil beauty and brilliancy of the ocean's skin, one forgets the tiger heart that pants beneath it; and would not willingly remember, that this velvet paw but conceals a remorseless fang" (114: *405*). This mirror-like placidity can be totally deceptive, as when the *Pequod's* crew waits for the uprising of an harpooned whale. "As the three boats lay there on that gently rolling sea, gazing down into its eternal blue noon; and as not a single groan or cry of any sort ... came up from its depths; what landsman would have thought, that beneath all that silence and placidity, the utmost monster of the seas was writhing and wrenching in agony!" (81: *300*). But it is in the penultimate paragraph of Chapter 58, "Brit," that Ishmael most successfully integrates color and non-color, skin and under-the-skin, surface and under-the-surface:

> Consider the subtleness of the sea; how its most dreaded creatures glide under water, unapparent for the most part, and treacherously hidden beneath the loveliest tints of azure. Consider also the devilish brilliance and beauty of many of its most remorseless tribes, as the dainty embellished shape of many species of sharks. (58: *235*)

If the interface is often semi-opaque, an "envelope" or "wrapper" to ultimate reality, it is also often reflective. In the opening chapter, after describing the "thousands upon thousands" of water-gazers that line the ocean's shore, Ishmael attempts to explain their "reveries" by the story of Narcissus who, "because he could not grasp

the tormenting, mild image he saw in the fountain, plunged into it
and was drowned. But that same image, we ourselves see in all rivers
and oceans. It is the image of the ungraspable phantom of life; and
this is the key to it all" (1: *14*).[16] Every page of *Moby-Dick* is shaped
by the idea of water-as-mirror. The Narcissus story expresses the
fact that man can, on the intuitional level, glimpse himself in nature, just as Ishmael must have seen himself mirrored in the primal
waters in which the *Pequod* floats. It implies that the external quest
is an internal quest, that outer knowledge is inner knowledge, and
that both can be very dangerous. As Narcissus plunged into the
fountain, so does Ishmael go to sea. As Narcissus drowned, so does
Ishmael—almost. The ungraspable phantom is as much within man
as without man, and for Ishmael the voyage of the *Pequod* is as
much a voyage into the interiorities of his own soul as it is a voyage
into the exteriorities of the ocean-world.

Ishmael slips easily from the Narcissus figure into a more generalized formulation when he speaks of "that deep, blue, bottomless soul, pervading mankind and nature" (35: *140*). The phrase
suggests that intuitional *transparency* of the oceanic interface which
makes it possible for him to see beyond mere surfaces to the inner
reality of things. Ishmael, fascinated by this transparency, speaks
of how the *Pequod's* "three boats lay there on that gently rolling sea,
gazing down into its eternal blue noon":

> In that sloping afternoon sunlight, the shadows that the three boats
> sent down beneath the surface, must have been long enough and
> broad enough to shade half Xerxes' army. Who can tell how appalling
> to the wounded whale must have been such huge phantoms flitting
> over his head! (81: *300*)

Such transparency engages even Ahab, committed though he is to
pasteboard opacity. "Slowly crossing the deck from the scuttle,
Ahab leaned over the side, and watched how his shadow in the water
sank and sank to his gaze, the more and the more that he strove to
pierce the profundity" (132: *443*). Starbuck, too, seeks vainly for
some glimpse of the ontological realities which the ocean's transparency seems to make accessible. "Loveliness unfathomable, as ever
lover saw in his young bride's eye!—Tell me not of thy teeth-tiered
sharks, and thy kidnapping cannibal ways. Let faith oust fact; let

fancy oust memory; I look deep down and do believe" (114: *406*). But it is only object-oriented Ishmael, gifted with true intuition, who is able to learn from these phenomenological transparencies. In Chapter 87, "The Grand Armada," peering over the boat's side, he gazes down through the surface of an "enchanted pond" into "watery vaults" of a "wondrous world" where "Some of the subtlest secrets of the seas" are revealed to him (87: *325–26*).

The full significance of the water-mirror does not come clear, however, until one realizes that on one symbolic level Ishmael does not go to sea at all. Yvor Winters has remarked that "The symbolism of *Moby-Dick* is based on the antithesis of the sea and the land: the land represents the known, the mastered, in human experience; the sea, the half-known, the obscure region of instinct, uncritical feeling, danger, and terror."[17] In one sense this is true; but in another sense the sea is not the antithesis of the land, but rather its correlate and analogue. Leo Marx has pointed out the existence in *Moby-Dick* of a "complex pastoral motive,"[18] and there is no question that Melville frequently sees water as land. In the poem "Pebbles" from *John Marr*, he speaks of the "hollows of the liquid hills / Where the long Blue Ridges run."[19] Similarly, Ishmael speaks of "the illimitable Pine Barrens and Salisbury Plains of the sea" (53: *204*). He refers to the ocean as "watery pastures" (35: *139*), and speaks of "these sea-pastures, wide-rolling watery prairies and Potters' Fields of all four continents" (111: *399*). In another land-figure, these seas become the home of the Nantucket whaler, "to and fro ploughing ... his own special plantation" (14: *63*). In Chapter 58, "Brit," Ishmael describes how the *Pequod* encounters "vast meadows of brit ... so that we seemed to be sailing through boundless fields of ripe and golden wheat." Right whales soon appear: "As morning mowers, who side by side slowly and seethingly advance their scythes through the long wet grass of marshy meads; even so these monsters swam, making a strange, grassy, cutting sound; and leaving behind them endless swaths of blue upon the yellow sea" (58: *234*). Indeed, the sea is so much like the land that Ishmael confesses that at times he "feels a certain filial, confident, land-like feeling towards the sea ..., [regarding] it as so much flowery earth" (114: *405*).

This elaborate analogy has a central epistemological significance.

When Ishmael launches forth upon the primordial waters, he is not so much going to sea as he is going to the *land-made-transparent*. Aboard the *Pequod* Ishmael does not abandon the realities of land-life; he only abandons—or escapes—their phenomenal opacity. At sea the facts of existence which have caused a "damp, drizzly November" (1: *12*) in Ishmael's soul imperceptibly soften and melt until he is able to glimpse, through that "minute opening" which intuition affords, those noumenal verities which loom in lambent and oneiric whiteness beneath the phenomenal sea-surface.

Two other constitutive analogues in *Moby-Dick* are the metaphor of the *ocean-island*, and the metaphor of the *thought-diver*. The island imagery of the novel provides a vehicle for rising above the interfacial surface, and the diver imagery provides a similar vehicle for getting below that surface. The crucial ocean-island passage occurs in the "Brit" chapter where Ishmael, after developing the sea as the "foe to man," and a "fiend to its own offspring," a "savage tigress" or "mad battle steed" that "overruns the globe" with "universal cannibalism," goes on to establish an antithesis between sea and land which expresses a parallel dualism in the soul of man:

> Consider all this; and then turn to this green, gentle, and most docile earth; consider them both, the sea and the land; and do you not find a strange analogy to something in yourself? For as this appalling ocean surrounds the verdant land, so in the soul of man there lies one insular Tahiti, full of peace and joy, but encompassed by all the horrors of the half known life. (58: *235–36*)

Ishmael is saying that the "universal cannibalism" of the external world finds its terrifying correlate in man himself. The "appalling ocean" of the soul is a metaphorical rendering of Ishmael's neurotic awareness of man's ineluctable immersion in natural process, an immersion which makes man the supreme shark, and human life and human behavior a "shocking sharkish business" (64: *249*). The Tahiti-island image, on the other hand, offers an avenue of possible melioration for Ishmael's radical, despairing naturalism. On this point, the extracetological evidence is of substantial help. Melville, in a journal entry, asserts that "J[esus] C[hrist] should have appeared in Taheti,"[20] and as described in *Omoo* the island becomes a symbol of inviolate sanctuary. The narrator speaks of the island's "uninhabited interior, ... almost impenetrable from the densely wooded glens, frightful precipices, and sharp mountain ridges absolutely inaccessible." The heart of Tahiti is "but little known, even to the natives themselves." But what seems to have struck Melville the most is the astonishing *height* that this Eden rises above the sharkish sea: he makes a point of the fact that the mountains of Tahiti "rise nine thousand feet above the level of the ocean."[21] In a similar passage, the narrator of *Mardi* speaks of "the nine thousand feet of Pirohitee's tall peak, which, rising from out the warm bosom of Tahiti, carries all summer with it into the clouds."[22] In *Moby-Dick* this sense of *elevation* becomes a visual analogue for the distance that man can rise above the terrible imperatives of his own inner being. Man may be a shark, but there is something in him that rises above insensate biological process, something which Ishmael calls "That immaculate manliness we feel within ourselves, so far within us, that it remains intact though all the outer character seem gone" (26: *104*). The same image of island-innerness occurs again when Ishmael finds his boat at the still, secret center of the gallied whale-herd:

> And thus, though surrounded by circle upon circle of consternations and affrights, did these inscrutable creatures at the centre freely and fearlessly indulge in all peaceful concernments; yea, serenely revelled in dalliance and delight. But even so, amid the tornadoed Atlantic of my being, do I myself still for ever centrally disport in mute calm; and while ponderous planets of unwaning woe revolve round me, deep down and deep inland there I still bathe me in eternal mildness of joy. (87: *326*)

The Tahiti of man's soul, however, is not transcendental in the usual sense. As the cannibalistic ocean has its upper limit, so also does Tahiti itself which, while it may "carry all summer with it into the clouds," nevertheless *stops* at the clouds. The island *is* an island, rooted ineluctably in the vitalistic biological broth out of which it rises. Ishmael's insular Tahiti, thrusting up through the surface of the "appalling ocean" of man's soul, is thus an image, not of etherealized transcendentalism such as Emerson would recognize, but rather of a naturalistic transcendentalism, a truncated or terminal transcendentalism perhaps best termed *metanaturalism*. Tahiti expresses Ishmael's paradoxical conviction that man is *naturally* more than merely natural. The island image in *Moby-Dick* articulates what Milton Stern has called "Melville's poetically antimaterialistic statements," which are not "antimaterialistic *in se* as much as they are a suggestion that man must accept the independent, amoral, and ultimate reality of the material world as the stuff from which he can fashion for himself an identity which is nobler than the merely physical."[23]

In an 1849 letter to Evert Duyckinck, Melville anticipates the metaphor of the *thought-diver* in *Moby-Dick*. "I love all men who *dive*. Any fish can swim near the surface, but it takes a great whale to go down stairs five miles or more; & if he dont attain the bottom, why, all the lead in Galena can't fashion the plumet that will." Melville deeply admires "the whole corps of thought-divers, that have been diving & coming up again with bloodshot eyes since the world began."[24] Ishmael is one of these divers: "The more I dive into this matter of whaling, and push my researches up to the very springhead of it, so much the more am I impressed with its great honorableness and antiquity" (82: *304*). Similarly, after being nearly lost in the squall that interrupted the first lowering, the diving image expresses Ishmael's attitude toward his own possible sudden demise: "Now then, thought I, unconsciously rolling up the sleeves of my frock, here goes for a cool, collected dive at death and destruction, and the devil fetch the hindmost" (49: *197*). He even prefigures the destruction of the *Pequod* as a dive; aboard the *Moss*, he watches Queequeg dive to the rescue of the bumpkin knocked overboard by the flying boom. "From that hour," Ishmael tells us, "I clove to Queequeg like a barnacle"—and then he gives the first anticipative reference to the final catastrophe: ". . . yea, till poor Queequeg took his last long dive" (13: *61*). Ahab, too, thinks in diving images. Brooding at the cabin-window, he sees the setting sun plunging through the water surface: "The gold brow plumbs the blue. The diver sun—slow dived from noon,—goes down; my soul mounts up!" (37: *147*). Apostrophizing the whale's head hoisted at the *Pequod's* side, Ahab makes Leviathan a diver:

Speak, thou vast and venerable head...; speak, mighty head, and tell us the secret thing that is in thee. Of all divers, thou hast dived the deepest. That head upon which the upper sun now gleams, has moved amid this world's foundations.... O head! thou hast seen enough to split the planets and make an infidel of Abraham, and not one syllable is thine! (70: *264*)

There are risks in any dive through the surface of appearances. The "sunken-eyed young Platonist" at the mast-head who allows himself to be lulled into "unconscious reverie" by "the blending cadence of waves with thoughts" may suddenly find himself taking a dive from which there is no return:

...move your foot or hand an inch; slip your hold at all; and your identity comes back in horror. Over Descartian vortices you hover. And perhaps, at mid-day, in the fairest weather, with one half-throttled shriek you drop through that transparent air into the summer sea, no more to rise for ever. Heed it well, ye Pantheists! (35: *140*)

Pip's psychic dive is also trans-phenomenal, carrying him "down alive to wondrous depths, where strange shapes of the unwarped primal world glided to and fro before his passive eyes" (93: *347*). Tashtego experiences a similar dive while bailing the oil out of the whale's head, suddenly dropping "head-foremost down into this great Tun of Heidelberg, and with a horrible oily gurgling, [going] clean out of sight!" At this moment the tackles part and the head itself starts a last long dive of its own: "... with a thunder-boom, the enormous mass dropped into the sea, like Niagara's Table-Rock into the whirlpool;... poor, buried-alive Tashtego was sinking utterly down to the bottom of the sea!" Finally, the dive of the whale-head precipitates a third dive, again by the redoubtable Queequeg. "But hardly had the blinding vapor cleared away, when a naked figure with a boarding-sword in its hand, was for one swift moment seen hovering over the bulwarks. The next, a loud splash announced that my brave Queequeg had dived to the rescue" (78: *288–89*). Of the three, it is Tashtego's dive which is most clearly a plunge into the white region of the noumenon, the "secret inner chamber and sanctum sanctorum" of Leviathan. In earlier passages Ishmael makes much of the white interiority of the Sperm Whale,

132112

describing Leviathan's "chaste-looking" mouth, "from floor to ceiling, lined, or rather papered with a glistening white membrane, glossy as bridal satins" (74: *280*). The same whiteness is emphasized after the vast body has been peeled of its surtout of blubber; under the black phenomenal skin *any* whale exhibits the noumenal white of Moby Dick. At the "funeral" of this tremendous corpse, "The peeled white body . . . flashes like a marble sepulchre"; the "vast white headless phantom" floating away from the ship is an appalling "great mass of death" (69: *261–62*). Tashtego's dive is similarly trans-phenomenal: to plunge into Leviathan's inner regions is to enter a world the "very whitest and daintiest" (78: *290*), a "silken pearl-colored membrane, like the lining of a fine pelisse, forming the inner surface of the Sperm Whale's case" (77: *287*).

Not only do the constitutive metaphors of *Moby-Dick* develop organically out of the protometaphor of *color: interface: non-color*. They also intersect in the definitive figure of Narcissus with which Ishmael begins his story. The pallidly beautiful image which Narcissus sees glimmering beneath the fountain's surface resembles himself because it is a product of the illuminating *lamp-mind* which, in the act of perception, stamps the world with the features of the unique self. By the same token, the noumenal *me* which peers back at Narcissus out of the watery *not-me* stands as the aboriginal *primal form*, the anteperceptual substrate for all the other primal forms which loom and glide through *Moby-Dick*. Similarly, the *reflective transparency* of Narcissus' fountain parallels the intuitive transparency of Ishmael's ocean, and the dive of Narcissus provides the model for Ishmael as *thought-diver*. Finally, if Narcissus and Ishmael are able to dive at all, it is because of the existence of a metanaturalistic inner Tahiti, a psychic *ocean-island* which furnishes a sense of elevation and separateness, and consequently the requisite sense of self. Thus the figure of Narcissus is the vehicle for the coalescence of the five constitutive metaphors which shape every succeeding page of the novel. It is this coalescence which gives *Moby-Dick* its underlying unity, its conceptual cohesion, its tonal consistency.

THE UNIVERSAL THUMP
Jehovah's Winter World

WE HAVE EXAMINED the existence in *Moby-Dick* of a protometaphorical substrate, out of which five constitutive metaphors develop. But such an analogue-system is structural rather than dynamic, conceptual rather than dramatic. It provides the ideational vehicle of the novel, but it does not make that vehicle "go." What *does* make the vehicle go is the presence of a protodynamic to match the protometaphor. Once again the opening chapter is of definitive importance, giving us the initial adumbration of the protodynamic. Ishmael always goes to sea, he tells us, "as a simple sailor, right before the mast." As such, he becomes the target for directives emanating from everyone over him in the ship's hierarchy. "True, they rather order me about some, and make me jump from spar to spar, like a grasshopper in a May meadow." At first he finds all this "unpleasant enough": to be everybody's lackey "touches one's sense of honor," especially if one comes from an "old established family," and "if just previous to putting your hand into the tar-pot, you have been lording it as a country schoolmaster, making the tallest boys stand in awe of you. The transition is a keen one, I assure you, from a schoolmaster to a sailor, and requires a strong decoction of Seneca and the Stoics to enable you to grin and bear it." But Ishmael commands such humorous stoicism:

> What of it, if some old hunks of a sea-captain orders me to get a broom and sweep down the decks? . . . Who aint a slave? Tell me that. Well, then, however the old sea-captains may order me about— however they may thump and punch me about, I have the satisfaction of knowing that it is all right; that everybody else is one way or other served in much the same way—either in a physical or metaphysical point of view, that is; and so the universal thump is passed round, and all hands should rub each other's shoulder-blades, and be content. (1: *14–15*)*

This characteristically casual passage would be of no importance were it not that the "universal thump," on both the "physical" and "metaphysical" levels, is a central preoccupation of *Moby-Dick* from first page to last. Ishmael encounters it in one of its most pedestrian forms, the physical kick, before the voyage is well begun. When he makes the mistake of mentioning his experience in the merchant service to old Peleg, that old hunks makes it clear that he is accustomed to communicating his desires to the ship's underlings in ways other than purely verbal. "Marchant service be damned," he roars. "Talk not that lingo to me. Dost see that leg?—I'll take that leg away from thy stern, if ever thou talkest of the marchant service to me again. Marchant service indeed!" (16: *68–69*). Peleg means what he says. Manning the capstan that cold Christmas day as the *Pequod* gets under way, Ishmael gets a taste of that physical suasion which is part of life on a whaler. "I felt a sudden sharp poke

* The number before the colon in all parenthetical references in the text indicates chapter, which will be the same for most American editions of *Moby-Dick*; the italicized numbers after the colon indicate page in the Norton Critical Edition of *Moby-Dick*, edited by Harrison Hayford and Hershel Parker (New York: W. W. Norton & Company, 1967).

in my rear, and turning round, was horrified at the apparition of
Captain Peleg in the act of withdrawing his leg from my immediate
vicinity. That was my first kick":

> "Is that the way they heave in the marchant service?" [Peleg] roared.
> "Spring, thou sheep-head; spring, and break thy backbone!" ... And
> so saying, he moved along the windlass, here and there using his leg
> very freely.... Thinks I, Captain Peleg must have been drinking
> something to-day. (22: *95*)

A "situational" version of the universal thump occurs earlier, when
Peter Coffin tricks Ishmael into sharing a bed with a cannibal. Ishmael recognizes that the landlord has been "skylarking with me
not a little," but again he draws upon Seneca and the Stoics:

> However, a good laugh is a mighty good thing, and rather too scarce
> a good thing; the more's the pity. So, if any one man, in his own
> proper person, afford stuff for a good joke to anybody, let him not
> be backward, but let him cheerfully allow himself to spend and be
> spent in that way. (5: *35*)

During the first lowering, when Starbuck's boat, with Ishmael
aboard, is separated from the *Pequod* during a squall, the crew is
recovered from almost certain death by sheer luck. In the subsequent chapter entitled "The Hyena," and as a consequence of this
brush with death, Ishmael develops a "free and easy sort of genial,
desperado philosophy," the central premise of which is that a man
must take "this whole universe for a vast practical joke, though the
wit thereof he but dimly discerns, and more than suspects that the
joke is at nobody's expense but his own." Death and destruction
become wryly comic expressions of the "universal thump." "And
as for small difficulties and worryings, prospects of sudden disaster,
peril of life and limb; all these, and death itself, seem ... only sly,
good-natured hits, and jolly punches in the side bestowed by the
unseen and unaccountable old joker"—which cosmic funny-man,
the chapter title suggests, laughs at man's plight as the hyena laughs,
a sort of scavenger humor with, perhaps, a trifle too much tooth to
it (49: *195–96*).

This preoccupation with the physical and metaphysical "hits" and
"punches" of life furnishes another of the Yankee simplicities of
Moby-Dick, the dramatic relation we may somewhat inelegantly

call the protodynamic of *thumper: thumpee*. Melville does not
achieve the definitive statement of the relation until Billy Budd delivers a consummate thump to Claggart's forehead some forty years
after *Moby-Dick*. But "The Town-Ho's Story" provides the requisite parallel. The "brutal overbearing" of Radney, and the "bitterly provoked vengeance" of Steelkilt are expressed in a series of
thumps and counter-thumps. Radney demands that Steelkilt, who
has just finished an exhausting turn at the ship's pumps, sweep down
the planks and clean up after a pig running loose on the decks, tasks
normally reserved for the lowly ship's boys. This is precisely the
humiliating situation which Ishmael anticipated in Chapter I, when
he asked what it would really matter "if some old hunks of a sea-
captain orders me to get a broom and sweep down the decks? . . .
Who aint a slave?" (1: *15*). The answer must be: Steelkilt aint. He
quietly refuses Radney's command, whereupon the enraged mate
pursues him around the windlass with an "uplifted cooper's club
hammer" in his hand until Steelkilt warns "that if the hammer but
grazed his cheek he (Steelkilt) would murder him. . . . Immediately
the hammer touched the cheek; the next instant the lower jaw of
the mate was stove in his head; he fell on the hatch spouting blood
like a whale" (54: *209–14*). Steelkilt does *not* react to the thumps
of life with the stoical good humor which Ishmael cultivates. This
difference in attitude highlights one of the central concerns of
Moby-Dick, the thumpish nature of life and the question of what
reactive stance the individual, in the role of *thumpee*, ought to take
toward the "unaccountable old joker" or whatever else in the cosmos appears to play the role of *thumper*.

Ahab, for example, consistently images his thoughts as physical
blows. He will "strike through the mask"; he will be like the prisoner
"thrusting through the wall"; he would "strike the sun if it insulted
[him]" (36: *144*). In an especially vivid articulation of the *thumper:
thumpee* protodynamic, the *Pequod's* Captain makes topical reference to Jem ("Deaf") Burke, English boxing champion in 1833,
and William Thompson, called "Bendigo," champion from 1839 to
1845, using these figures to express the thumpish stance of the "great
gods" of the universe.[1]

I laugh and hoot at ye, ye cricket-players, ye pugilists, ye deaf
Burkes and blinded Bendigoes! I will not say as schoolboys do to

bullies,—Take some one of your own size; don't pommel *me*! No, ye've knocked me down, and I am up again; but *ye* have run and hidden. (37: *147*)

But if the bully-gods of the universe mask themselves behind phenomena, great Leviathan is a visible articulation of the untrammeled power they invisibly possess. Ishmael devotes a whole chapter to just the tail of the whale, whose "Titanism of power" can, when "smiting the surface" of the sea, produce a "thunderous concussion [which] resounds for miles"; the "gigantic tail" is "simply irresistible": nothing in this world can stand before "the measureless crush and crash of the sperm whale's ponderous flukes" (86: *315–17*). Another chapter is devoted to the "Battering-Ram" of the whale's head, an "enormous boneless mass" of "compacted collectedness," a "dead, impregnable, uninjurable wall" displaying such "concentrations of potency" that "though the Sperm Whale stove a passage through the Isthmus of Darien, and mixed the Atlantic with the Pacific, you would not elevate one hair of your eye-brow" (76: *284–85*). A third chapter, "The Affidavit," is devoted to the whale's historical ability to "stave in, utterly destroy, and sink" large ships by "vertical bumps," cosmic "thwacks," and "terrible shocks" of "great power and malice" (45: *178–81*). All this prepares one for the climactic thump when "the solid white buttress" of Moby Dick's forehead crushes the *Pequod's* starboard bow, "till men and timbers reeled" (135: *468*). But even this predestinated shock is not the last thump of the novel. As the *Pequod* sinks beneath the surface, out of the waves in mute gesture rises Tashtego's "red arm and a hammer hover[ing] backwardly uplifted in the open air, in the act of nailing the flag faster and yet faster to the subsiding spar." The final *thumpee* is the "sky-hawk" which interposes "its broad fluttering wing between the hammer and the wood," and, victim of Tashtego's last defiant blow at the cosmos, is pulled down with the ship into the abyss (135: *468–69*).

This concentration in *Moby-Dick* on the *physical blow as philosophical analogue* takes on moral significance when articulated as *vengeance*. Bildad and Peleg are "Quakers with a vengeance" (16: *71*); the "vengeful" Radney of the *Town-Ho* faces the "bitterly provoked vengeance" of Steelkilt, who has "complete revenge" when the White Whale himself becomes his "avenger," seizing

Radney in his jaws and taking him to the bottom (54: *209, 221*). Starbuck tells Ahab that he has shipped on the *Pequod* "to hunt whales, not my commander's vengeance. How many barrels will thy vengeance yield thee even if thou gettest it, Captain Ahab?" he asks. When Ahab retorts that "my vengeance will fetch a great premium *here!*," smiting his breast, Starbuck is appalled. "Vengeance on a dumb brute ... that simply smote thee from blindest instinct! Madness!" (36: *143–44*). The supreme expression of insensate and unbridled vengeance in *Moby-Dick*, however, is the Christian God Himself. The vast ocean He has made and on which the *Pequod* sails is a visible, pervasive symbol for the vengeful retribution which He visits on those who offend Him. Noah's Ark, Ishmael reminds us, "the first boat we read of, floated on an ocean, that with Portuguese vengeance had whelmed a whole world without leaving so much as a widow." To Ishmael that vast ocean is daily and hourly reminder of the enormity and cosmic totality of God's vengefulness. "That same ocean rolls now; that same ocean destroyed the wrecked ships of last year. Yea, foolish mortals, Noah's flood is not yet subsided; two thirds of the fair world it yet covers" (58: *235*).

The Christian God thus becomes a central source of the "universal thump." He bears, in fact, a suspicious resemblance to Ishmael's "unaccountable old joker" delivering "hits" and "punches" to man —except that man's relation to God is no joking matter. The pivotal statement of this relationship is Father Mapple's sermon on Jonah, which offers the Christian explanation of the pervasive tragedy of life, the universality of the "universal thump." Mapple's God is a God "chiefly known to me by Thy rod" (9: *51*), and Jonah, after three days' encounter with the "hard hand of God" (9: *48*), is the archetypal thumpee. The hymn which prefaces the sermon suggests why Ishmael would listen with focused intensity to the paradigm of life's meaning which Father Mapple offers. Ishmael's soul is full of "damp, drizzly November," his "hypos" have gotten the "upper hand" of him, he is obsessively fascinated by coffin warehouses and funerals (1: *12*)—and so he would be certain to identify with Jonah, himself in "black distress" and "plunging to despair." It would inevitably occur to Presbyterian Ishmael that his "unbidden infidelities" (7: *41*) might be the result of his failure to find, as Jonah finds, the "Deliverer God" of the hymn, in all His "mercy and . . . power" (9: *44*). Melville may, as Lawrance Thompson suggests, have written the sermon tongue-in-cheek—we will probably never know about that—but it is unlikely that Ishmael would have *listened* tongue-in-cheek.[2]

Instead, as Jonah takes his dive, Ishmael, raptly attentive to Mapple's rhetoric, would dive with him, to surface at the end of the sermon with some truths different from what the orthodox Mapple intended or what the sermon overtly conveys. Ishmael, because he was telling his story to a nineteenth-century American audience, does not take us into his confidence concerning these insights. In fact, one of the most significant things in these early chapters is Ishmael's refusal to comment upon the sermon, even though he is generally the most garrulous and digressive of narrators. As Mapple waves a final benediction, Ishmael simply tells us that "He said no more, but . . . covered his face with his hands, and so remained, kneeling, till all the people had departed, and he was left alone in the place" (9: *51*). Nothing could be more devastatingly eloquent than this lack of comment. It signals the failure of the last attempt Ishmael will make to achieve intellectual repose through the orthodox Christian explanation of the Leviathanism of the cosmos, a Leviathanism which Ishmael sees as a constitutive element of all external nature, in the ocean, the land, the mountains, and even the stars (57: *231–33*). Father Mapple's sermon has if anything probably intensified—rather than meliorated—those hypos which drove Ishmael to the Whaleman's Chapel in the first place. Nor is there anything mysterious about how the intended words of consolation and delight which Father Mapple delivers could fall with such leaden coldness upon Ishmael's heart. For the sermon is actually the supreme statement in *Moby-Dick* of the protodynamic of *thumper: thumpee.* Ishmael, obsessively concerned with the problem of the "universal thump," and particularly with its Leviathanic manifestations, would find the sermon profoundly engrossing—and profoundly disappointing. The reason is simple: the prefatory hymn speaks of a God of "mercy"—but the sermon itself is about a God of vengeance. The Christian explanation, or at least Father Mapple's explanation, is that the Leviathanism which surrounds man and so often overwhelms him is simply God's vengeful response to man's guilt. The sermon is only a superbly articulated version of that deific "Portuguese vengeance" of which the boundless diluvian ocean is perpetual reminder.

This vengeful aspect of the Jonah sermon is not apparent so long as one reads it from the vantage-point of a comfortable Christian orthodoxy. All one has to do is suspend critical judgment and marshal an habitual acceptance when Mapple asserts that his sermon will retail the story of "the sin, hard-heartedness, suddenly awakened fears, the swift punishment, repentance, prayers, and finally the deliverance and joy of Jonah" (9: 45). Since Ishmael says nothing which might serve as a guide in evaluating the sermon, we might be inclined to settle for a conventional reading, were it not for the fact that we know that Ishmael never views anything with conventional eyes. He has just finished reading the despairing cenotaphs masoned into the Chapel walls, graveless gravestones which document in "lines that seem to gnaw upon all Faith" (7: 41) the violence, the titanic power of the whale, resulting so often in the "speechlessly quick chaotic bundling of a man into Eternity" (7: 41). He would almost certainly be struck by a parallel violence at work in the Jonah story. With "endless processions of the whale" (1: 16) floating through his soul, Ishmael would be bound to ponder Father Mapple's assertion that "God came upon [Jonah] in the whale," so that Leviathan, by sheer brute power plunging Jonah all helpless into "living gulfs of doom . . . ten thousand fathoms down," becomes the direct, concrete expression of an equivalent brute power in God.

Similarly, Ishmael would inevitably be struck by the gross disproportion between means and ends which seems to characterize the activities of the Christian God. Jonah's "wilful disobedience" of God's "hard command" is in the deific moral economy sufficient to justify a "dreadful storm," a maelstrom of "black sky and raging sea" and "reeling timbers" which brings not only the guilty Jonah to the brink of destruction, but a ship, "like to break," and her innocent crew as well. Ishmael tells his story a century before the development of nuclear-war technology and its special, ghastly nomenclature, but we may borrow a pair of terms from that technology to characterize the storm-brewing and whale-dispatching

God of Father Mapple's sermon. He is an *overkill* God, a *megaton* God, achieving His ends by the broadcast application of brute power in quantities nearly sufficient to destroy a world, and therefore certain to reduce "frighted Jonah" to the "cringing attitudes" which are the only possible response of minuscule man to Jehovah's moral imperatives. It is no wonder that "Terrors upon terrors run shouting through [Jonah's] soul." Neither would the analytical Ishmael be likely to overlook the fact that the "true and faithful repentance" which "aghast Jonah" discovers in the belly of the whale is the direct consequence of the animal terror which God's storm and God's whale have generated in him. Father Mapple's God is, like the God of the sharks and in Queequeg's phrase, "one dam Ingin."[3]

The correlation of Father Mapple's Whale-God with Queequeg's Shark-God is more than superficial. The Ishmael who listens to the sermon is the same Ishmael who later will speak of the "universal cannibalism" of the sea (58: *235*), who will see much of human life as a "shocking sharkish business," and who, watching the "countless numbers" of sharks ravaging the whale tied alongside the *Pequod*, will obliquely suggest that there may after all be a certain "propriety" in "conciliating the devil" (64: *249–50*). Surely *this* Ishmael, neurotically sensitive to whatever "half-formed, foetal suggestions" (41: *156*) may lie under the surface of Father Mapple's rhetoric, would have experienced a rising sense of horror, an exacerbation of an already almost psychotic hypo, when he realized that the vehicle of God's vengeance upon Jonah is a sharkishness of which file-toothed Queequeg, sitting a few pews away, is a visible emblem. Jonah is *eaten alive* by God, or at least by God's agent. In the midst of "masterless commotion" Jonah "drops seething into the yawning jaws awaiting him," whereupon "the whale shoots-to all his ivory teeth, like so many white bolts, upon his prison." "Swallowed down to living gulfs of doom," Jonah is *devoured* by God.

This is an admittedly neurotic reading of the sermon, but Ishmael, our "only true lamp," *is* neurotic. If we define neurosis as the capacity to realize certain truths with an incandescent verity from which most of us are protected, then we can conclude that hypo-ridden Ishmael arrives at a level of truth concerning the Christian explanation of Leviathanism from which Father Mapple's less perceptive auditors are happily insulated. That this truth which Ishmael almost certainly perceived is also what Melville himself intended is suggested by the mute presence of Queequeg. Melville brings the cannibal to the Whaleman's Chapel for the sermon, even though he has no dramatic function in the scene, and never refers to the sermon he has shared with Ishmael. Concerning the Christian cannibal-God, cannibal Queequeg is as silent as Christian Ishmael.

On the most fundamental level, however, the wrathful Jehovah of the sermon is a special sort of primal form. It may be objected that the Christian God can hardly be included among the other primal forms of *Moby-Dick* because, unlike the anteformal squid or the White Whale, Jehovah is visually inaccessible and therefore perceptually formless. But this is just the point: existing outside the "sensuous manifold," beyond nature, inaccessible, invisible, and incomprehensible, Jehovah is the primal form reduced to formlessness by the transcendentalism implicit in the Christian world-view. Because He *is* transcendental, Jehovah becomes the central statement of the agentistic problem which is part of the Christian world-view. Since *Moby-Dick* is a book about the natural world and man's relation to it, and since Ishmael's sensibility is so overwhelmingly nature-oriented, the question of the place of nature in Father Mapple's sermon is relevant. Viewed through the vehicle of Ishmael's sensibility, it becomes obvious that nature, both animate and inanimate, must act and does act in the Christian world-view as the *agent* of a transcendentally conceived God who cannot act for Himself in this world because He is so radically and intractably in another. Hence, in Father Mapple's sermon, sea and storm are God's agents, and the whale is God's agent. The consequence is the alienation and separation of *man from nature*. Nature, viewed agentistically, inevitably becomes the antagonist of man. Jonah coming on deck during the height of the storm is "sprung upon by a panther billow"; and the storm itself is a consequence of nature's revulsion: "The sea rebels; he will not bear the wicked burden" of Jonah.

Just as important is the way in which the agentistic world-view implicit in the Christian paradigm causes the alienation and separation of *man from man*. Steeped like Ahab in agentism, the crew of Jonah's beleaguered ship cast lots to discover "for whose cause this great tempest was upon them." When the lot falls to Jonah, the terrified crew themselves become part of the agentistic continuum: "... then, with one hand raised invokingly to God, with the other they not unreluctantly lay hold of Jonah," flinging him overboard and into the whale's maw. Being God's agents, the crew cannot be Jonah's friends, much less his brothers—although before God's "hard hand" forces them into the agentistic role the crew, while listening to Jonah's story, are "still ... pitiful," and "mercifully turn from him, and seek by other means to save the ship." The Christian Jehovah apparently finds this merciful response to Jonah's plight intolerable, for immediately "the indignant gale howls louder" until the crew is forced to knuckle under to megaton force. "Woe to him," Father Mapple later warns, "who seeks to pour oil upon the waters when God has brewed them into a gale!" Human brotherhood and human mercy have no place in Mapple's sermon-world.

On the deepest level of all, the need of a transcendentally conceived God for agents in a world above which He must stand, results in the separation and alienation of *man from himself.*[4] If man must be God's agent, then he cannot be his own agent. To the extent that he is true to God, he must be untrue to himself—although Father Mapple phrases the idea somewhat differently. "And if we obey God," the preacher insists, "we must disobey ourselves; and it is in this disobeying ourselves, wherein the hardness of obeying God consists." Guilt, in this schema, is man's awareness of the extent to which he has failed to subordinate his inner and personal voice to an outer and transcendental voice. With guilt comes self-alienation: Jonah, waiting in a windowless cabin while the ship takes on cargo, is appalled by the way a gimbal-lamp appears to be hanging out-of-true in the heeled-over vessel. His sense of guilt and fear cause him to take the misalignment of the cabin walls as symbolic of a similar misalignment or disjunction within himself. "Oh! so my conscience hangs in me! ... straight upward, so it burns; but the chambers of my soul are all in crookedness!" The inexorable pressures of the "hard hand of God" result in a deep and debilitating inner malaise, a pervasive sense of psychic distortion, of "crookedness" of self.

Thus the Christian imperatives demand the unequivocal dissociation of man from nature, from other men, and from himself.

It is no accident that this triple alienation precisely describes Captain Ahab, Christian and Quaker, the "crooked" or "ugly" Narcissus whom we will examine two chapters hence. As recompense for such terrible distortions, Father Mapple can only offer an eventual, other-worldly "Delight"—a word that with thudding repetitiveness he uses ten times in the closing paragraph of the sermon, and a word which takes on bitterly ironic overtones when, in Chapter 131, the *Pequod* finally encounters a vessel called the *Delight*. All of this suggests that the central intention of the opening "land" chapters of *Moby-Dick*, that substantial portion of the book which takes place before the *Pequod* makes its symbolic break with the Christian shore, has to do with these distortions, this "crookedness," this de-naturalizing of man which Christian belief, centered on a tran-scendental Godhead as primal form, makes possible. For if the Christian Jehovah is not Himself perceptually accessible, His world —Christian New England—is entirely so. Wintry, ice-locked, snow-covered New England—typified in New Bedford and Nantucket—is as much a noumenally pallid primal form as the squid or the spirit-spout.

Ishmael is aware that summer-time New Bedford is "sweet to see; full of fine maples—long avenues of green and gold." "So omnipotent is art," he continues, that the phenomenal flower-curtain is exquisitely developed in this prosperous whaling town. In "many a district" in the summer months "bright terraces of flowers" match the beauty of New Bedford women, who "bloom like their own red roses" (6: *38–39*). But Ishmael chooses to make his break with the land in December when the vernal flower-curtain is stripped away by Euroclydon's cold blasts so that we may glimpse the nou-menal verities which lie hidden beneath the sensuous surface. In winter New Bedford (and Nantucket) become these "Puritanic sands," this "scraggy scoria of a country," composed of "the barren refuse rocks thrown aside at creation's final day" (6: *38–39*). The "packed snow and ice" of a bitter New England winter, with the whole country locked in "congealed frost lay[ing] ten inches thick in a hard, asphaltic pavement" of "flinty projections" (2: *17*) turns this Christian stronghold into a kind of geographical noumenon, an impression which Ishmael reinforces when, gliding down the Acush-

net river aboard the *Moss* on their way to Nantucket, he and Queequeg look back on the "terraces of streets" of New Bedford, "their
ice-covered trees all glittering in the clear, cold air" (13: *59*).

In fact, Jehovah's New England is unutterably inhospitable. Ishmael arrives in New Bedford on a "howling night," finds himself in
a "dreary street" with "gloom towards the north" and "darkness
towards the south," finally discovers the Spouter-Inn standing on a
"sharp bleak corner, where that tempestuous wind Euroclydon kept
up a worse howling than ever it did about poor Paul's tossed craft,"
proceeds to "scrape the ice from [his] frosted feet," pauses in the
entry-way to contemplate a picture which reminds him of a "Hyperborean winter scene" or "the breaking-up of the ice-bound stream
of Time," and is shortly ushered with others into a dining room
"cold as Iceland" where "We were fain to button up our monkey
jackets, and hold to our lips cups of scalding tea with our half
frozen fingers." After this polar meal he spends some time in the bar-
room, where the crew of the *Grampus* appears like "an eruption of
bears from Labrador," with their beards "stiff with icicles" (2: *17–
20*; 3: *20–23*). On the Sunday morning following Ishmael goes to
the Whaleman's Chapel through "driving sleet and mist" (7: *39*),
listens to the "howling of the shrieking, slanting storm" while Father
Mapple delivers his sermon (9: *49*), and brings to a close this frigid
encounter with the arctic Christian world when the *Pequod* sails on
a "short, cold Christmas." As "the short northern day merged into
night, we found ourselves almost broad upon the wintry ocean,
whose freezing spray cased us in ice, as in polished armor" (22: *95*).

This repetitive stress on coldness is more than merely meteorol-
ogical. The boreal frigidity of Jehovah's Christian world is visual
and tactile analogue of a deeper, far more terrible coldness in the
hearts of New England's people. Physical iciness in *Moby-Dick*
is a correlate of moral iciness. Ishmael speaks of the "ice of indifference" between himself and Queequeg which a brief acquaintance
"soon thawed," leaving them "cronies," in bed together on a "hearts'
honeymoon, . . . a cosy, loving pair." "I felt," Ishmael confesses, "a
melting in me." But the thaw is due to Queequeg's tropical pagan
warmth. Ishmael stresses that "Christian kindness has proved but
hollow courtesy," nothing more than "civilized hypocrisies and
bland deceits" (10: *53–54*). The extracetological evidence rein-

forces this reading. William H. Gilman has pointed out that Mel-
ville's "principal target" in writing *Redburn* "was the appalling
dearth of real brotherhood, human sensitivity and charity in the
Christian world of mid-nineteenth century,"[5] a point confirmed by
Redburn's assertion that "We talk of the Turks, and abhor the can-
nibals; but may not some of *them*, go to heaven, before some of *us*?
We may have civilized bodies and yet barbarous souls."[6] Certainly,
Melville saw a frightening reality lurking under the surface of
Christianity. Tyrus Hillway remarks on how Melville was struck
by the "dull barrenness and unfruitfulness of [the] land of the
Gospel" during his tour of the Middle East; "its atmosphere seemed
not godly but somehow diabolic"[7]—a diabolism prefigured in the
New England of *Moby-Dick*. Before Ishmael meets his pagan
roommate at the Spouter-Inn, landlord Peter Coffin explains that
this yet-to-be-seen harpooneer has returned from the South Seas
with a large stock of embalmed "New Zealand heads" which are
"great curios, you know," in Christian New Bedford. Trade has
been brisk, the landlord assures Ishmael, "and he's sold all on 'em
but one, and that one he's trying to sell to-night, cause to-morrow's
Sunday, and it would not do to be sellin' human heads about the
streets when folks is goin' to churches." Apparently Jehovah's
people freely engage with Queequeg in such "cannibal business," as
Ishmael calls it—except, of course, on the Lord's Day (3: *26–27*).

If the Christians of New Bedford and Nantucket are willing to
engage in "cannibal business" ashore, they are much more so inclined when at sea. The Quakers of Nantucket "are the most
sanguinary of all sailors and whale-hunters. They are fighting Quakers; they are Quakers with a vengeance" (16: *71*). Pious Captain
Bildad has been, as Ishmael tells us, "originally educated according
to the strictest sect of Nantucket Quakerism," and has remained true
to these rigid principles throughout his life and despite many tempta-
tions. Ishmael remarks, however, a certain "lack of common consistency" in the Bible-reading and hymn-singing Bildad who, though
"refusing, from conscientious scruples, to bear arms against land
invaders, yet himself had illimitably invaded the Atlantic and
Pacific; and though a sworn foe to human bloodshed, yet had he in
his straight-bodied coat, spilled tuns upon tuns of leviathan gore"
(16: *72*).

What Bildad is, is *sharkish*. Significantly, this word is furnished us by Bildad's Quaker partner, Captain Peleg, who expresses his suspicion to Ishmael that the latter's lungs may be soft: "...thou dost not talk shark a bit," the old whaleman complains (16: *69*). Peleg uses the same term again when Bildad attempts to introduce Queequeg to the Christian religion. "Avast there, avast there, Bildad, avast now spoiling our harpooneer," Peleg roars. "Pious harpooneers never make good voyagers—it takes the *shark* out of 'em; no harpooneer is worth a straw who aint pretty *sharkish*" (18: *85*; italics mine). Old Bildad and Peleg, Quakers though they are, in finding a crew for the *Pequod* have made sharkishness their prime criterion. Horrified Starbuck describes the men they have signed for the voyage as "a heathen crew that have small touch of human mothers in them! Whelped somewhere by the sharkish sea" (38: *148*). Nor is the sharkishness of the *Pequod's* owners confined to the professional and dispassionate pursuit of whales. Ishmael tells us that crabbed Bildad, during his sea-days, had the reputation of an "incorrigible old hunks" and a "bitter, hard task-master" whose crews "were mostly all carried ashore to the hospital, sore exhausted and worn out." With characteristic understatement, Ishmael adds: "For a pious man, especially for a Quaker, [Bildad] was certainly rather hard-hearted, to say the least" (16: *72*). There is a strong resemblance between Bildad's hard-handed treatment of his crews, and Jehovah's hard-handed treatment of "bruised and beaten" Jonah. If Bildad and Peleg are sharkish, they can refer to a well-established, indeed unimpeachable, precedent for a severity which is hardly distinguishable from unabashed brutality.

All of this comes to sharp focus in that central symbol of Christian sharkishness in *Moby-Dick*, the *Pequod* herself. The name is no accident. In his initial description of this "cannibal of a craft," Ishmael makes explicit references to the Pequod War and its consequences. "*Pequod*, you will no doubt remember, was the name of a celebrated tribe of Massachusetts [actually Connecticut] Indians, now extinct as the ancient Medes" (16: *67*). From various sources,[8] both Melville and Ishmael would have known of the overkill vengeance which Jehovah's people wreaked upon the Pequods for relatively minor depredations, and in particular the attack by these Christians upon the Indian fort near Mystic, Connecticut. All the wigwams were set on fire, most of the Indians burning to death, and the rest, with the exception of a few girls, being put to the sword as they attempted to flee. Estimates indicate that between 500 and 800 warriors were slain in a single night. Not satisfied with this butchery, the English pursued those Pequods not caught in the Mystic massacre into the Unquowas swamp near Fairfield and exterminated them. The result was, in Timothy Dwight's words, a "tribe . . . so far annihilated as to be thenceforth without a government and without a name."

Ishmael stresses that the *Pequod* is even more sharkish than her name. For "more than half a century," the vessel has been engaged in the "wild business" of whaling. During his own term as chief mate, Peleg, indulging a cannibal taste which belies his Quakerism, had decorated and fitted her with a barbarity which makes this "rare old craft" the external symbol of an internal moral condition:

> She was apparelled like any barbaric Ethiopian emperor, his neck heavy with pendants of polished ivory. She was a thing of trophies. A cannibal of a craft, tricking herself forth in the chased bones of her enemies. All round, her unpanelled, open bulwarks were garnished like one continuous jaw, with the long sharp teeth of the sperm whale, inserted there for pins, to fasten her old hempen thews and tendons to. (16: *67*)

The *Pequod* is one great, predacious *jaw*, expressive of a savagery underlying Christianity which the savages themselves would be hard-pressed to emulate. Moreover, Melville exploits the pallid connotations of the word *ivory* to turn the *Pequod* into another primal form. While her "old hull's complexion was darkened like a French grenadier's," the overall impression is one of whiteness. Her rigging-sheaves are of "sea-ivory," and so is her tiller, carved "from the long narrow lower jaw of her hereditary foe" (16: *67*). Ahab's cabin-table is "ivory-inlaid" (34: *131*); so indeed are the cabins (81: *302*). As the *Pequod* plunges into the frigid Atlantic on Christmas night "The long rows of teeth on the bulwarks glistened in the moonlight; and like the white ivory tusks of some huge elephant, vast curving icicles depended from the bows" (22: *95*). Ishmael again recalls this picture of tusked ferocity in the next chapter, speaking of the *Pequod's* "vindictive bows" thrusting into the "cold malicious waves" (23: *97*). Approaching Cape Horn, it is the "ivory-tusked Pequod [which] sharply bowed to the blast, and gored the dark waves in her madness" (51: *201*). Repeatedly, the ship is for Ishmael the "ivory Pequod" (48: *193*; 51: *199*; 67: *257*).

Because all of this ivory and noumenal whiteness is the work of Peleg, the *Pequod* is another example of the illuminating and shaping lamp-mind at work, and an instance of the metaphor of the sculptured noumenon. Just as Queequeg by his carving imposes his bodily *self* upon the carpenter's "box," endowing its rough-hewn noumenal neutrality with definitive moral meaning and final ontological finish, so does Peleg shape the original *Pequod* to a sharkishness which is a projection of the predacious imperatives of his own moral being. Just as Peleg shapes the *Pequod* in his own moral image, so do the Christians of Jehovah's New England shape God to *their* image. Captain Peleg's *Pequod* suggests that if predatory Jehovah is "one dam Ingin," it is because the people who worship him are mostly dam Ingins.

Sharkish Jehovah is not the only god who moves through the early "land" pages of *Moby-Dick*. There is also Queequeg's little god Yojo, a radically different product of man's tendency toward anthropomorphic projection. Nothing could be more symbolically eloquent than the scene which greets Ishmael when he returns to the Spouter-Inn after Father Mapple's sermon. He discovers Queequeg (who had rather impolitely left the Chapel in the middle of the sermon) ensconced in the bar-room:

> He was sitting on a bench before the fire, with his feet on the stove hearth, and in one hand was holding close up to his face that little negro idol of his; peering hard into its face, and with a jack-knife gently whittling away at its nose, meanwhile humming to himself in his heathenish way. (10: *51*)

As in the case of Queequeg's coffin and Captain Peleg's *Pequod*, a carving metaphor is used to express the projective and shaping powers of the lamp-mind. The language of the passage is carefully structured to stress the face-to-face, *vis-à-vis* relationship between Queequeg and Yojo, so that the little "Congo idol" (3: *30*), his nose being reshaped to Queequeg's satisfaction, becomes an expressive bit of Kantian skrimshander. Yojo is what Queequeg wants him to be, and nothing more.

Yojo is another primal form, and in fact part of a tripartite cluster of primal forms. It is no accident that like humpbacked Moby Dick, Yojo is a "curious little deformed image with a hunch on its back" (3: *30*)—and it is even less of an accident that Yojo shares this deformity with yet another primal form, the "badger-haired old merman, with a hump on his back" of Stubb's "Queen Mab" dream (31: *115*). Unlike most of the other primal forms in *Moby-Dick*—the squid, the spirit-spout, and the White Whale—Yojo is an intense *black* instead of noumenal white, a fact which Ishmael stresses. Yojo is, he tells us, "exactly the color of a three days' old Congo baby" (3: *30*), a "bit of black wood" (10: *54*). This blackness places Yojo in man's epistemological color-world, the world of natural, sensuous, immediate, often Adamic apprehension. Yojo is a deific projection accessible to touch and sight, to feel and heft, to tactile realization, so that he stands in polar opposition to the transcendental Jehovah, invisible and metaphenomenal, arrogantly above and beyond the world that man actually knows. Yojo is, like the Tahiti ocean-island image, counter-transcendental. Accustomed by his Christian and Presbyterian background to a God who is separated from nature, Ishmael cannot as yet see that Yojo is expressive of a healthy union with the physical world which sets Queequeg apart from all the Christians in the novel. Queequeg derives his humanizing warmth from Yojo: the "shrine" or "chapel" which Queequeg chooses for Yojo at the Spouter-Inn is the fireplace; Yojo is ensconced, "like a tenpin, between the andirons" (3: *30*). Similarly, just as wooden Yojo sustains the union of Queequeg with nature, so he sustains the union of Queequeg with his fellow men. Ishmael in the Whaleman's Chapel worshipped, if that is the word, in isolation. But back at the Spouter-Inn when he decides to "turn idolator" at Queequeg's behest, the result is human union rather than disunion:

> So I kindled the shavings; helped prop up the innocent little idol; offered him burnt biscuit with Queequeg; salaamed before him twice or thrice; kissed his nose; and that done, we undressed and went to bed, at peace with our own consciences and all the world. (10: *54*)

Yojo thus brings Ishmael the peace his hypo-ridden psyche seeks, a unity with both man and nature which is in sharp contrast to the alienation he found in the Whaleman's Chapel.

Most significant is the contrast between Jehovah and Yojo in terms of the protodynamic of *thumper: thumpee*. Jehovah's power is transcendental and unlimited; He is an overkill God whose "Portuguese vengeance" swamps the world with megaton force. Little Yojo is subject to the same contingencies with which man himself must cope. He is no omnicompetent deity, but instead, as Queequeg explains to Ishmael, "a rather good sort of god, who perhaps meant well enough upon the whole, but in all cases did not succeed in his benevolent designs" (16: *66*). He is a human god—and because he is human, he keeps Queequeg human, just as Jehovah, being inhuman, forces His worshippers to inhumanity. That Yojo is no terrifying thumper is suggested by the casual way in which, worship over, Queequeg dumps him into his grego pocket, "as carelessly as if he were a sportsman bagging a dead woodcock" (3: *30*).

While the point is not developed in *Moby-Dick*, Yojo probably stands in about the same relation to his worshippers as the Polynesian gods of the early *Typee* stood in relation to theirs. A typical instance is the doll-god Moa Artua who, when he did not promptly come up with answers to the questions posed to him by Kolory, was beaten about the head, stripped of his tappa and red cloth, and covered from sight; he was a "poor devil of a deity, . . . cuffed about, cajoled, and shut up in a box." When another island deity, a "grotesquely shaped log," accidentally fell over on Kory-Kory, the latter "leaped furiously to his feet, and seizing [a] stick, began beating the poor image: every moment or two pausing and talking to it in the most violent manner, as if upbraiding it for the accident." The gods of *Typee* are "luckless idols, . . . receiv[ing] more hard knocks than supplications." The narrator concludes: "I do not wonder that some of them looked so grim, and stood so bolt upright as if fearful of looking to the right or the left lest they should give anyone offense."[9] *Typee* gives us a total reversal of the protodynamic of *thumper: thumpee*, with natural man thumping his gods rather than the other way around. Similarly, it has never occurred to Queequeg that he should *fear* Yojo. The Congo idol, contingent deity that he is, will never force Queequeg into those "cringing attitudes" (9: *48*) which characterize Jonah's relation to Jehovah. Jehovah is man's enemy. Yojo is his friend.

V

QUEEN MAB
The Pyramid and Merman as Primal Forms

THUMP AND COUNTER-THUMP, the physical blow as philosophical analogue: here is another of those Yankee simplicities which gleam steadily beneath the multiplex surface of *Moby-Dick*. Ahab tells Starbuck that "I'd strike the sun if it insulted me" (36: *144*) *—and one of the central questions of the novel is whether this counter-strike philosophy represents a viable way of responding to the "uni-

* The number before the colon in all parenthetical references in the text indicates chapter, which will be the same for most American editions of *Moby-Dick*; the italicized numbers after the colon indicate page in the Norton Critical Edition of *Moby-Dick*, edited by Harrison Hayford and Hershel Parker (New York: W. W. Norton & Company, 1967).

versal thump" implicit in much cosmic activity. Although it has been ignored in most critical estimates, Chapter 31, dealing with second-mate Stubb's "Queen Mab" dream, provides an exhaustive analysis of the question well *before* Ahab persuades the hypnotized crew to become parties to his vengeful counter-thump against Moby Dick. The *Pequod's* Captain, who will brook no insult nor abide any affront to his own Sultan ego, is nevertheless quick enough to thump others in this way, as Stubb is one of the first to learn. When the second mate lodges a mild complaint because Ahab is thoughtlessly pacing the nighttime quarter-deck, his ivory leg by its reverberant thumping keeping Stubb from sleep, Ahab turns on him in sudden anger, dismissing both him and his complaint with brutal abruptness: "Down, dog, and kennel!" When Stubb persists, asserting that "I am not used to be spoken to that way, sir; I do but less than half like it, sir," Ahab increases the magnitude of the verbal blow he has already delivered: "Then be called ten times a donkey, and a mule, and an ass, and begone, or I'll clear the world of thee!" Stubb places this exchange within the overarching *thumper: thumpee* paradigm of the novel: "I was never served so before," he mutters while hastily retreating below-decks, "without giving a hard blow for it" —and he then reconceptualizes Ahab's verbal blow as a physical kick, thus relating the insult directly to Ishmael's own earlier experience at the capstan with Captain Peleg's broad foot:

> But how's that? didn't he call me a dog? blazes! he called me ten times a donkey, and piled a lot of jackasses on top of *that*! He might as well have kicked me, and done with it. Maybe he *did* kick me, and I didn't observe it, I was so taken all aback with his brow, somehow. It flashed like a bleached bone. (29: *113–14*)

Then, "turned . . . wrong side out" by the experience, Stubb returns to his bunk to dream the dream which he recounts to third-mate Flask the next day. "Such a queer dream, King-Post, I never had. You know the old man's ivory leg, well I dreamed he kicked me with it; and when I tried to kick back, upon my soul, my little man, I kicked my leg right off! And then, presto! Ahab seemed a pyramid, and I, like a blazing fool, kept kicking at it." While Stubb indefatigably kicks away at this oneiric pyramid, he speculates concerning the precise significance of a kick delivered, not by a "real leg," but rather by a "false leg" such as Ahab's. As if emphasizing the relationship of his dream to Ishmael's earlier thoughts on the attitude one ought to take toward both the "physical" and "metaphysical" varieties of "universal thump" (1: *15*)—as well as prefiguring the thumpishly vengeful antagonism of Radney and Steelkilt in "The Town-Ho's Story" (54: *208–24*)—Stubb burdens little Flask with a careful distinction between *two sorts of thumps*:

> And there's a mighty difference between a *living thump* and a *dead thump*. That's what makes a blow from the hand, Flask, fifty times more savage to bear than a blow from a cane. The living member— that makes the living insult, my little man. (31: *115*; italics mine)

All the while Stubb is working this problem out in his dream, he continues "stubbing my silly toes against that cursed pyramid." But he is suddenly interrupted. "While I was battering away at the pyramid, a sort of badger-haired old merman, with a hump on his back, takes me by the shoulders, and slews me round. 'What are you 'bout?' says he.... 'And what business is that of yours, I should like to know, Mr. Humpback?'" Stubb somewhat combatively inquires. "'Do *you* want a kick?'"

> By the lord, Flask, I had no sooner said that, than he turned round his stern to me, bent over, and dragging up a lot of seaweed he had for a clout—what do you think, I saw?—why thunder alive, man, his stern was stuck full of marlinspikes, with the points out. Says I, on second thoughts, 'I guess I won't kick you, old fellow.' 'Wise Stubb,' said he, 'wise Stubb;' and kept muttering it all the time, a sort of eating of his own gums like a chimney hag. (31: *115*)

The dream concludes with the merman advising Stubb to quietly suffer Ahab's kicks: "... account his kicks honors; and on no account kick back; for you can't help yourself, wise Stubb. Don't you see that pyramid?" (31: *116*).

Now, how seriously are we to take this apparently nonsensical oneiric sequence? Flask dismisses it with the remark that "it seems a sort of foolish to me" (31: *116*), and most students of Melville appear to have come quietly to the same conclusion. The problem is that *Stubb* is the source of the dream, and for over a century readers of *Moby-Dick* have felt themselves to be on safe ground in not taking the second mate very seriously. Tyrus Hillway dismisses

Stubb as "easy-going," and Edward H. Rosenberry sees him simply as the source of the "comic ballast" of the novel, contrapuntal to Ahab's "tragic intensity."[1] There is some sanction for such a casual view. Ishmael, speaking rather enviously, one suspects, of "the invulnerable jollity of indifference and recklessness in Stubb" (41: *162*), characterizes him in an early chapter as "A happy-go-lucky":

> ...neither craven nor valiant; taking perils as they came with an indifferent air; and while engaged in the most imminent crisis of the chase, toiling away, calm and collected as a journeyman joiner engaged for the year. Good-humored, easy, and careless, he presided over his whale-boat as if the most deadly encounter were but a dinner, and his crew all invited guests.... Long usage had, for this Stubb, converted the jaws of death into an easy chair. (27: *105*)

The narrator of *Pierre* remarks that "some men refuse to solve any present problem, for fear of making still more work for themselves in that way,"[2] and this seems at first glance to be Stubb's case: "Think not, is my eleventh commandment," he roundly asserts; "and sleep when you can, is my twelfth" (29: *114*).

Such flippancy, however, may be nothing more than Stubb's *manner*, a face he puts on to deceive Ahab, and Ishmael—and even, perhaps, the reader. It is possible that his off-handedness finds its source not in a crass superficiality, but rather in a wise, instinctive, shrewdly humorous acceptance of things-as-they-are. It may be that Stubb is actually closer to a true estimate of the Leviathanic cosmos than anyone else on the *Pequod*; he may, indeed, be the healthiest man in the crew excepting only Queequeg. Certainly, it becomes obvious that Stubb is not nearly so "careless" and "indifferent" as Ishmael's early-on estimate would suggest. It is Stubb who is responsible for Pip's insanity, since Pip jumped from Stubb's boat, and it was the second mate's decision to abandon him in the midst of the ocean's "heartless immensity"—though it is often forgotten that Stubb thought that one or the other of two following boats would immediately rescue the child (93: *347*). But the searing guilt which Stubb feels hardly suggests an easy-going superficiality. As he watches Pip, the last of the seven interpreters, approach the doubloon to give his reading from Murray's *Grammar*, Stubb can hardly bear to look upon that "unearthly idiot face.... I can stand the rest," he mutters, "for they have plain wits; but he's too crazy-

witty for my sanity." Tortured by both guilt and pity, he indulges
in self-recrimination: "Pip—poor boy! would he had died, or I; he's
half horrible to me." And again: "... poor lad!—I could go hang
myself" (99: *362–63*).

Equally revealing is Stubb's reaction to the "wide-slaughtering
Typhoon" (116: *409*) which assails the *Pequod*. He lightly asserts
that "it's all in fun," and sings a ditty the burden of which is that "a
joker is the whale," and the ocean "a funny, sporty, gamy, jesty,
joky, hoky-poky lad." When pious Starbuck, who values a pre-
tentious high seriousness almost as much as some readers, chides the
second mate, telling him to be quiet if he is a brave man, Stubb's
reply suggests a depth of seasoned self-awareness which vindicates
the merman's description of him as "wise Stubb." "But I am not
a brave man," he flatly tells Starbuck; "never said I was a brave
man; I am a coward; and I sing to keep up my spirits" (119: *413–
14*). Moreover, he has the sensitivity to know when "hoky-poky"
humor is no longer an appropriate response. When the "tri-pointed
trinity of flames" appears on the *Pequod's* masts, it is he who expresses immediate, heart-felt, and reverent awe: "The corpusants
have mercy on us all!" he cries (119: *415*). Finally, when Captain
Gardiner of the *Rachel* appeals to Ahab to help him find his sea-
lost son, it is Stubb's humane response which is juxtaposed to Ahab's
brutal refusal: "We must save that boy," he unhesitatingly exclaims (128: *434–35*).

I make these efforts to rescue the *Pequod's* second mate from a
century-long pejorative estimation because it is essential to see that
beneath a mask of flippancy Stubb stands as a serious figure of
consummate realism, and that his "Queen Mab" dream is an expression of that realism, indispensable to an understanding of later
dramatic developments in *Moby-Dick*. If the novel can be said to
have a "key" (I would not want to push such an idea very far),
Stubb's dream is it. In the opening lines, for example, having been
kicked by Ahab, Stubb counter-thumpishly kicks back. The moment he does this, he sustains the same physical loss that Ahab has
already sustained: "... upon my soul, ... I kicked my leg right off!"
Moments later, Ahab turns into a *pyramid*. This metamorphosis
suggests that the dream is *really about Leviathan*, since the novel is
studded with carefully-placed references which relate the whale to

the pyramid figure. Ishmael describes Moby Dick as having "a peculiar snow-white wrinkled forehead, and a high, pyramidical white hump" (41: *159*). Later he speaks of the whale's hump as a "solid pyramid of fat" (65: *255*). Still later he refers to the Sperm Whale's "pyramidical silence" (79: *292*). Finally, Ishmael complains that American portrayers of whaling "seem entirely content with presenting the mechanical outline of things, such as the vacant profile of the whale; which . . . is about tantamount to sketching the profile of a pyramid" (56: *230–31*).

But the whale-pyramid figure is only the first link in a knotted *chain* of images. The pyramid which Stubb kicks is linked to the merman because the pyramid which is the Sperm Whale's hump reappears in the dream as the merman's hump. Stubb, fearful that we will miss the connection, pointedly calls the merman "Mr. Humpback." The range of connection extends even further: while Ahab is not literally humpbacked, the image nevertheless becomes associated with him when he complains that Starbuck "takes me for the hunchbacked skipper of some coasting smack" (120: *418*), and when he asks the blacksmith to fabricate "a pair of steel shoulder-blades," referring to himself obliquely as "a pedlar aboard with a crushing pack" (108: *390*). Finally, this series of "linked analogies" and "cunning duplicate[s]" (70: *264*) is resonantly amplified when we recall that Queequeg's Yojo is "a curious little deformed image with a hunch on its back" (3: *30*).

Of all these interlaced elements—Ahab-to-pyramid-to-whale-to-merman-to-Yojo—it is the last, hunchbacked Yojo, examined in the last chapter, who may provide the requisite clue for solving Stubb's oneiric puzzle. For Yojo is above all a naturalistic figure, sign and symbol of Queequeg's identification with the natural world. Since the hunchbacked idol appears to be linked to both the humpbacked merman and the humpish pyramid of the dream, we must examine the possibility that both pyramid and merman are also in some sense *images of the natural world*. It is suggestive, for example, that a form of pyramid appears in Melville's first book, and on—of all places—a Pacific island. Tommo remarks on a series of huge stone terraces hidden in the jungle:

> As I gazed upon this monument, doubtless the work of an extinct and forgotten race, thus buried in the green nook of an island at the

ends of the earth, the existence of which was yesterday unknown, a
stronger feeling of awe came over me than if I had stood musing at
the mighty base of the Pyramid of Cheops. There are no inscriptions,
no sculpture, no clue, by which to conjecture its history; nothing but
the dumb stones.[3]

This passage should be placed alongside later references to the
pyramid-form, such as the two which occur in *Mardi*. Taji remarks that "like a pyramid, the past shadows over the land," and
Babbalanja asserts that "It is not the Pyramids that are ancient, but
the eternal granite whereof they are made; which had been equally
ancient though yet in the quarry."[4] These references provide a
pyramid-figure which was clearly for Melville an image of a dimly
intuited past which, while it "shadows" and thereby shapes the
present, is nevertheless antechronical in the same sense that the
"pre-adamite" whale, the "ante-chronical Leviathan," is an "antemosaic, unsourced existence" which was "before all time" (104:
380). Moreover, while the pyramid is unmistakably artifactual, the
consequence of an apparently intelligent shaping process, it is
uniquely inscrutable with regard to the nature of that intelligence.
The pyramid consists only of "dumb stones," tantalizingly suggestive, but bearing "no inscriptions," furnishing "no clue, by
which to conjecture its history." This geometric blankness is identical to the "dead, impregnable, uninjurable wall" (76: *285*), the
"dead, blind wall" (76: *284*) of the whale, who "has no face" (86:
318), "no nose, eyes, ears, or mouth; . . . nothing but that one broad
firmament of a forehead" (79: *292*). Finally, the pyramid, made
of "eternal granite," exhibits the same ontological perdurability as
the ship-shattering berg of the *John Marr* poem. The battering-ram
forehead of the Sperm Whale possesses the same terrible intractability: ". . . this whole enormous boneless mass is as one wad, . . .
of a boneless toughness, inestimable by any man who has not
handled it. . . . It is as though the forehead of the Sperm Whale were
paved with horses' hoofs. I do not think that any sensation lurks in
it" (76: *284–85*).

These pyramidical meanings are amplified in Melville's story, "I
and My Chimney," the narrator of which owns a house his wife is
intent on rebuilding, but which boasts a huge central chimney stand-

ing in the way of such plans. The chimney has already had its upper reaches removed; the remainder is of a "pyramidal shape" which "pyramidically diminished as it ascended." It strikes its owner as primally antechronical. "Very often I go down into my cellar, and attentively survey that vast square of masonry. I stand long, and ponder over, and wonder at it. It has a druidical look, away down in the umbrageous cellar there, whose numerous vaulted passages, and far glens of gloom, resemble the dark, damp depths of primeval woods." When the wife engages an architect to cope with this immense obstacle to her plans, the narrator takes him on a guided tour. "We seemed in the pyramids; and I, with one hand holding my lamp over head, and with the other pointing out, in the obscurity, the hoar mass of the chimney, seemed some Arab guide, showing the cobwebbed mausoleum of the great god Apis." The meaning is clear: the narrator's wife, egotistically intent upon her own ideas of how reality should be ordered, cannot reconcile herself to the fact that reality reposes upon a substrate of ontological intractability which cannot be wished, dreamed, talked, or planned away. "At last," the narrator tells us, "I gently reminded her that, little as she might fancy it, the chimney was a fact—a sober, substantial fact, which, in all her plannings, it would be well to take into full consideration." The narrator's wife must learn the lesson that the hunchbacked merman teaches to Stubb; kicking at pyramids is not generally a productive endeavor.[5]

Most revealing of all, however, in establishing the meaning of Stubb's "Queen Mab" dream, are those passages from Melville's *Journal of a Visit to Europe and the Levant*, a trip taken during 1856–57, which concern his confrontation with the veritable Egyptian pyramids about which he had already thought and written so much. Howard C. Horsford points out that the entries in the *Journal* are not the off-hand jottings of the casual traveller. "Melville read through and worked over the journal, not once or twice but many times." Significantly, the facsimiles which Horsford chooses to reproduce to illustrate this intensive revision process have to do with the most sustained passage in the *Journal* concerning the pyramids. It is this and other pyramid-passages which elicited Melville's greatest effort to successfully express the inexpressible, to give verbal articulation to the primally anteverbal. The brooding tension of this effort, the tortured struggle for expression, are evident in every line:

> Scamper to them with officers on donkeys.... Kites sweeping & soaring around, hovering right over apex.... Looks larger midway than from top or bottom. Precipice on precipice, cliff on cliff. Nothing in Nature gives such an idea of vastness. A balloon to ascend them.... Resting. Pain in the chest. Exhaustion. Must hurry. None but the phlegmatic go deliberately. Old man ... oppressed by the massiveness & mystery of the prymds. I myself too. A feeling of awe & terror came over me.... The dust.... I shudder at idea of ancient Egyptians.

Melville immediately associates this geometric vastness with the Jehovah whose agent-whale figured so largely in Father Mapple's sermon. "It was in these pyramids that was conceived the idea of Jehovah. Terrible mixture of the cunning and awful.... The idea of Jehovah born here." Moreover, the pyramids stand as something antithetical to natural life:

> *No vestige of moss upon them. Not the least. Other ruins ivied. Dry as tinder. No speck of green....* Line of desert & verdure, plain[er] than that between good & evil. An instant collision of alien elements. ... Grass near the pyramids, but will not touch them—as if in fear or awe of them. (italics Melville's)

Later in the *Journal* Melville compulsively returns to the same topic, obviously dissatisfied with his first effort to say what he meant:

> *The Pyramids.* The lines of stone look less like courses of masonry, than like strata of rocks. The long slope of crags & precipices. The vast plane. No wall, no roof. In other buildings, however vast, the eye is gradually innured to the sense of magnitude, by passing from part to part. But here there is no stay or stage. It is all or nothing. It is not the sense of heigth, or breadth or length or depth that is stirred, but the sense of immensity that is stirred. After seeing the pyramid, all other architecture seems but pastry.... It refuses to be studied or adequately comprehended. It still looms in my imagination, dim & indefinite.[6]

The passage has at least two central meanings. First, this reworking makes clear that for Melville the Egyptian pyramids are, despite their mathematical form, closer to a manifestation of nature than a work of man. The "precipice on precipice, cliff on cliff" idea of the first passage is here expanded to give the pyramids a geological and antediluvian massiveness, composed of "strata of rocks" shaped into a "long slope of crags and precipices." Melville is seeking to express, not the measure of man's accomplishment, but rather some quality he finds in the cosmos. The pyramids, man-made though they are, are a figure for the essence of the natural world.

The second meaning has to do with the utter inscrutability, the conceptual inaccessibility, the monolithic muteness of these "dumb stones." Their ordered geometricity, the abstractive trigonometry of their form, seem to speak in the most self-evident way of the existence of some sort of shaping intelligence. This is why Melville suggested in the earlier passage that the "idea of Jehovah" must have been born there. The three-cornered triangularity of each face carries an obvious trinitarian tonality. In this sense the pyramids exhibit something more than the random naturalness of mountains and cliffs—but beyond this suggestion of intelligent creation, Melville senses that nothing else can be inferred: the pyramids are utterly blank. They refuse "to be studied or adequately comprehended." The pyramids contain nothing so human or comprehensible as a "wall" or a "roof"—their monolithic totality has "no stay or stage," no "parts" to make rational analysis possible. "It is all or nothing." All that can be inferred is an "immensity," possibly intelligent but certainly non-human, alien and threatening.

It seems likely that these meanings, articulated five years after *Moby-Dick*, were in Melville's mind in inarticulate form while he was writing his whale story. If this is the case, then the pyramid in *Moby-Dick*—and especially in Stubb's dream—becomes (we use once again the phrase Ishmael applies to the *Pequod*'s carpenter) a "script abstract; an unfractioned integral" (107: *388*) which is visually expressive of the nature of substrative reality. As primal form, the pyramid is anteverbal manifestation of the essential *thingness of things*. On the one hand, its geometricity represents that subliminal, inchoate *hint* of intelligent artifactuality which is pervasive in the natural world, in snow-crystal and rainbow, in bird-wing and flower-bud, in sun and storm, in solstice and ecliptic, and indeed in the whole vast swing of the turning cosmos. On the other hand, the

pyramid in its static, insensate, adamantine perdurability gives visual adumbration to that total unawareness in the physical universe,
that basaltically primordial unconsciousness, which is so terrifying
to the thoughtful observer, and which Ishmael speaks of as "the
general stolidity discernible in the whole visible world; which . . .
still eternally holds its peace, and ignores you, though you dig
foundations for cathedrals" (107: *388*). And this is the ambiguity:
the berg-stolid indifference of stone, of tree, of water, and of wind
belies the simultaneous hint—it is never more than a hint—of intelligence and artifice, and indeed almost obliterates it. All of these
meanings coalesce when Ishmael repeatedly refers to the Sperm
Whale as "pyramidical." Moby Dick—and all the other whales of
the novel—reflect in a condensed way this cosmic ambiguity. Their
actions seem to suggest intelligence and volition, but these evidences
of awareness are almost obliterated by their blank facelessness and
the insensate ponderosity of their mastodon-massiveness. The great
Leviathan of *Moby-Dick* is simply a sentient, flesh-and-blood version of the pyramid.

Read in this way, the meaning of the pyramid in Stubb's "Queen
Mab" dream seems reasonably clear. When Stubb kicks back at
Ahab, he is kicking at what he takes to be a directive, *thumper* intelligence which has chosen to kick him as *thumpee*. When Ahab suddenly turns into a pyramid, the appearance of focused intelligence
is abruptly merged—and almost submerged—in a much broader substrate of stolid indifference. The meaning of this metamorphosis is
that Ahab, intelligent though his actions appear to be, is in an ultimate sense *of a piece with* the whole natural world—Stubb's particular and personal not-me—any part of which may "kick" Stubb
at any moment. In terms of causation, Ahab stands at only a single
remove from the pyramid—is indeed essentially, from Stubb's point
of view, pyramidical.

Moreover, Stubb kicking back at the pyramid becomes a direct
analogue of Ahab kicking back at Moby Dick, who has himself a
pyramidical hump. Stubb's personal attack on Ahab-as-pyramid is
paralleled by Ahab's first deeply personal attack on Moby Dick, an
assault which in its intensity and purblind animosity far exceeded
the professionally dispassionate demands of the whale-hunt. For
when Moby Dick, during their first encounter, crushed his boat and

threw him into the water, the frenzied Ahab, "seizing the line-knife from his broken prow, had dashed at the whale, as an Arkansas duellist at his foe, blindly seeking with a six inch blade to reach the fathom-deep life of the whale" (41: *159*). As Ahab lost a leg in consequence of this personal and vindictive counter-thump, so does Stubb kick his leg "right off" in the dream. The parallel stands as direct comment upon Ahab's intention of converting the voyage of the *Pequod* into a counter-strike against Moby Dick. Nature, despite signs and hints of intelligence, is so totally and stolidly indifferent, so monolithically unaware, and so incapable, because of the ontological pyramidism which underlies it, of sustaining injury, that any attempt at counter-thump is certain only to bring death or injury to anyone who attempts it. Ahab's failure is prefigured by Stubb's failure to damage the pyramid. Unlike Ahab, however, Stubb will utilize his failure to achieve wisdom.[7]

But this is only half the story—and half the dream. Nature presents itself in aspects other than that of pyramidical stolidity. Nature is also process and event, "pauselessly active in uncounted modes" (107: *388*). On the highest level this event-and-process aspect may become sentient, often apparently aware. Thus, as the pyramid in Stubb's dream is a primal form representing *inanimate nature*, in a parallel fashion the humpbacked merman is a primal form representing *animate nature* in all its manifestations, living and non-living, sentient and non-sentient. It would be a mistake to assume that "Mr. Humpback" is a person, or even in the traditional sense a personification, even though he walks and talks like one. The details of the dream suggest that Melville is not proposing any sort of personality or intelligence in nature. The merman is only minimally anthropomorphic for the same reason that the pyramid is only minimally artifactual: he represents that subliminal *hint* of personality that we glimpse occasionally in nature. But he is horribly alien—courageous Stubb is momentarily terrified by him ("Such a phiz!"). He is oneirically bisexual, half sea-man and half like a "chimney hag." Finally, he boasts a decidedly un-anthropomorphic posterior stuck full of marlinspikes. He is simply, therefore, the pyramid (nature-as-being) recast as an active principle (nature-as-process), the basic and ineluctable pyramidism reappearing in the

primal sea-creature's hump. Stubb's merman is kin to the blind vitalism of the "formless" squid (59: *237*), or Ahab's "personified impersonal" (119: *417*), or Ishmael's "generic or Pantheistic vitality"
(66: *257*) which is far more fundamental than individual or organic
life. He is, in short, simply a visual manifestation of an immanent
and constitutive cosmic dynamism.

We can offer this analysis of the merman with considerable confidence because he reappears later, thinly disguised as the *Pequod's*
carpenter. The carpenter is, Ishmael tells us, a "pure manipulator,"
an "omnitooled, open-and-shut carpenter" who works, not "by
reason or by instinct," but rather by a "kind of deaf and dumb,
spontaneous literal process." He does not stand distinctly apart from
the ontological matrix in the sense that a real person stands apart
from the physical environment which surrounds him. Rather, the
carpenter *blends*, metaphysically speaking, with his surroundings,
so that it is sometimes difficult to tell him from the stool on which
he sits or the bench at which he works. As Ishmael phrases it, he is
more *thing* than *person*, characterized by a "half-horrible stolidity,"
and by "an all-ramifying heartlessness" which "shaded off into the
surrounding infinite of things" (107: *388–89*). Heartless though
he is, he has a sense of humor of sorts. We become certain that we
are again encountering the merman of Stubb's dream when Ishmael tells us that the carpenter's stolidity is "dashed at times, with
an old, crutch-like, antediluvian, wheezing humorousness, not un-
streaked now and then with a certain grizzled wittiness; such as
might have served to pass the time during the midnight watch on
the bearded forecastle of Noah's ark" (107: *388*). Indeed, the carpenter sounds suspiciously like the "hyena" of Chapter 49, the "unseen and unaccountable old joker" who thumps man, often to death
and destruction, by means of "sly, good-natured hits" and "jolly
punches in the side" (49: *195*).

The merman-as-carpenter is important to an understanding of
Stubb's dream because, in a brilliant reversal of points of view, we
get from him some idea of how a sentient creature such as man would
appear to unaware nature *were it somehow made aware*. Thanks to
the carpenter we get, not man's view of the pyramid, but rather
the pyramid's view of man. And the view is, as Ishmael senses, "half-
horrible." The carpenter is appallingly unaware of any difference

between living flesh and bone on the one hand, and dead wood or steel on the other. All things are simply undifferentiated *matter* to him, to be held firmly in the jaws of his innumerable vices and worked on indifferently with his innumerable tools. As Ishmael describes his work, the living and the dead, the sentient and the non-sentient, are inextricably mixed:

> A belaying pin is found too large to be easily inserted into its hole: the carpenter claps it into one of his ever-ready vices, and straightway files it smaller.... An oarsman sprains his wrist: the carpenter concocts a soothing lotion. Stubb longs for vermillion stars to be painted upon the blade of his every oar: screwing each oar in his big vice of wood, the carpenter symmetrically supplies the constellation. A sailor takes a fancy to wear shark-bone ear-rings: the carpenter drills his ears. Another has the toothache: the carpenter out pincers, and ... whirling round the handle of his wooden vice, ... signs to clap his jaw in that, if he would have him draw the tooth. (107: *387–88*)

Belaying pins, human wrists, oars, ears, aching jaws: it is all one to the pyramidical carpenter, who is "prepared at all points, and alike indifferent and without respect in all. Teeth he accounted bits of ivory; heads he deemed but top-blocks; men themselves he lightly held for capstans" (107: *388*). When Queequeg lies dying, the merman-carpenter is called forward to measure the cannibal for a coffin. Moving with what Ishmael calls "indifferent promptitude," he applies his rule to the savage's still-living body, taking "Queequeg's measure with great accuracy, regularly chalking Queequeg's person as he shifted the rule" (110: *396–97*). To the carpenter Queequeg in all his vibrant and complex humanity is simply a linear fact, indistinguishable from rock or tree or cloud, merely another vehicle for the insensate workings of blind process. Such is the pyramid's view of man, in its full "all-ramifying heartlessness."

This pyramidical indifference is of decisive significance for the larger meanings of *Moby-Dick*. Ahab's attention has been engaged, not by the "pasteboard" object-world, but rather by the event-world of the "undoubted deed." It is in the world of process, especially when viewed concatenatively, that Ahab thinks he sees "some unknown but still reasoning thing [putting] forth the mouldings of its features from behind the unreasoning mask." He will, he tells Starbuck, wreak his hate upon this manifestation of directive intelligence, "sinew[ed]" as it is by "inscrutable malice" (36: *144*). But the merman-carpenter seems to belie Ahab's assumption that concatenative process presupposes directive intelligence. Ishmael points out that although the carpenter's "liveliness of expertness . . . would seem to argue some uncommon vivacity of intelligence," this is not the case: the carpenter does *not* have a "common soul," but only an "unaccountable, cunning life-principle" which keeps him in motion in the same sense that an "unreasoning wheel" is kept in motion. The carpenter is a "pure manipulator; his brain, if he ever had one, must have early oozed along into the muscles of his fingers" (107: *388-89*). Cosmic process, despite its incredible complexity, would appear to be mindless process, and Ahab would appear to be tragically and ironically mistaken in assuming the existence of some "still reasoning thing" behind the phenomenal mask. Ahab may be girding for battle with a dead void.

Because of this mindlessness, cosmic process is enormously dangerous; if a man gets in the way, he is crushed. This may happen at any time and any place: man is inextricably enmeshed in the inscrutable movement of the animate universe which the merman-carpenter represents. In one of those subterranean linkages which give *Moby-Dick* its internal coherence, the process-carpenter and the aboriginal merman are re-articulated as the labyrinthine whale-line. The oarsman is surrounded by its "perilous contortions," which fold "the whole boat in its complicated coils, twisting and writhing around it in almost every direction." Ishmael continues: "Nor can any son of mortal woman, for the first time, seat himself amid those hempen intricacies, and while straining his utmost at the oar, [not] bethink him that at any unknown instant the harpoon may be darted, and all these horrible contortions be put in play like ringed lightnings." Such ringed lightnings, whipping about the boat and everyone in it can, due to the "least tangle or kink, . . . infallibly take somebody's arm, leg, or entire body off" in an instant. It is "like being seated in the midst of the manifold whizzings of a steam-engine in full play, when every flying beam, and shaft, and wheel, is grazing you":

> But why say more? [Ishmael concludes]. All men live enveloped in whale-lines. All are born with halters round their necks; but it is

only when caught in the swift, sudden turn of death, that mortals realize the silent, subtle, ever-present perils of life. And if you be a philosopher, though seated in the whale-boat, you would not at heart feel one whit more of terror, than though seated before your evening fire with a poker, and not a harpoon, by your side. (60: *239–41*)

The application seems clear: Ahab, attacking Moby Dick with a six-inch blade "like an Arkansas duellist," was swiftly caught up by such a causal "kink" or "tangle" in the play of cosmic process. Interposing himself among the "manifold whizzings" of natural activity, he was thumpishly deprived of his leg. But it can be argued —it is certain that Ahab would argue—that it is a gross oversimplification to treat Moby Dick or any other Leviathan with such reductiveness. The whale must be something more than a mere death-dealing kink or grazing whiz. The point is substantive, and meeting it takes us finally back to the aboriginal merman of Stubb's dream. Perhaps the most significant part of the "Queen Mab" sequence is the passage in which the startled Stubb, suddenly and unexpectedly spun around and confronted by the merman, offers to thump *him* as he had been, until interrupted, thumping the pyramid. "Do *you* want a kick?" he asks "Mr. Humpback":

> By the lord, Flask, I had no sooner said that, than he turned round his stern to me, bent over, and dragging up a lot of seaweed he had for a clout—what do you think, I saw?—why thunder alive, man, his stern was stuck full of marlinspikes, with the points out. Says I, on second thoughts, 'I guess I won't kick you, old fellow.' 'Wise Stubb,' said he, 'wise Stubb.' (31: *115*)

The porcupine impregnability which this array of marlinspikes affords queer Mr. Humpback reminds one of that device of classical warfare, consisting of slanted rows of pointed timbers sunk in a ditch-bottom, on which the horses of attacking cavalry inevitably impale themselves. The analogy provides precisely the term needed: the marlinspikes, located just where one might be tempted to deliver a kick, comprise an *ontological cheval-de-frise*, some quality inherent in the thingness of both animate and inanimate nature, designed into the being of being to fend off counter-thumps of all sorts. The merman's marlinspikes therefore stand for the fact that animate nature, whether manifested in typhoon, or flood, or earthquake, or shark, or—to come fully to the point—Leviathan himself, is *not equipped offensively, but only defensively*. The *cheval-de-frise* is a totally passive arrangement. Thus, even when some part of animate nature appears on the superficial event- or process-level to be engaged in malign and focused attack, this is *only an appearance*. On the ontological level all that is manifested is the blind, metaphysically passive, marlinspike perdurability of the active not-me, which is concerned with nothing, aware of nothing, discommoded by nothing, but only imperturbably and hummingly engrossed in the on-going maintenance of its own internal processes and modes, many of which are, of course, "sharkish." The ultimate, massively subtle message of Stubb's "Queen Mab" dream, then, is that the whale (or the shark or squid) is nothing more than an *uncommonly energetic pyramid*—which is, of course, why Ishmael so pointedly and repeatedly describes him as "pyramidical." It is greatly to Stubb's credit that he grasps this elusive metaphysical subtlety, refrains from kicking the merman as he kicked the pyramid, and earns from Mr. Humpback the sobriquet of "wise Stubb."

This admittedly difficult point of Stubb's dream is brilliantly supported by the figure of Ahab himself, who walks on two sorts of legs. One leg is living flesh and blood; this is Ahab's phenomenal leg. The other is made of pale ivory; this is Ahab's noumenal leg. One leg resides in the Lockean "primary" world; the other resides in the Lockean "secondary" world. Ahab, in terms of the overarching protometaphor of *color: interface: non-color*, has one foot planted firmly in the sensuous color world and the other planted just as firmly in the non-color world. The spiritual split and psychic dissociation which is the consequence of such a straddling philosophical stance is signified by the "slender rod-like mark, lividly whitish" (28: *110*), which courses out of Ahab's gray hair and down across his face and neck, disappearing into his clothing. The ivory leg is a "stript abstract" or "unfractioned integral" of that which may loosely be termed "legness." The ivory leg, in other words, makes visible the noumenally substrative pyramidism of the flesh-and-blood leg. As the living whale is substratively a pyramid, so Ahab's living leg is substratively a whalebone peg, part of the bergstolid not-me.

Such a reading of the "leg-and-foot problem" in Stubb's dream throws valuable light on that central portion of the chapter which makes "Queen Mab" a limited sort of "key" to the rest of the novel. Stubb tells himself that Ahab's kick was really "not much of an insult." Ahab did not, he recalls, kick him with the "real leg." Rather, the thump was delivered with the "false leg." This consideration leads Stubb to distinguish between *two sorts of thumps*:

> And there's a mighty difference [he tells Flask] between a *living thump* and a *dead thump*. That's what makes a blow from the hand, Flask, fifty times more savage to bear than a blow from a cane. The *living member*—that makes the *living insult*, my little man. (31: *115*; italics mine)

The fundamental issue raised here, coming *before* Ahab makes his quarter-deck speech to the *Pequod's* crew, is of obvious application. The thump which Moby Dick delivered in the past to Ahab, shearing off his leg, and the thump which Moby Dick will deliver to the *Pequod*—these are both either live thumps or dead thumps, the result either of a malignly focused intelligence, or of blind cosmic process. Ahab thinks in terms of live thumps, delivered by a "living member" and therefore constituting a "living insult" to which a living and vengeful counter-thump is a viable response. But the whole tenor of the "Queen Mab" chapter seems to suggest that Ahab is *wrong*. The pyramid, of course, is not "live" in the sense that Stubb uses the term. But neither is the merman "live" in this sense; he is only active as process is active. Therefore the reader who takes the trouble to unravel Stubb's dream must keep in mind the possibility that the climactic thump which Moby Dick delivers at the end of the novel *may be only a "dead thump."*

Such an interpretive possibility is suggested by the metamorphosis of Ahab into a pyramid at the beginning of the dream. When one is confronted with what seems to be a thumper, be it Ahab or the whale, even the briefest of causal regressions will bring one back, not to a malign and intending intelligence, but rather back to the pyramid, and only the pyramid. Ultimately, then, *there is no thumper*, though there are indeed thumps, the inexorable consequence of blind process. This is why the merman tells Stubb to consider the kick which Ahab has given him a sort of compliment, "an honor," in the same way that "In old England the greatest lords think it great glory to be slapped by a queen, and made garter-knights of." The thumps of life are never of low derivation, never meanly sourced: the whole stupendous cosmos is behind every one of them. There is a certain "honor" in being kicked by something so vast and so ultimate (31: *116*). Thus, all thumps are, in Ishmael's wry phrase, "*universal* thumps," and the only appropriate response for suffering humanity is, as Ishmael suggests in the first chapter of *Moby-Dick*, to have "all hands . . . rub each other's shoulder-blades, and be content" (1: *15*).

AHAB
The Ugly Narcissus

CAPTAIN AHAB, in all his "Nantucket grimness and shagginess" (33: *130*),* stands in *Moby-Dick* as the central expression of the pro- todynamic of *thumper: thumpee*. For Ahab has been twice thumped by the great albino whale. Not only has his living leg been, in Peleg's vivid phrase, "devoured, chewed up, [and] crunched by the mon- strousest parmacetty that ever chipped a boat" (16: *69*), so that, as Ahab says, he has been "made a poor pegging lubber . . . for ever

* The number before the colon in all parenthetical references in the text indicates chapter, which will be the same for most American editions of *Moby-Dick*; the italicized numbers after the colon indicate page in the Norton Critical Edition of *Moby-Dick*, edited by Harrison Hayford and Hershel Parker (New York: W. W. Norton & Company, 1967).

and a day" (36: *143*). Just as important, the loss of his leg leads directly to a second wound, an additional violation of his person:

> For it had not been very long prior to the Pequod's sailing from Nantucket, that he had been found one night lying prone upon the ground, and insensible . . . his ivory limb having been so violently displaced, that it had stake-wise smitten, and all but pierced his groin; nor was it without extreme difficulty that the agonizing wound was entirely cured. (106: *385*)

Ahab is already insane when he suffers this second visitation: during the homeward voyage following the loss of his leg, laced tight into his hammock, "his torn body and gashed soul bled into one another; and so interfusing, made him mad" (41: *160*). Consequently, this second violation only exacerbates an already established monomania; it is perhaps what Ahab means when he speaks of himself as "madness maddened" (37: *147*).

That the groin wound would result in lunacy piled upon lunacy seems likely when one recalls that Ahab, in the seasoned vigor of an indurated old age has three voyages earlier married him a wife—"a sweet, resigned girl," Peleg calls her—and had a child by this child. This May-and-December union leads Peleg to insist that "Ahab has his humanities" (16: 77). Thus, Moby Dick has not only deprived Ahab of his leg, but also indirectly struck at the most vital point of a relationship which is the primary humanizing influence of his old age. Ahab regards this second and psychologically much more profound violation as the direct consequence of the first. To him, "all the anguish of that then present suffering was but the direct issue of a former woe," part of a malign continuum of evil and pain brought down upon him by the White Whale. He sees that "as the most poisonous reptile of the marsh perpetuates his kind as inevitably as the sweetest songster of the grove; so, equally with every felicity, all miserable events do naturally beget their like" (106: *385*). The loss of his leg has threatened Ahab's *life*; the subsequent groin wound has threatened his *life-source*.

It is no mere hunter of whales who has been immersed in this tragic continuum. Even Peleg is aware that Ahab stands apart. "Ahab's above the common," he tells Ishmael; "Ahab's been in colleges, as well as 'mong the cannibals; been used to deeper wonders than the waves; fixed his fiery lance in mightier, stranger foes than whales" (16: 76). Ishmael himself explains how such superiority is possible in a profession which would hardly seem fertile ground for such qualities. The answer is the Quaker tradition, richly Biblical. There are men "named with Scripture names" who, having grown up in "the stately dramatic *thee* and *thou* of the Quaker idiom," retain this mode of expression and conceptualization intact through the "audacious, daring, and boundless adventure of their subsequent lives." The result of this mixture of the Biblical and bloody is "a thousand bold dashes of character, not unworthy a Scandanavian sea-king." Moreover, when this pregnant synthesis occurs

> in a man of greatly superior natural force, with a globular brain and a ponderous heart; who has also by the stillness and seclusion of many long night-watches in the remotest waters ... been led to think untraditionally and independently; receiving all nature's sweet or savage impressions fresh from her own virgin, voluntary, and confiding breast, and thereby ... to learn a bold and nervous lofty language— that man makes one in a whole nation's census—a mighty pageant creature, formed for noble tragedies. (16: 71)

The reference here, though indirect, seems unmistakable. Ahab is "that man"; Ahab, plunged by Leviathan into a self-regenerating continuum of mortal grief and pain, must be that "mighty pageant creature."

Or is he? For there is a strange, almost furtive obliqueness in Ishmael's references to "a man" and "that man," when it is obvious— or has always seemed obvious—that he is speaking of Ahab. It is true that this passage occurs in an early chapter, and is anticipatory, Ahab having yet to appear upon his quarter-deck. But this fact does not account satisfactorily for the passage's odd indirection. There are rhetorical means sufficient to talk, should Ishmael wish to, of Ahab before Ahab appears. A rigorous formulation must state the whole double-edged case: the "mighty pageant creature, formed for noble tragedies" may be, as traditional opinion proposes, the Ahab of *Moby-Dick*—or he may *not* be.

As a matter of common sense, of course, it is obvious that Ishmael *is* talking about Ahab here, however tangentially—but it does not follow that Ahab, the "mighty pageant creature," is automatically

the Ahab of *Moby-Dick*. The Ahab that Ishmael speaks of here is a
pre-textual Ahab, existing before the novel begins and only up to
that moment when the White Whale, in some pre-literary limbo
outside the textual continuum, sheared off his leg. This Ahab cannot
be assumed to be the Ahab of *Moby-Dick* any more than the Hamlet
who was away at school when the King his father was murdered
can be assumed to be the Hamlet of the play. This is the reason, one
suspects, that Ishmael never mentions Ahab by name here. The
events of *Moby-Dick* will have to establish whether the actualized
Ahab of the novel lives up to the advance billing of this anticipatory
passage or not.

   This is an admittedly Byzantine reading of a passage which has
always been taken at face value. But then, there is no mind in American literature more Byzantine, more attracted to subterranean sinu-
osities of meaning, than Melville's. Obviously, the way in which the
reader identifies the "mighty pageant creature" is crucial to an
understanding of the entire novel. Taken straight, the passage makes
Ahab the hero of *Moby-Dick*. Taken more cautiously, the passage
leaves the whole question open. Whether, in fact, the Ahab of
Moby-Dick is identical with the pre-literary Ahab—"one in a whole
nation's census"—is the main consideration of this chapter.

   There can be no question of the heroic nature of Ahab's pain: he
comes to us "with a crucifixion in his face," as Ishmael says, "in all
the nameless regal overbearing dignity of some mighty woe" (28:
111). Neither can there be any question of the titanic dimensions of
his ends and purposes. His "globular brain and . . . ponderous heart"
(16: *71*) have achieved a magnificent universalization of his suffering. As the brilliance of his madness grows, he finally identifies Moby
Dick, not only with "all his bodily woes, but all his intellectual and
spiritual exasperations," so that

> All that most maddens and torments; all that stirs up the lees of
> things; all truth with malice in it; all that cracks the sinews and
> cakes the brain; all the subtle demonisms of life and thought; all evil,
> to crazy Ahab, were visibly personified, and made practically as-
> sailable in Moby Dick. He piled upon the whale's white hump the
> sum of all the general rage and hate felt by his whole race from Adam

down; and then, as if his chest had been a mortar, he burst his hot heart's shell upon it. (41: *160*)

Ahab is "intent on an audacious, immitigable, and supernatural revenge" (41: *162*). He will chase Moby Dick "round Good Hope, and round the Horn, and round the Norway Maelstrom, and round perdition's flames . . . till he spouts black blood and rolls fin out" (36: *143*). This is his "grand, monomaniac object" (64: *248*)—and this is, at least in conventional terms, splendidly heroic, a fit endeavor for a "mighty pageant creature."

The question is: does Ahab, in the textual continuum of *Moby-Dick*, meet the challenge of his pain, lifting *himself* up to the level of heroic greatness demanded by his ends and purposes? Does he, on the intellectual, volitional, and moral levels, become in fact the "mighty pageant creature" which his role as avenger of "his whole race from Adam down" demands? The pre-textual Ahab's "globular brain and . . . ponderous heart" signal extraordinary intelligence and broad, humane sympathies; one must inquire whether it is upon these heroic resources that the *textual* Ahab actually draws as he launches himself upon the "fiery hunt" (42: *170*).

Such questions have to do with the inner Ahab rather than the perfervidly histrionic outer Ahab. Seeking answers to them forces us to attend to that handful of extremely complex passages in which Ishmael develops Ahab's (and simultaneously Starbuck's) psychology. There is, for example, a developed theory of the personality implicit in that passage in which Ishmael defines what part of Starbuck is under Ahab's control, and what part is not:

> [Ahab] knew, for example, that however magnetic his ascendency in some respects was over Starbuck, yet that ascendency did not cover the complete spiritual man any more than mere corporeal superiority involves intellectual mastership; for to the purely spiritual, the intellectual but stands in a sort of corporeal relation. Starbuck's body and Starbuck's coerced will were Ahab's, so long as Ahab kept his magnet at Starbuck's brain; still he knew that for all this the chief mate, in his soul, abhorred his captain's quest, and could he, would joyfully disintegrate himself from it, or even frustrate it. (46: *183*)

The passage suggests that the "complete spiritual man" is comprised of four psychological areas: (1) soul; (2) mind; (3) will; (4)

body. The focus of attention here is Starbuck's will, which has been "coerced" by Ahab. But in order to coerce Starbuck's will, Ahab has had to hold the "magnet" of his own overwhelming personality to Starbuck's "brain"—meaning, of course, mind. A hierarchical sequence is implied: the mind magnetically coerced, the will is consequently coerced; coercion of the will, in turn, makes possible coercion of the body. This leaves the soul of Starbuck. It is this which is "purely spiritual" and in relation to which mind "but stands in a sort of corporeal relation." It is, Ishmael thinks, the soul which would frustrate Ahab's intention. Such frustration is out of the question so long as Ahab controls the three more "corporeal" faculties which are the normal vehicles through which the soul acts. The passage thus suggests a psychological chain-of-command moving from spirit to mind, from mind to will, and from will to body. The single apparently inviolate element, the spirit or soul, corresponds neatly to Ishmael's "insular Tahiti" (58: *236*), the area "deep down and deep inland" at the center of "the tornadoed Atlantic of my being" (87: *326*), where resides "That immaculate manliness we feel within ourselves, so far within us, that it remains intact though all the outer character seem gone" (26: *104*).

It is this psychic paradigm which must be brought to bear on that pair of passages in which Ishmael attempts to explain the nature and source of Ahab's monomania. Ishmael insists that Ahab's is a "broad madness," meaning that "not one jot of his great natural intellect had perished" as his monomania grew. Rather, Ahab's mind, which in his saner days had been his freely responding "living agent," had been raised to another order of power in the process of becoming, paradoxically, a debased and imprisoned "living instrument":

> If such a furious trope may stand, his special lunacy stormed his general sanity, and carried it, and turned all its concentrated cannon upon its own mad mark; so that far from having lost his strength, Ahab, to that one end, did now possess a thousand fold more potency than ever he had sanely brought to bear upon any one reasonable object. (41: *161*)

The passage reveals what became of the "globular brain" of the pre-textual Ahab. All its vast potentiality has been focused on a single objective, much as the diverse rays of the sun can be focused to a single point of blinding intensity. But this is to say that Ahab has been turned by his "special lunacy" into a moral and volitional *idiot savant*. He has lost that multidimensionality of intellect, that polyfaceted roundness of personality, which makes the human person human. Regardless of the "thousand fold" power of his focused intellect, the "globular brain" (and presumably the concomitant "ponderous heart") of the pre-textual "mighty pageant creature" no longer exist. The mind capable of only a single idea—"one unsleeping, ever-pacing thought" (36: *140*)—is no mind at all. Ahab admits that the singularity of his intention has made further thought impossible: "Here's food for thought," he mutters, "had Ahab time to think; but Ahab never thinks; he only feels, feels, feels; *that's* tingling enough for mortal man! to think's audacity" (135: *460*).

This reading is amplified by the vision of Ahab driven from his hammock in the night by the "hell in himself":

> For, at such times, crazy Ahab, the scheming, unappeasedly steadfast hunter of the white whale; this Ahab that had gone to his hammock, was not the agent that so caused him to burst from it in horror again. The latter was the eternal, living principle or soul in him; and in sleep, being for the time dissociated from the characterizing mind, which at other times employed it for its outer vehicle or agent, it spontaneously sought escape from the scorching contiguity of the frantic thing, of which, for the time, it was no longer an integral. (44: *174-75*)

This correlates well with the soul-mind-will-body psychology developed in the earlier discussion of Starbuck's "coerced will." Here, however, Ishmael refines the distinction between the "living principle or soul," and the "characterizing mind." In the normal personality the "soul" exists in an "integral" and presumably harmonious relationship with the "characterizing mind." The result, normally, is a single organic entity, *soul-mind*. Further, what each half of this duality contributes to the other is also clear, again if only by implication. The soul contributes the essential life, the fundamental dynamism, similar to what Ishmael on another page calls "generic or Pantheistic vitality" (66: *257*). Conversely, this generalized life-dynamism is given focus by the "characterizing mind." The soul is the source of vitality without which the mind could not live or function. Reciprocally, the soul would be only so much diffuse energy without the "characterization" given it by the normal mind.

But Ahab's is not a normal personality. Ahab's mind is now a "frantic thing," whose only "characterizing" consists in turning all the "concentrated cannon" of Ahab's vast intellect on a single objective. During the waking day, in a complete inversion, the "living principle or soul" becomes the helpless "instrument" of this monstrosity, instead of being, as it normally is, the source of natural impulse and vitality. At night, however, when the enveloping unawareness of sleep relaxes the bond, the soul attempts to escape the "scorching contiguity"—and so what appears somnambulistically on the midnight deck is *another* Ahab than the one "that had gone to his hammock." In short—and this is the essential point deeply buried in Ishmael's labyrinthine syntax—there are actually *two Ahabs* on the *Pequod*.

The central problem of Melville's psychology now begins to take shape. The text implies that the eternal soul, the vitalizing dynamism of nature, does *not* animate the daytime Ahab. Yet Ishmael reminds us that "the mind does not exist unless leagued with the soul." We must perforce conclude that Ahab's on-deck mind derives its immense vitalism from some source other than the natural soul, which it is now pervertedly using only as an "instrument." The question is: what *is* supplying the vitality of the *Pequod's* Captain, he who strides the quarter-deck, controls absolutely both ship and crew, delivers soliloquies and makes speeches, and stands as the central dramatic figure of *Moby-Dick?* What impels the *textual* Ahab? Ishmael has, he thinks, the answer:

> ... it must have been that, in Ahab's case, yielding up all his thoughts and fancies to his one supreme purpose; that purpose, by its own sheer inveteracy of will, forced itself against gods and devils into a kind of self-assumed, independent being of its own. Nay, could grimly live and burn, while the common vitality to which it was conjoined, fled horror-stricken from the unbidden and unfathered birth. (44: 175)

There is in Ahab, then, a "common vitality," the generic "soul" of earlier passages. But opposed to this natural vitality is a monstrous "unbidden and unfathered birth." This is Ahab's "supreme purpose," which in a kind of frightful psychological parthenogenesis has, through Ahab's will, become independent and self-sustaining, divorced altogether from the soul. The daytime, commanding Ahab, in short, does not draw on what we think of as "life," does not "live" in the traditional sense at all.

Instead of living, Ahab *burns*. This burning is the unnatural source of his vitality, but fire-vitality is not life-vitality. Ahab's vitalism is not a *living* vitalism, but only an *actve* vitalism in the sense that fire is active and metaphorically "alive." This is the meaning of the heat images in the passage, centered on a "supreme purpose" which can "grimly live and burn" in "scorching contiguity" to the organic "common vitality." This is the meaning of the tale which Dough-Boy, the *Pequod's* steward, carries to Stubb, and which Stubb repeats, about how Ahab's pillow is, each morning, "sort of frightful hot, as though a baked brick had been on it. A hot old man!" Stubb exclaims (29: *113*)—a conclusion which the carpenter also comes to: Ahab is "fiery hot, I tell ye!" (127: *432*). This is also the meaning of Ishmael's assertion in "The Try-Works" chapter that the "rushing Pequod, . . . laden with fire, and burning a corpse, . . . seemed the material counterpart of her monomaniac commander's soul" (96: *354*).

The volitional Ahab is, moreover, as perverted as the vital Ahab. If the mind "characterizes" the generalized dynamism of the soul, it also "characterizes" the activities of the will. The mind, to extend Ishmael's "cannon" metaphor, "aims" the will and then, in the act of free choice, redirects this volitional "aim." The will remains free only so long as it enjoys a full range of possible direction and possible focus. But the unnatural "frantic thing" which is Ahab's mind confines his will to a single characterization. While Ahab's will is hyperintensely active, it is not free. The Ahab of the textual continuum is therefore not only an intellective but a volitional zombie, the empty husk of the magnificent pre-literary Ahab. The waking, on-deck Ahab has achieved a total dissociation from his own soul, and severed at its root his connection with the vitalism of the natural world. He is the supreme expression in *Moby-Dick* of that separation from nature, that alienation from other men, and that corrosive destruction of self demanded in megaton imperatives by the Jehovah of Father Mapple's sermon. This accounts for the atrophy of what he contemptuously calls the "low, enjoying power" (37: *147*), and also for his rejection of the natural world as mere "pasteboard" (36: *144*). It is this divorce from the sensuous manifold which explains the event-centered, rather than object-centered, Ahabian epistemology and the inferential, rather than intuitive, processes which are its concomitant.

This destruction of the natural Ahab is one that Ahab has freely chosen. Ishmael makes it clear that the White Whale did not make Ahab mad. Neither did the loss of his leg. What made Ahab mad was Ahab. The crucial lines bear repeating. Ahab, Ishmael explains, "yielding up all his thoughts and fancies to his one supreme purpose; that purpose, by its own sheer inveteracy of will, forced itself . . . into a kind of self-assumed, independent being" (44: *175*). Ahab *yielded* himself to his purpose, deliberately sacrificed the "thoughts and fancies" of his broad humanity and globular brain to his single intention, and in one final, terrible act of will, *willed the functional destruction of his will*, placing himself permanently (somewhat like Hawthorne's Ethan Brand) beyond the possibility of further choice or retraction. It is in the light of these facts that Ahab's climactic confrontation with the corpusants must be read. Here he most clearly affirms the inviolate freedom of the individual in the face of cosmic power. "Though but a point at best," he tells the corpusants, "whencesoe'er I came; wheresoe'er I go; yet while I earthly live, the queenly personality lives in me, and feels her royal rights" (119: *417*). This is superb rhetoric, but it is false fact. Ahab has wilfully destroyed his "personality," and obliterated its "queenly" freedom. As Newton Arvin points out, the Ahab who confronts the corpusants "is not, in the high sense, a personality, but only a proud and defiant will. . . . He is no longer a free mind: his thought has become the slave to his insane purpose."[1] Ahab assiduously cultivates this dehumanization, protecting it from any influence which might mitigate its terrible singularity. He carefully keeps Pip at arm's length because he fears that the little black boy's devotion will cure his madness. "There is that in thee, poor lad," he tells Pip, "which I feel too curing of my malady. Like cures like! and for this hunt, my malady becomes my most desired health" (129: *436*). Those who see Ahab's relationship with Pip as evidence that the *Pequod's* Captain remains human to the end overlook the fact that Ahab actually threatens Pip's life. The old man tells Pip that in the coming conflict with Moby Dick he will not permit Pip to be by him. When Pip's importunate weeping shakes him, Ahab's dehumanization becomes unequivocally clear: "Weep so," he cries, "and I will murder thee! have a care, for Ahab too is mad" (129: *436*).

The external sign of Ahab's "malady" is his terrible scar, the "slender, rod-like mark" which threads "its way out from among his grey hairs, . . . continuing right down one side of his tawny scorched face and neck," a scar which, if the Manxman is to be believed, runs from "crown to sole" (28: *110*). It is expressive of that dichotomization of Ahab's psyche and person which is also suggested by the "Iron Crown of Lombardy" which Ahab tells us he wears: " 'Tis split, too—that I feel; the jagged edge galls me so, my brain seems to beat against the solid metal" (37: *147*).

These meanings are deepened when one realizes that two other members of the crew are also scarred. The most important is Perth, the ship's "begrimed [and] blistered old blacksmith" (112: *400*). Like Ahab, Perth had married in his old age "a youthful, daughter-like, loving wife," and like Ahab he had had children by this child. Like Ahab, like Stubb kicking his pyramid, and like the Captain of the *Samuel Enderby*, hunchbacked old Perth has suffered a physical loss in his extremities. Years before, he had drunkenly fallen asleep in a dilapidated barn in the dead of winter. The outcome was the loss of all his toes to frostbite, so that the old man, as he moves about the ship, exhibits a "slight but painful appearing yawing in his gait," not unlike Ahab's own "crippled way" (112: *400-01*; 29: *112*). This deformity, however, is not Perth's tragedy, but only its sign. The happiness of his May-and-December marriage had been earlier destroyed when a "desperate burglar," the "Bottle Conjurer" of drink, "slid into his happy home, and robbed them all of everything." As a consequence, "the house was sold; the mother dived down into the long church-yard grass; her children twice followed her thither; . . . the houseless, familyless old man staggered off a vagabond in crape," and destroyed by "the hideous rot of life," Perth "went a-whaling" aboard the *Pequod* (112: *400-02*).

The blacksmith is a victim, like Ahab, of the "malicious agencies" of life, of "all the subtle demonisms of life and thought" (41: *160*). Perth has been "heaped" by life as Ahab has been "heaped" by Moby Dick (36: *144*). Like Ahab, he is deeply scarred. Ahab watches the old man hammering a piece of hot iron, "the red mass sending off the sparks in thick hovering flights, some of which flew close to Ahab."

The *Pequod's* Captain remarks that the spark-shower goes unnoticed by Perth: "... look here, they burn; but thou—thou liv'st among them without a scorch." Perth's response is resonantly significant. "Because I am scorched all over, Captain Ahab," he answers; "I am past scorching; not easily can'st thou scorch a scar" (113: *402–03*). The blacksmith is *all scar*, a walking cicatrix tempered in the fire of human agony to an ultimate toughness. Ahab, subjected to the same ordeal, has cracked cleanly down the middle like a badly wrought pot that fractures in the kiln. Perth's absolute stolidity astonishes the fractured Ahab, who knows his history. "Thy shrunk voice sounds too calmly, sanely woful to me. In no Paradise myself, I am impatient of all misery in others that is not mad. Thou should'st go mad, blacksmith; say, why dost thou not go mad? How can'st thou endure without being mad?" (113: *403*). When Perth boasts that he can fix "all seams and dents but one," Ahab responds passionately. "Look ye here, then," he cries, indicating his own scarred visage, "look ye here—*here*—can ye smooth out a seam like this, blacksmith[?] ... If thou could'st, ... glad enough would I lay my head upon thy anvil, and feel thy heaviest hammer between my eyes." But sundered Ahab is beyond Perth's skill: "Oh! that is the one, sir!" he replies. "Said I not all seams and dents but one?" (113: *403*). Perth suggests that it is possible to undergo the agony of existence without cracking as Ahab has; the blacksmith's wholeness hints at the existence of a deep-seated flaw in Ahab. That this is what Melville had in mind when he scarred Ahab's face and body seems probable in view of his characterization, in an 1849 letter to Evert Duyckinck, of what he called the "gaping flaw" in Emerson: "These men," Melville asserted, "are all cracked right across the brow."[2]

As Perth is all-over scar, so is Queequeg. A sailor of Melville's background, who had lived among seafaring men who willingly underwent the tortures of tattooing as a badge of their trade, and who spent months among Polynesians equally inclined to embellish their features with scar-patterns, would certainly be aware of the symbolic resonances of Queequeg's tattoos, and the sustained suffering he would experience while the various hieroglyphic figures were being applied. These tattoos, covering nearly all of the cannibal's person, are "the work of a departed prophet or seer of his island, who, by these hieroglyphic marks, had written out on [Queequeg's] body a complete theory of the heavens and earth, and a mystical treatise on the art of attaining truth" (110: *399*). Thus Queequeg's tattoos achieve universal significance: the meaning of life and the truth of existence are incised upon man's living body in the fleshly cuneiform of the scar, using the common idiom of pain. Some men, like Ahab, are shattered in the process, and some men, like Perth and Queequeg, are not.

We can now provide answers to the rhetorical questions which Ahab poses in "The Symphony," when Starbuck again appeals to him to abandon the pursuit of Moby Dick—and Ahab refuses:

> What is it, what nameless, inscrutable, unearthly thing is it; what cozening, hidden lord and master ... commands me, ... recklessly making me ready to do what in my own proper, natural heart, I durst not so much as dare? Is Ahab, Ahab? Is it I, God, or who, that lifts this arm? (132: *444-45*)

What lifts his arm is his psychically parthenogenetic "supreme purpose," here characterized as a "nameless, inscrutable, unearthly thing." But if natural Ahab does not lift his own arm, he is nevertheless responsible for the fact that he does not lift it. This is a lack of will which he himself has willed. This fact makes Ahab's attempts to place the blame for his actions elsewhere carry an air of shabby and trimming retraction. Stubb overhears him complain that "some one thrusts these cards into these old hands of mine; swears that I must play them, and no others" (118: *413*). But the "some one" is the "frantic thing" he has permitted to take the place of self. Consequently, Ahab-the-man must take responsibility for Ahab-the-automaton. The same tendency to dodge responsibility is apparent when he tells Starbuck that "This whole act's immutably decreed. 'Twas rehearsed by thee and me a billion years before this ocean rolled. Fool! I am the Fates' lieutenant; I act under orders" (134: *459*). The statement contains a grain of truth. He is under orders, but they emanate from nothing so ultimate as "Fate." Fate need not bother to direct a mere machine; it helplessly directs itself.

Moby-Dick is in fact studded with figures which stress the mechanical consequences of the unnatural vitality which impels Ahab forward to destruction. If Starbuck stands for "the soft feeling of the human" (38: *148*), Ahab is associated with metallic hardness. He paces his cabin with "iron brow" (109: *394*); he wears an "Iron Crown" upon a "steel skull" (37: *147*); he stands "like an iron statue," his "firm lips [meeting] like the lips of a vice" (111: *400*). Ishmael speaks of "Ahab's iron soul" (130: *438*), and Starbuck of his "Heart of wrought steel" (135: *463*). It is this metallic heart which makes it possible for him to stand "like an anvil" as Captain Gardiner of the *Rachel* appeals for help in finding his son (128: *435*). Ahab's conception of the ideal man is one "fifty feet high in his socks; . . . no heart at all; [and a] brass forehead" (108: *390*).

Melville further exploits his metallic dehumanization in a sustained electromagnetic metaphor. At the end of the quarter-deck scene, when the three mates have crossed their lances before Ahab, he touches the "crossed centre," and

> while so doing, suddenly and nervously twitched them; meanwhile, glancing intently from Starbuck to Stubb; from Stubb to Flask. It seemed as though, by some nameless, interior volition, he would fain have shocked into them the same fiery emotion accumulated within the Leyden jar of his own magnetic life. (36: *145–46*)

This "fiery emotion," which Ahab calls "mine own electric thing," is so inimical to natural life that Ahab asserts that had "the full-forced shock" of it actually been conveyed to the three mates along their extended lances, "Perchance . . . it would have dropped ye dead" (36: *146*). Mere men are thus to lethal Ahab nothing more than mechanical ancillaries to his electric will. " 'Twas not so hard a task," he reflects after the quarter-deck scene. "I thought to find one stubborn, at the least; but my one cogged circle fits into all their various wheels, and they revolve" (37: *147*). The ease with which he has achieved this debasing gear-tooth interlock makes Ahab contemptuous: "The permanent constitutional condition of the manufactured man, thought Ahab, is sordidness" (46: *184*).

It is this contempt, plus the heady feeling that he has "manufactured" his crew, encouraging in Ahab a "certain sultanism of his brain" which, as Ishmael says, "became incarnate in an irresistible dictatorship" over the crew (33: *129*). Just as the ship, though made of many materials, is one thing, so also "all the individualities of the crew, this man's valor, that man's fear; guilt and guiltlessness, all varieties were welded into oneness, and were all directed to that fatal goal which Ahab their one lord and keel did point to" (134: *455*). Ahab makes the point explicitly during the battle with Moby Dick. "Ye are not other men," he tells his terrified boat-crew, "but my arms and my legs; and so obey me" (135: *465*). Their humanity and dignity magnetically drawn out of them, the *Pequod's* crew, "Like machines . . . dumbly [move] about the deck, ever conscious that the old man's despot eye [is] on them" (130: *438*). If Ahab is a Prometheus, a man-maker, as Ishmael calls him (44: *175*), it is only in the ironic sense that he makes mechanical men of real men, imposing upon them his mogul-will to effect their destruction.[3]

Undemocratic arrogance and overweening dominance, however, do not of themselves preclude the development of heroic character *if* they are the consequence of a refinement of conception and insight, and a complexity of execution all far above the capacities of the ordinary man. The subtle villain can easily become heroic: Macbeth and Richard III come immediately to mind. Such considerations bring us to the heart of the "Ahab problem" in *Moby-Dick*: the question of Ahab's *subtlety*, or lack of it. Ishmael raises the issue himself, in a passage of shrouded ambiguity which comes near the end of Chapter 33, "The Specksynder" (*128–30*). Having noted that "even Captain Ahab was by no means unobservant of the paramount forms and usages of the sea" in maintaining his magnetic control over the crew, Ishmael goes on to remark that such a "practical, available supremacy over other men" cannot be achieved or maintained simply through the exercise of "intellectual superiority," no matter how great. Even the supreme intellect can maintain its leadership only with "the aid of some sort of *external arts and entrenchments*, always, in themselves, more or less paltry and base" (italics mine). A few lines later Ishmael touches again on such "arts" and "entrenchments," noting that they are generally "small things" which nevertheless have "large virtue" to sway when "extreme political superstitions invest them." Because of the paltry nature of these devices certain rare persons, whom Ishmael calls "God's true princes of the Empire," refuse to interpose themselves in the sphere of action, kept by their fastidiousness from the "world's hustings."

This "choice hidden handful" are Ishmael's "Divine Inert"—and Melville has given us a full-dress study of a supremely immobile specimen of the Divine Inert in Bartleby, the scrivener who, when confronted with life's exigencies, simply "prefers not," and dies for his preference. But Ishmael is concerned in "The Specksynder," not with the Bartlebys of this world, but with the active leader. He is proposing that the relative superiority of leadership carries with it a concomitant and absolute *inferiority*, so that "the highest honors that this air can give" end up being awarded to men of equivocal quality who "become famous more through their infinite inferiority to the choice hidden handful of the Divine Inert, than through their undoubted superiority over the dead level of the mass."

But there is more. The inferiority of the active leader is seldom or never perceived. So efficacious—if "paltry and base"—are the "external arts and entrenchments" of leadership that the capacity or incapacity of the leader is of relative unimportance. Ishmael offers two contrastive examples of this anomaly. At one extreme there is a leader such as "Nicholas the Czar": in such instances, "the ringed crown of geographical empire encircles an imperial brain," so that the immense efficacy of the leader's "arts" and "entrenchments" is enhanced by a commensurate capacity to rule. Then, Ishmael asserts, "the plebian herds crouch abased before the tremendous centralization." And then there is the antipodal instance, where the leader is bereft of capacity to rule. In this case the "external arts and entrenchments" of leadership display their efficacy in a peculiarly vivid way: "Such large virtue lurks in these small things when extreme political superstitions invest them," Ishmael asserts, "that in some royal instances *even to idiot imbecility they have imparted potency*" (33: *129*; italics mine).

This discussion of internal political capacity and external political potency could be taken as another of those digressions which occur so often in *Moby-Dick*. In a chapter devoted to the relationship between captain and crew, Ishmael has simply wandered off the track. One can then conclude that the labyrinthine pair of paragraphs which conclude Chapter 33 have nothing to do with Ahab. Ishmael, in fact, seems eager to help us to such a conclusion. He has been speaking of kings and czars, and such "royal instances" of leadership are not to be found on a lowly American whaler. "But Ahab," Ishmael concludes, ". . . still moves before me in all his Nantucket grimness and shagginess; and in this episode touching Emperors and Kings, I must not conceal that I have only to do with a poor old whale-hunter like him; and, therefore, all outward majestical trappings and housings are denied me." Ahab is another matter; any application of Ishmael's political analysis to him would be inappropriate.

And yet . . . the last sentence of the paragraph immediately preceding Ishmael's apparent digression refers to Ahab's own employment of "external arts and entrenchments," which Ishmael calls his not "unobservant" exploitation of "the paramount forms and usages of the sea." Such a pointed contiguity of both topic and phrasing cannot be overlooked. The application of Ishmael's analysis to Ahab, "poor old whale-hunter" though he is, is inescapable. Ishmael's demurrer must be discounted just as one discounts that much more famous one which asserts that *Moby-Dick* must never be assumed to be anything remotely like a "monstrous fable, or still worse and more detestable, a hideous and intolerable allegory" (45: *177*). This being the case, we are obliged to determine in what sense Ishmael's shrouded analysis applies to Ahab. One possibility is that Ahab is an instance of the "imperial brain" which distinguished Nicholas the Czar. Such a reading is reinforced by Ishmael's discussion of "that man" of "globular brain and . . . ponderous heart" who "makes one in a whole nation's census." But we have established that this is the Ahab of the pre-literary limbo, in relation to which the Ahab of the textual continuum is an empty husk. Thus we are brought to the antipodal alternative: that Ahab in all his "potency" of command represents an "idiot imbecility" effectively masked by "external arts and entrenchments." To suggest that this kind of out-and-out assertion is Ishmael's intention would be to push the evidence too far. We must not convert Ishmael's hints into facts. But this much can be said: the weight of the textual evidence of *Moby-Dick* places Captain Ahab much closer to the "royal instance" of "idiot imbecility" than to the instance of "imperial" intelligence. Ishmael's intention is to implant such equivocal, "half-formed, foetal suggestions" (41: *156*) in the reader's mind in the slyly ambiguous close of "The Specksynder." "Oh, Ahab!" he exclaims in the last sentence, "what shall be grand in thee, it must needs be plucked at from the skies, and dived for in the deep, and featured in the unbodied air!" (33: *130*). The sentence has generally been taken in its obvious sense. It can, however, be read in a different and more pejorative way.

The point is important because those things in Ahab which are *not* "grand," those things which are crudely mean or grossly dehumanized, need not be searched for in the "unbodied air." They are embedded in the tactile matrix of the textual continuum. The most important is a pervasive crudity of conception. Ahab's assertion, that "I'd strike the sun if it insulted me" (36: *144*), carries with it, beneath the obvious resonance of Promethean defiance, a less obvious suggestion of crude reliance on brute force. We have already remarked Ahab's tendency to images of physical violence— "striking," "thrusting," and "shoving." It is in these terms alone that his "supreme purpose" is cast. Intent upon harpooning the malign enigma he sees behind the cosmos, he attempts to effect an impact on the metaphysical world through the palpable devices of the physical world. This is a foredoomed effort so profoundly American that it relates him to our entire literature, aligning him with such distant figures as Jay Gatsby of Fitzgerald's great novel. Gatsby's grossness of realization is Ahab's grossness of realization. This lack of conceptual subtlety manifests itself most clearly in Ahab's address to the corpusants. They signify only "speechless, placeless power," an empirically realized force which for Ahab reaches its highest manifestation quantitatively, when it "launchest navies of full-freighted worlds" (119: *417*). Similarly, Leviathan is simply gross power to Ahab. The subtle perplex of meanings with which bookish Ishmael invests Moby Dick highlights the crudity of Ahab's own conceptualizations.

A similar grossness is apparent in the various devices—"external arts and entrenchments"—by which Ahab keeps his crew in subjection. They are all, in Ishmael's telling phrase, "paltry and base" (33: *129*). "I crush the quadrant," Ahab boasts to his gape-mouthed underlings, "the thunder turns the needles, and now the mad sea parts the log-line. But Ahab can mend all" (125: *427*). The ignorant crew rewards such pomposities with "glances of servile wonder" (124: *425*), but there is some question as to whether Ishmael expects the reader to be equally susceptible. Ishmael mentions that Ahab, when making a new needle for the turned-around binnacle compass, goes "through some small strange motions with it—whether indispensible to the magnetizing of the steel, or merely intended to augment the awe of the crew, is uncertain." When this mumbo-jumbo succeeds, then, says Ishmael, "In his fiery eyes of scorn and triumph, you . . . saw Ahab in all his fatal pride" (124: *425*). If Ishmael is not taken in, neither is "wise Stubb." During the typhoon Ahab grasps the chains which terminate the mast-mounted lightning-rods of the *Pequod.* "Hand me those main-mast links there; I would fain feel this pulse, and let mine beat against it; blood against fire!" (119: *416*). Stubb's commentary on this performance is definitive:

> What's the mighty difference [he asks overawed Flask] between holding a mast's lightning-rod in the storm, and standing close by a mast that hasn't got any lightning-rod at all in a storm? Don't you see, you timber-head, that no harm can come to the holder of the rod, unless the mast is first struck? What are you talking about, then? Not one ship in a hundred carries rods, and Ahab,—aye, man, and all of us,—were in no more danger then, in my poor opinion, than all the crews in ten thousand ships now sailing the seas. (121: *419*)

Wise Stubb suggests that timber-headed Flask "be sensible" concerning such paltry mummeries (121: *419*). One suspects that Melville meant this good advice for readers and critics too.

To analyze Ahab's monomania and the self-induced dehumanization which is its concomitant is not, however, to account truly for the genesis of either. Why does Ahab set out to harpoon the cosmic enigma embodied in the White Whale? One answer is that were he not a *man of faith,* an unvitiated product of his Nantucket, Christian-Quaker background, Ahab could not act as he does. Only a thoroughgoing theist can contemplate, much less attempt, deicide. The point is made by placing Ahab in conjunction with that other man of faith in *Moby-Dick,* the chief mate Starbuck. Because Melville deals with the officers of the *Pequod* in symmetrically arranged trinities, with the "light" triumvirate of Starbuck, Stubb, and Flask contrasted to the "dark" triumvirate of Queequeg, Tashtego, and Daggoo—these "Knights and Squires" relationships (26, 27: *102–108*) obscure the fact that Starbuck stands in a much closer relationship to Ahab than to the other two mates or the three harpooneers.

In grim confrontation, Ahab and Starbuck understand one another, and in this mutual understanding is subterranean union.

While Stubb is a Cape-Cod-man (27: *105*), and Flask a Vineyard-man (27: *106*), it is Starbuck whose roots are identical with Ahab's. He, like Ahab, is "a native of Nantucket, and a Quaker by descent" (26: *102*). Ishmael makes much of the aridity and sterility of Nantucket. "Look at it—a mere hillock, and elbow of sand; all beach, without a background. . . . Some gamesome wights will tell you that they have to plant weeds there, they don't grow naturally; that they import Canada thistles; . . . that one blade of grass makes an oasis, three blades in a day's walk a prairie" (14: *62*). The desiccation of this particular spit of the "Puritanic sands" (6: *39*) is reflected in those of the *Pequod's* officers who come from the dour Puritan-Quaker tradition which dominates the island. Ahab, when he first appears, "looked like a man cut away from the stake, when the fire has overrunningly wasted all the limbs without consuming them, or taking away one particle from their compacted aged robustness" (28: *109–10*). Similarly, Starbuck "must have been born in some time of general drought and famine, or upon one of those fast days for which his state is famous. Only some thirty arid summers had he seen; those summers had dried up all his physical superfluousness" (26: *102*). In both Starbuck and Ahab this aridity is a sign of "inner health and strength." As Ahab is robustly "compacted," Starbuck's "thinness" is "merely the condensation of the man." As Ahab seems "made of solid bronze, and shaped in an unalterable mould," so also Starbuck's economy of form seems to insure that he will "endure for long ages to come, and to endure always, as now" (26: *102–03*; 28: *110*). In such figures does uncertain and bedeviled Ishmael pay tribute to the sturdy religious certainties which have toughened both Starbuck and Ahab. In their aridly Lenten essentiality, they have, like the Jonah of Father Mapple's sermon (9: *45*), learned to disobey themselves. Living their lives upon the world's waters, they are nonetheless oddly waterless, induratedly desiccative, marked in common by a kind of ontological dehydration which is at once the measure of their tough commitment to other-worldly realities, and their tragic dissociation from the sensuous natural world through which the *Pequod* sails. They are Jehovah's men, not Nature's. Starbuck and Ahab are paired by an identity of thought and emotion which no mere surface antagonism can override.

Paradoxically, the theistic faith of Ahab and Starbuck is best measured by the corrosive doubts that gnaw upon that faith. Their belief is manifested by the steady rejection of unbelief. Ishmael, pondering the cenotaphs in the wintry light of the Whaleman's Chapel, remarks that "Faith, like a jackal, feeds among the tombs, and even from these dead doubts she gathers her most vital hope" (7: *41*). Faith derives its vitality from "dead doubts"—and Ahab admits the presence of such doubts. "Sometimes I think there's naught beyond," he confesses (36: *144*). The same fear of the void reappears late in the novel as the carpenter's calking mallet causes Queequeg's coffin to reverberate hollowly. The carpenter urges Ahab to "hark" to the music of the mallet:

> Aye [Ahab retorts], and that's because the lid there's a sounding-board; and what in all things makes the sounding-board is this—*there's naught beneath*. And yet, a coffin with a body in it rings pretty much the same, Carpenter. Hast thou ever helped carry a bier, and heard the coffin knock against the church-yard gate, going in? (127: *432*; italics mine)

Full or empty, a coffin *sounds* empty. Sound itself becomes here the expression of nothingness. A definition of how faith must function when confronted by such atheistical hints from the void immediately follows. The carpenter begins to respond to Ahab's query—"Faith, sir, I've—"—whereupon Ahab interrupts him, leaping upon this crucial word. "Faith?" he interjects, cutting the carpenter off, "What's that?" "Why, faith, sir," the carpenter responds, disconcerted by Ahab's suddenness, "it's only a sort of exclamation-like—that's all, sir." In other words, faith is essentially expletory, a creedal exercise based on the conviction that "saying makes it so." In the carpenter's words, "that's all" faith is or ever can be (127: *432*).

To emphasize the tenuous nature of faith, Ahab, who has already noted that Queequeg's coffin, resting on two line-tubs, resembles a catafalque ("Middle aisle of a church!"), now draws on his Quaker knowledge of the Bible to make further ironic comment upon the nature of religious belief. Recalling Isaiah 6, *9* ("Listen carefully, but you shall not understand! Look intently, but you shall know nothing!") and the constant references to Isaiah's looking-and-hearing paradigm in the New Testament,[4] Ahab suggests that true sight and true hearing—the "high perception" of his "Sunset" soliloquy (37: *147*)—can only destroy faith rather than reaffirm it. "There's a sight! There's a sound!" he mutters as the void of Queequeg's coffin reverberates under the mallet. "The greyheaded woodpecker tapping the hollow tree! *Blind and dumb* [one is certain Melville meant to write *deaf*] *might well be envied now!*" (127: *432*; italics mine). The whole tableau gives Ahab intimations that he may be pursuing nothing at all. He thus finds the reverberations of the coffin unbearable. "Will ye never have done, Carpenter, with that accursed sound? I go below; let me not see that thing here when I return again" (127: *433*). But despite these persistent intimations of a nullity behind nature, Ahab steadfastly maintains his agentistic view. "Look!" he exclaims, "see yon Albicore! *who* put it into him to chase and fang that flying-fish?" (132: *445*; italics mine). But Ahab knows very well Who this "who" is. His whole Nantucket heritage has told him. It is the Christian God, the Jehovah of pallid New England. Indeed, it is this Jehovah Who is Ahab's exemplar: as Jehovah downed Jonah, so Ahab will down Jehovah. The "fiery hunt" is an act of Christian faith.

Nor is Ahab the only person on the *Pequod* to give the issues of *Moby-Dick* a Christian cast. Just as Ahab confronts the "tri-pointed trinity of flames" (119: *416*), so also does Starbuck conceptualize the powers of the universe in trinitarian terms. Reading the golden doubloon nailed to the mast, the pious first mate comes up with an interpretation which sounds like a primer of Christian faith: "A dark valley between three mighty, heaven-abiding peaks, that almost seem the Trinity, in some faint earthly symbol. So in this vale of Death, God girds us round; and over all our gloom, the sun of Righteousness still shines a beacon and a hope." But Starbuck, like Ahab, is assailed with doubts. No sooner does he decide that the Quito sun embossed upon the doubloon is the "beacon" and "hope" of Christian faith, than it occurs to him that even suns are mutable. "Yet, oh, the great sun is no fixture; and if, at midnight, we would fain snatch some sweet solace from him, we gaze for him in vain!" The conclusion is that God is not always in His Heaven. Starbuck cannot face the implications of this. He admits that the coin speaks "truly" to him but nevertheless he turns away. "I will quit it," he mutters, "lest Truth shake me falsely" (99: *360*).

The chief mate thus becomes a figure of that man of faith who knows there are things he cannot allow himself to know. When the squid appears, Starbuck, sensing that this sucking and writhing epiphany of Prime Life is a "thing of portents" (61: *241*), cries out in a "wild voice" against those meanings of the squid which, as a man of faith, he must at all costs avoid. "Almost rather had I seen Moby Dick and fought him," he exclaims, "than to have seen thee, thou white ghost!" (59: *237*). The squid represents unacceptable fact. If Starbuck is forced to choose between faith and fact, he will choose faith and reject fact. He makes this clear while gazing over the boat's side into the blue depths of the tranquil ocean:

> Loveliness unfathomable, as ever lover saw in his young bride's eye! Tell me not of thy teeth-tiered sharks, and thy kidnapping cannibal ways. *Let faith oust fact; let fancy oust memory; I look deep down and do believe.* (114: *406*; italics mine)

Implicit here is Starbuck's covert recognition that faith is a fragile thing demanding protection and insulation. Ishmael remarks that Starbuck was one of those men who, "while generally abiding firm in the conflict with seas, or winds, or whales, or any of the ordinary irrational horrors of the world, yet cannot withstand those more terrific, because more spiritual terrors, which sometimes menace you from the concentrating brow of an enraged and mighty man" (26: *104*). Ishmael suggests that such "spiritual terrors," impinging on Starbuck, might "burn all his courage up." And this is what happens: in the quarter-deck scene Starbuck capitulates before Ahab's "concentrating brow." "My soul is more than matched," he later tells himself; "she's overmanned; and by a madman! Insufferable sting, that sanity should ground arms on such a field!" (38: *148*). The nature of this capitulation needs careful attention. It must not be assumed that Ahab has simply reduced Starbuck to passivity so that he and the crew can pursue Moby Dick without hindrance. Starbuck is not to be merely neutral. Rather, he is to *actively aid* Ahab, and this despite the fact that "in his soul" he "abhorred his captain's quest" (46: *183*). "I think I see his impious end," he confesses to himself, *"but feel that I must help him to it"* (38: *148*; italics mine). Starbuck, whatever the revulsion in his soul, is in some sense actively willing the thing Ahab wishes to achieve.

Such a reading of the chief mate's role is reinforced by Ishmael's later remark, that "Starbuck's body and Starbuck's coerced will were Ahab's, so long as Ahab kept his magnet at Starbuck's brain" (46: *183*). A superficial reading of both this passage and his "Dusk" soliloquy might suggest that Starbuck is being forced to do something (as the traditional phrase has it) *against his will*. But this is not what Ishmael is saying. The passage states that Starbuck's *will itself* had been "coerced." A "coerced will," if the phrase means anything at all, must mean a will that is willing that which the coercer wishes it to will. Starbuck, despite all his protestations, is intending that revenge upon the White Whale which he called "blasphemous."

How did Ahab achieve this startling psychological inversion? Starbuck has habitually let faith oust fact. Ahab, by sheer power of personality, reverses this process, so that fact has ousted faith. Ahab has forced Starbuck, despite his faith, *to knowledge.* This is why the chief mate remarks on the "sharkish" sea, the animalistic "long howl" of the rioting crew, and the "wolfish gurglings" of the ship as it careens through the darkening water. "Oh, life!" he exclaims, " 'tis in an hour like this, with soul beat down and held to knowledge, —as wild, untutored things are forced to feed—Oh, life! 'tis now that I do feel the latent horror in thee!" (38: *148*). A man of faith, force-fed such knowledge, can only conclude like Ahab that behind the "latent horror" of a demonic world must stand a God who is Himself a horror. Thus Starbuck is reluctantly convinced of the validity of Ahab's grudge against God. Behind a facade of antagonism and opposition, the first mate secretly hopes for the success of Ahab's quest. It is this subterranean sympathy which causes him to pray desperately to the gathering darkness. "Stand by me, hold me, bind me, O ye blessed influences!" (38: *148*). The prayer is oddly phrased. Starbuck prays, one suspects, to be "bound" and "held" from becoming another Ahab—and another would-be deicide. Because Ahab and Starbuck share a common faith they also share a common faithlessness, and are bound together by a common doom. Ahab is the overt rebel; Starbuck is the clandestine rebel, piously masking his rebellion even from himself.

The reverberations of Queequeg's coffin under the carpenter's mallet suggest what the cenotaphs suggest: that there is *nothing* behind appearances. Yet Ahab insists he has seen *something*, and Ahab must be taken seriously on this point. What is it, then, that he has seen? One possible answer can be derived from the Ahabian epistemology adumbrated in the doubloon. Gazing at the golden Quito coin nailed to the mast, Ahab takes it for an image of physical reality: ". . . this round globe is but the image of the rounder globe," he asserts, "which, like a magician's glass, to each and every man in turn but mirrors back his own mysterious self" (99: *359*). Such a solipsistic epistemology, reducing reality to a mirror-like opacity, makes it possible to suggest that what Ahab sees or thinks he sees in nature is not the Christian God—or any other god—but rather only the image of himself, thrown back upon himself by "reflective" reality. That Ahab himself dimly suspects such a possibility is suggested when, during his address to the corpusants, he asserts that "In the midst of the personified impersonal, a personality stands here" (119: *417*). The phrase "personified impersonal" accords well with Ahab's mirror-epistemology. The "impersonal" world *appears* to be instinct with personality because we are constantly *glimpsing ourselves* in nature. In the act of perception, we "person" the "impersonal." Ahab, then, is not attacking God. Rather, he is *attacking himself*. If he detects "inscrutable malice" in the comings and goings of natural process, this must be his own malice imaged back at him. The world that Ahab sees is a world the moral coloration of which is supplied by his own lamp-mind. Ahab thus is another Narcissus—but with a crucial difference. The Narcissus of Ishmael's opening pages dove into the reflective fountain in pursuit of the "tormenting, mild image" of beauty that he saw there (1: *14*). Ahab's frantic plunge is made in hate, in horror and revulsion. Ahab is thus best understood as the Ugly Narcissus, and the circumnavigative voyage of the questing *Pequod* can only bring him back upon himself.

But if Ahab sees only ugliness and malice in life, other percipients, even when similarly circumstanced and looking into the same reality-mirror, see something else. This is the meaning of Captain

Boomer and Doctor Bunger of the *Samuel Enderby*, an English whaler with which the *Pequod* gams. In an encounter with the White Whale, Captain Boomer has lost an arm to match Ahab's leg. Melville relates this deprivation to the *thumper: thumpee* protodynamic by replacing (or rather by having Dr. Bunger replace) Captain Boomer's lacerated arm, not with the traditional hook, but rather with "a white arm of sperm whale bone, terminating in a wooden head like a mallet" (100: *363*). The genial Boomer's reaction to this loss is just the opposite of Ahab's. When the *Pequod's* Captain asks him if he succeeded in harpooning Moby Dick in two subsequent encounters, Boomer calmly retorts: "Didn't want to try to: ain't one limb enough?" (100: *367*). Captain Boomer has cultivated a philosophical imperturbability to match the imperturbability of the pyramidical cosmos he confronts. Because he will not counter-thump, he stands as another expression of the wisdom of Stubb.

While Ahab's suffering has isolated him from all men, Boomer's pain has had the opposite effect. Ishmael advises that the only panacea for the "universal thump" is for "all hands . . . [to] rub each other's shoulder-blades, and be content" (1: *15*). Dr. Bunger's shoulder-rubbing takes an alcoholic form. When the sober-sided physician tells Ahab that "I did all I could; sat up with him nights; was very severe with him in the matter of diet," Captain Boomer cannot contain himself. "Oh, very severe," he agrees, and then, altering his voice in the face of Dr. Bunger's droll solemnity:

> Drinking hot rum toddies with me every night, till he couldn't see to put on the bandages; and sending me to bed, half seas over, about three o'clock in the morning. Oh, ye stars! he sat up with me indeed, and was very severe in my diet. Oh! a great watcher, and very dietetically severe, is Dr. Bunger. (Bunger, you dog, laugh out! why don't ye? You know you're a precious jolly rascal.) (100: *366*)

Nothing could be more striking, in contrast to Ahab's humorless isolation, than Captain Boomer's deep affection for his dead-pan ship's surgeon. "Oh, you solemn rogue, you—you Bunger! was there ever such another Bunger in the watery world? Bunger, when you die, you ought to die in pickle, you dog; you should be preserved to future ages, you rascal" (100: *367*). The thumps of cosmic process, if taken in stoical good humor and mutual charity, should forge rather than sever the bonds of human affection. Boomer and Bunger have been humanized by Moby Dick to just the extent that Ahab has been dehumanized. Victims of that overwhelming "universal thump" which only Moby Dick can deliver, they have looked into Ahab's mirror—but they have not seen there what Ahab has seen.[5]

VII

ISHMAEL'S HYPOS
The Propriety of Devil-Worship

IN A LETTER to Evert Duyckinck, written in 1849, two years before
the publication of *Moby-Dick*, Melville expressed his sense of the
galling limitations which inhibit intimacy between reader and writer.
"What a madness & anguish it is," he complained, "that an author
can never—under no conceivable circumstances—be at all frank with
his readers."[1] The remark strikes an odd note, coming as it does
from the creator of Ishmael, who appears to be the most frank
and accessible of men. "Call me Ishmael," he begins, with the hearty
abruptness of a sailor, and after the manner of a man who has nothing to hide. The initial handful of chapters in particular are delivered
to us in the off-hand, throw-away tone one expects from a simple
seaman. He went on a whaling voyage, Ishmael tells us, because
there was "no money in my purse, and nothing particular to interest

me on shore." He decides upon a four years' cruise, if we may believe him, as if he were planning to row a dinghy across an inland pond of a summer's afternoon: "I thought I would sail about a little and see the watery part of the world" (1: *12*).* He pretends to find it impossible to take the whole business seriously, and it is clear he hopes the reader too will assume his casual attitude. In the "grand programme of Providence," he assures us, the voyage of the *Pequod* was to be merely a "brief interlude and solo between more extensive performances" (1: *16*). For something so trivial, elaborate preparations were hardly necessary. "I stuffed a shirt or two into my old carpet-bag, tucked it under my arm, and started for Cape Horn and the Pacific" (2: *16*). Thus does Ishmael work hard—perhaps a trifle *too* hard—to convince us that there are no depths to *him*, and that his listeners need anticipate nothing more than a casually entertaining sailor's yarn in what follows. Melville may have found the impossibility of frankness with his readers a "madness & anguish," but a convivial openness appears to be the most natural thing in the world for Ishmael.

And this is precisely the point. We should be suspicious of a creature who finds frankness so easy when his creator finds it so difficult. We should respond to Ishmael's instant camaraderie with the reserve immediate intimacy deserves. For the fact is that Ishmael's off-hand tone is a screen deliberately thrown up to distract us from certain terrible urgencies of his inner being. He is, in relation to the reader, in the position of the man who pays out quantities of hard-earned cash he can ill afford to unburden himself to a psychoanalyst, and who then lies steadily and desperately to him in session after session. Ishmael too knows that he who speaks of the Gorgon must confront the Gorgon. We can therefore expect from him what he himself gets from the cryptic Elijah, an "ambiguous, half-hinting, half-revealing, shrouded sort of talk" (19: *88*). Ishmael will speak the truth and reveal his soul to us, but only by imperceptible stages, always reluctantly, and frequently with a

* The number before the colon in all parenthetical references in the text indicates chapter, which will be the same for most American editions of *Moby-Dick*; the italicized numbers after the colon indicate page in the Norton Critical Edition of *Moby-Dick*, edited by Harrison Hayford and Hershel Parker (New York: W. W. Norton & Company, 1967).

duplicity of meaning which finds its source in the furtive hope that we will, after all, miss or misunderstand what he is really trying to tell us. It is this "shrouded" idiom—what C. C. Walcutt calls "double- and triple-talk"—which makes *Moby-Dick* the supreme example of underground fiction in American literature.[2]

What Ishmael is trying to tell us in the first paragraph of his tale, for example, is entirely inconsonant with the slapdash tone he assumes in the telling of it. The beginning is pure froth: he went a-whaling because there was "nothing particular to interest me on shore." We reach an only slightly deeper level when he explains that such sea-voyages are his way of "driving off the spleen, and regulating the circulation." It is only at this point, with the careless reader now off his guard, that Ishmael confesses to a soul filled with "damp, drizzly November," to an obsession with coffin warehouses and funerals, and to a hypochondria which frequently gets "an upper hand of me." And thus, by covert gradation, to his first shrouded revelation, that he is steeped in despair to the point of suicide. A sea-voyage is, he tells us off-handedly, "my substitute for pistol and ball." Fearful that we will miss what is being furtively conveyed, Ishmael says it twice: "With a philosophical flourish Cato throws himself upon his sword; I quietly take to the ship" (1: *12*).[3] Read in this way, the "humorous" opening of *Moby-Dick* darkens to a grim ambiguity. Our joking sailor friend is actually a suicidal neurotic, afflicted with what Melville, in an 1851 letter to Hawthorne, called "crotchetty and over doleful chimearas, the like of which men like you and me and some others, forming a chain of God's posts round the world, must be content to encounter now and then, and fight them the best way we can."[4] Melville's "chimearas" become Ishmael's "hypos": Ishmael will use the term once more, in the course of his tortured discussion of the meaning of whiteness. "But thou sayest, methinks this white-lead chapter about whiteness is but a white flag hung out from a craven soul; thou surrenderest to a hypo, Ishmael" (42: *168–69*). Ishmael's soul is not craven, however, but instead immensely courageous. Rather than surrendering, he battles his hypos, and eventually resolves them. It is this terrible psychological struggle which constitutes the central narrative thread of *Moby-Dick*.

Before examining the hypos that Ishmael *does* have, however, it is necessary to touch briefly on a hypo he does *not* have. Ishmael, to state the matter succinctly, is no Ishmael. He is no misanthrope, no hater of mankind, either when he tells his story, or at that indeterminately earlier period when the voyage of the *Pequod* took place. His name is misleading, for the Biblical Ishmael is a "wild man; and his hand will be against every man, and every man's hand against him" (Genesis 16, *11–12*). Melville gives the name this conventional meaning when he has Redburn remark that "at last I found myself a sort of Ishmael in the ship, without a single friend or companion; and I began to feel a hatred growing up in me against the whole crew."[5] The Ishmael of *Moby-Dick* seems to reveal himself as precisely this sort of Ishmaelite when he confesses that the friendship of Queequeg caused a "melting" in him, so that "No more my splintered heart and maddened hand were turned against the wolfish world" (10: *53*). It is only necessary to assume that the "wolfish world" is the world of Ishmael's fellow men, and we have the alienated outcast of established critical opinion.

The only difficulty is that all the evidence points in the opposite direction. It is difficult to believe that Ishmael is a man-hater when he gets on a first-name basis with his readers immediately, and later apostrophizes them as "sweet friends" (15: *65*). He has, moreover, his own sweet friends: we see two of them in Don Pedro and Don Sebastian of Lima, to whom he tells the story of the *Town-Ho*. The demeanor of these noble Dons toward Ishmael, and his toward them, is a model of urbane friendship and polished sociability (54: *208, 214–15*). Ishmael also devotes an entire chapter to the *gam*, retailing with unmistakable gusto the "friendly and sociable contact" which is carried on between whalers which have "dear domestic things to talk about." Unlike the stiff-necked man-of-war, the whaler is full of "right-down hearty good-will and brotherly love." There is nothing quite like "the godly, honest, unostentatious, hospitable, sociable, free-and-easy whaler" (53: *205–06*), of which the *Samuel Enderby* is a prime example: "... a jolly ship; of good fare and plenty; fine flip and strong; crack fellows all, and capital from boot heels to hat-band" (101: *370–71*). Indeed, Ishmael exhibits a most un-Ishmaelite sociability even *before* Queequeg causes a "melting" in him. In New Bedford, Ishmael goes to what he hopefully calls the "social breakfast table" of the Spouter-Inn, "preparing to hear some good stories about whaling." He is deeply disappointed when the shaggy-bearded "timid warrior whalemen" gathered about the table are sheepishly embarrassed by each other's presence, maintaining a "profound silence" like so many "bashful bears" (5: *36*). Similarly, when Peter Coffin offers him a share of an unknown harpooneer's bed, Ishmael's response does not suggest misanthropy: "I would put up with the half of any decent man's blanket" (3: *22*). Next morning, he is not offended by Queequeg's "bridegroom clasp," but instead finds it a "comical predicament" (4: *33*). Neither is he offended by Peter Coffin's joke. "I cherished no malice towards him, though he had been skylarking with me not a little in the matter of my bedfellow" (5: *35*). Melville's careful development of Ishmael's hearty taste for the company of his fellow men thus forces us to cast about for another explanation of his name, and another interpretation of the fact that his "splintered heart and maddened hand were turned against the wolfish world" (10: *53*). Whatever it is which has alienated him must be more ultimate, more fundamental, than the day-to-day fallibilities of his fellow-mortals. Misanthropy can be discounted in any analysis of Ishmael's hypos.

Though Ishmael approaches his fellows with gregarious affability, it does not necessarily follow that he *trusts* them entirely. In particular, he seems honestly doubtful concerning the degree of sympathy his unconventional hypos can be expected to elicit from the conventional reader. So he hedges his bets by salting the story with affirmations of conventional belief which often stand cheek-by-jowl with passages expressing the most pervasive doubt. Lifted out of context, these affirmative passages have been used to give the novel a positive thrust of meaning which only serves to obfuscate further what Ishmael is trying, by shrouded indirection, to convey. It would be a mistake, for example, to discount the possibility of irony in his assertion that "I was a good Christian; born and bred in the bosom of the infallible Presbyterian Church" (10: *54*). His straight-faced use of "infallible" here ought to make us wonder how, exactly, he wishes to be taken. The same problem arises when he comments on Father Mapple's prow-shaped pulpit. "What could be more full of meaning?" he rhetorically asks, "for the pulpit is ever this earth's foremost part; all the rest comes in its rear; the pulpit leads the world.... Yes, the world's a ship on its passage out, and not a voyage complete; and the pulpit is its prow" (8: *43–44*). Such sentiments, expressed in such terms, verge unmistakably toward caricature of conventional affirmation. They are out of consonance with the probing, skeptical, ironic tonalities of the preponderant Ishmaelian voice. This is clearly the case with the affirmation which concludes Ishmael's contemplation of the cenotaphs, memorializing the deaths of whalemen who have "placelessly perished without a grave," which line the walls of the Whaleman's Chapel. "It needs scarcely to be told," Ishmael confides to us, "with what feelings, on the eve of a Nantucket voyage, I regarded those marble tablets, and by the murky light of that darkened, doleful day read the fate of the whalemen who had gone before me. Yes, Ishmael," he gloomily tells himself, "the same fate may be thine." And then he pretends to an abrupt and positive change of mood:

> But somehow I grew merry again. Delightful inducements to embark, fine chance for promotion, it seems—aye, a stove boat will make me an immortal by brevet. Yes, there is death in this business of whaling —a speechlessly quick chaotic bundling of a man into Eternity. But what then? Methinks we have hugely mistaken this matter of Life and Death. Methinks that what they call my shadow here on earth is my true substance.... Methinks my body is but the lees of my better being. In fact take my body who will, take it I say, it is not me. And therefore three cheers for Nantucket; and come a stove boat and stove body when they will, for stave my soul, Jove himself cannot. (7: *41*)

It is difficult to believe that the man who is hastening to sea because of an obsession with coffin warehouses and funerals can so abruptly dismiss death as unimportant for the flaccidly orthodox reason that only the body dies while the soul, "my shadow here on earth," lives on immortally. Such sentiments cannot be reconciled with Ishmael's assertion, only two paragraphs earlier, that the cenotaphs, which "cover no ashes," seem to "refuse resurrections" to those who have anonymously died in distant seas. It will take more than the athletic Christian optimism of Ishmael's "three cheers for Nantucket" to resolve his doubts concerning death and the unknown bourne which lies beyond.

The caution with which the conventionally affirmative passages of *Moby-Dick* must be approached is best exemplified, however, in the pair of paragraphs at the end of Chapter 26, in which Ishmael asserts the existence of a conventional deity, the "Spirit of Equality," the "great democratic God," from whom the dignity of ordinary men eternally flows:

> But this august dignity I treat of, is not the dignity of kings and robes, but that abounding dignity which has no robed investiture. Thou shalt see it shining in the arm that wields a pick or drives a spike; that democratic dignity which, on all hands, radiates without end from God; Himself! The great God absolute! The centre and circumference of all democracy! His omnipresence, our divine equality! (26: *104*)

Ishmael cites Bunyan, Cervantes, and Andrew Jackson as examples of the "high qualities," the "tragic graces," and the "ethereal light" with which his God of Democracy invests the common man. "Thou who," he concludes, "in all Thy mighty earthly marchings, ever cullest Thy selectest champions from the kingly commons; bear me out in it, O God!" (26: *104–05*).

These are immensely comfortable sentiments, for the reader as well as for Ishmael. Howard P. Vincent is able to accept them without reservation, asserting that "Melville's words are not merely the rip tide of rhetoric. They are deep belief." Henry Nash Smith, similarly, sees them as "the central affirmation of the novel."[6] They parallel, moreover, the note of chauvinistic Christian optimism in Melville's essay on Hawthorne, where he refers ecstatically to "those writers who breathe that unshackled, democratic spirit of Christianity in all things, which now takes the practical lead in this world, though at the same time led by ourselves—us Americans."[7] But Ishmael is *not* Melville. What he says here must be reconciled, if that is possible, with the rest of the textual continuum which is the only vehicle for whatever being he enjoys. How, for example, to reconcile the conventionally democratic God of Ishmael's panegyric with the undemocratic God of Father Mapple's equally conventional sermon? Again, what are we to make of this apostrophe to an "absolute" and "omnipresent" God when we recall that Ishmael, having found the absolutist and omnipresent Christianity of New England "but hollow courtesy" (10: *53*), has chosen to "turn idolator" (10: *54*), accepting a heathen cannibal as his "bosom friend"? It is equally difficult to reconcile the "abounding dignity" of Ishmael's "kingly commons" with the way in which the *Pequod's* crew of common men becomes the subservient tool of Ahab's sultan will, merely "various wheels" which revolve obediently in response to their Captain's inexorable "cogged circle" (37: *147*). We can accept Ishmael's assertion that ideal man is a "noble and ... sparkling, ... grand and glowing creature" (26: *104*)—but there appear to be no ideal men aboard the *Pequod*, and the democratic God does not move in any apparent way through the *Pequod's* sharkish world. While Ishmael's conventional affirmations are not exactly false—we all entertain levels of belief which are mutually inconsistent—they are misleading, and perhaps deliberately so. The reader who accepts them at face value is in danger of underestimating the hypos, corrosive of all faith and inimical of all belief, which have driven Ishmael into desperate pursuit of the "gliding great demon of the seas of life" (41: *162*).

Ishmael's conventional affirmations do not ring true because he is the chagrined and reluctant host to "unbidden infidelities" (7: *41*), terrible doubts which Melville himself, in a note appended to Leaf 311 of the manuscript version of *Billy Budd*, called "an irruption of heretic thought hard to suppress."[8] Orthodoxy can no longer persuade Ishmael from the conviction that "Though in many of its aspects this visible world seems formed in love, the invisible spheres were formed in fright" (42: *169*). He tells how, once the blubber is stripped from the whale, and the vast, whitened body cast loose, it is frequently sighted at night by some other ship and set down in the log and on the charts as *"shoals, rocks, and breakers hereabouts: beware!"* For years after such a sighting, Ishmael asserts, all ships shun the place. Such sheep-like foolishness becomes a paradigm for the lack of realism of established faith. "There's your law of precedents," Ishmael bursts out; "there's your utility of traditions; there's the story of your obstinate survival of old beliefs never bottomed on the earth, and now not even hovering in the air! There's orthodoxy!" (69: *262*). It is Queequeg, early in the novel, who precipitates this rejection of traditional formulations—for

Queequeg too, like Ahab and Starbuck, is a man of faith. When, with the impenetrable stubbornness of the orthodox, he refuses to allow anything to interrupt his "Ramadan," Ishmael subjects the indifferent savage to a long lecture on the history of the world's religions, designed to prove that "Lents, Ramadans, and prolonged ham-squattings in cold, cheerless rooms were stark nonsense; bad for the health; useless for the soul; opposed, in short, to the obvious laws of Hygiene and common sense." It is not Queequeg's religion, but the disintegration of his own Christianity which Ishmael is talking about when he attempts to justify intruding in this way upon another man's faith. "But when a man's religion becomes really frantic," he explains, "when it is a positive torment to him; and, in fine, makes this earth of ours an uncomfortable inn to lodge in; then I think it high time to take that individual aside and argue the point with him" (17: *81*). It is not Queequeg, but Ishmael, who has been driven "frantic" by orthodoxy.

What has brought Ishmael to this pass is a terrible insight into the true nature of religious faith. He has come to see that faith, because it cannot be sustained on the basis of the facts of this "wolfish world," must be sustained in terms of another world. Since that other world can only be approached through death, the inexorable consequence is that conventional faith draws its vitality, not from life, but from death. This is what he means when, during his contemplation of the Chapel cenotaphs, he remarks despairingly that "Faith, like a jackal, feeds among the tombs, and even from these dead doubts she gathers her most vital hope" (7: *41*). But even the "vital hope" of faith is based on an underlying hopelessness. When, some chapters later and during the *Pequod's* first lowering for whales, Ishmael's boat is separated from the ship during a squall and lost in blackest night, Queequeg lights a lantern and hoists it on a waif-pole. Ishmael sees this gesture as emblematic of the true nature of hope. "There, then, [Queequeg] sat, holding up that imbecile candle in the heart of that almighty forlornness. There, then, he sat, the sign and symbol of a man without faith, hopelessly holding up hope in the midst of despair" (48: *195*). Faith, in short, lives on death, and hope on hopelessness. It is therefore essential for Ishmael's psychological survival that he abandon both faith and hope as, like Narcissus, he makes his suicide-dive into the primal ocean.

For in the elemental world into which the *Pequod* is sailing, to abandon faith is an act of faith; to give up hope is the beginning of hope. Ishmael, by the time he meets his first real whale, having moved already to the freezing center of despair, will be in a position to come out, gradually, on the other side.

This examination of Ishmael's loss of faith and hope makes it possible to offer an explanation other than the traditional one for the name Melville gives him. Ishmael is not an Ishmaelite in the misanthropic sense. But he *is* an Ishmael, an outcast, in Christian New England, a viper in the bosom of doctrinal orthodoxy, a speculative and intellectual traitor to his whole religious heritage. Instead of the benign world of the Christian vision, he now sees a "wolfish world," where faith lives on carrion flesh. If he suffers from a "splintered heart and maddened hand," what has splintered and maddened him is not his fellow men, but rather the predacious world in which men must live. Ishmael's name is an expression of the deep sense of guilt that he feels because he can no longer be the orthodox Christian which, as the novel begins, he pretends to be. Driven by this guilt he flees to sea, knowing as the unresting Bulkington knows that "all deep, earnest thinking is but the intrepid effort of the soul to keep the open independence of her sea" (23: *97*). What drives the wordless Bulkington to such intrepid effort we never know, but what drives Ishmael can be specified with some precision. As the *Pequod* sets sail on that frigid Christmas day, Ishmael, casting off from the lee shore of orthodoxy, carries with him into that howling infinite three major hypos. The first is concerned with *death*, the second with the *void*, and the third with the pervasive *sharkishness* of nature and of man. These hypos, which orthodoxy has only exacerbated, he must resolve in the primordial realm of landlessness, or die in the attempt, for there and there only, as he tells us, "resides the highest truth, shoreless, indefinite as God" (23: *97*).

Ishmael's first-paragraph assertion, that he went to sea because he found himself "involuntarily pausing before coffin warehouses, and bringing up the rear of every funeral" (1: *12*) is much more than a vaguely humorous expression of that fear of death which all men feel. It is rather the opening statement of a motif which gradually develops into a masterfully ambiguous and altogether uncom-

mon view of death. Ishmael sets the stage for this development by
frequent death-references scattered through the early chapters. As
he feels his way through the frozen blackness of a Saturday night in
New Bedford, he occasionally glimpses a light in a window, "like
a candle moving about in a tomb." Mistaking a Negro church for
an inn, he stumbles over an ash-box in the entry-way and, almost
choked in the cloud, asks himself if these are "ashes from that destroyed city, Gomorrah." The black congregation appears like
"the great Black Parliament sitting in Tophet," presided over by
a "black Angel of Doom" whose text is death, "the blackness of
darkness, and the weeping and wailing and teeth-gnashing there."
This black manifestation of Christianity he labels "The Trap." The
ramshackle Spouter-Inn engenders images of fire-and-death-deci-
mated Sodom; Ishmael remarks that the building looked as if it might
"have been carted here from the ruins of some burnt district." Nor
is he reassured by the name of the proprietor, Peter Coffin: "Coffin?—Spouter?—Rather ominous in that particular connexion,
thought I" (2: *18*). The December winds howling about the inn
bring to mind the coldness of a corpse, leading him to observe that
it makes a great difference whether you regard this frigid wind from
a warm hearth, "or whether thou observest it from that sashless
window, where the frost is on both sides, and of which the wight
Death is the only glazier" (2: *19*). Even inside the Spouter-Inn,
images of the grave pursue him. Called to the dinner-table, he finds
the room "cold as Iceland—no fire at all. . . . Nothing but two dismal tallow candles, each in a winding sheet" (3: *22*). His first glimpse
of Queequeg is with a shrunken New Zealand head in his hand—
"a ghastly thing enough"—and when his new bed-mate takes off
his hat, his "bald purplish head . . . looked for all the world like a
mildewed skull" (3: *29*).

Nantucket is little better. The cenotaphs of the Whaleman's
Chapel engender the most funereal considerations, and on his return to Hosea Hussey's Try-Pots Inn Ishmael notices that the sign
over the entry is gallows-shaped. "It's ominous, thinks I. A Coffin
my Innkeeper upon landing in my first whaling port; tombstones
staring at me in the whalemen's chapel; and here a gallows! and a
pair of prodigious black pots too!" (15: *64*). When he and Queequeg go aboard the *Pequod* on Christmas Day and find a hung-over

rigger asleep on two chests in the crew's quarters, the tableau reminds Ishmael automatically of a corpse. He "jocularly hinted to Queequeg that perhaps we had best sit up with the body; telling him to establish himself accordingly." They seat themselves like mourners at a wake, Queequeg at the head, Ishmael at the feet (21: *92*).

But these heavy-handed death-references do nothing to illuminate the complexity of Ishmael's death-hypo. They suggest only that Ishmael, like all of us, wants to live rather than die. On one level, this is precisely what he means. He is horrified by the "speechlessly quick chaotic bundling of a man into Eternity" (7: *41*). But what really obsesses Ishmael is not so much death as the thought of what may lie on the *other side* of death. The cenotaphs intensify an already agonizing hypo because they are markers marking no grave, headstones where no head will ever rest, memorials to men whose flesh and bones are immured forever, not in some circumscribed spot within human ken, but in alien and un-Christian seas. Because they have nothing behind them, the cenotaphs articulate Ishmael's fear that there is nothing beyond death. Resurrection of the body and life everlasting are conceivable for those who lie in a Christian grave—but what of these men, whose remains are dispersed along the kelpy bottoms of the seven seas?

> Oh! ye whose dead lie buried beneath the green grass; who standing among flowers can say—here, *here* lies my beloved; ye know not the desolation that broods in bosoms like these. What bitter blanks in those black-bordered marbles which cover no ashes! What despair in those immovable inscriptions! What deadly voids and unbidden infidelities in the lines that seem to gnaw upon all Faith, and refuse resurrections to the beings who have placelessly perished without a grave. As well might those tablets stand in the cave of Elephanta as here. (7: *41*)

For if the living really believed in the after-life, would they not act differently than in fact they do?

> In what census of living creatures [Ishmael sardonically asks], the dead of mankind are included; why it is that a universal proverb says of them, that they tell no tales, though containing more secrets than the Goodwin Sands; how it is that to his name who yesterday departed for the other world, we prefix so significant and infidel a word

[Ishmael has a horror of becoming the "late" Ishmael], and yet do
not thus entitle him, if he but embarks for the remotest Indies of this
living earth[?] (7: *41*)

The answers are obvious. We do not include the dead in the census
of the living because in our heart of hearts we do not really believe
that they are *anywhere* living. The proverb asserts that the dead tell
no tales, not because the dead are so uniformly silent, but because
there is no tale to tell. We call the dead the "late" dead because the
term obliquely suggests a finality in death we cannot directly admit.
Such ideas are not confined to the Ishmael of *Moby-Dick*. "But
why this gloom at the thought of the dead?" Redburn asks. "And
why should we not be glad? Is it, that we ever think of [the dead]
as departed from all joy? Is it, that we believe that indeed they are
dead? They revisit us not, the departed; their voices no more ring
in the air."[9] The dead, for both Redburn and Ishmael, are "indeed
... dead." Such is the effect of unbidden infidelities on orthodox
belief and conventional affirmation.

Nevertheless, the reader who assumes that a simple fear of annihilation is the sum of Ishmael's necrophobia has fallen victim to
the shrouding, the persistent verbal masking, which makes the idiom
of *Moby-Dick* so extraordinarily deceptive. Ishmael does indeed
entertain misgivings concerning the Christian doctrine of the immortality of the soul. Overtly, he is fearful that he *will not* live
forever. Covertly, however, he is terrified that he *will*. On the surface, he yearns for immortality. Under the surface, where the dark
things move, he finds immortality a concept too horrible to contemplate. This subterranean fear accounts for the odd shift in
meaning which occurs halfway through the paragraph of ironic
questions which the cenotaphs generate:

... in what eternal, unstirring paralysis, and deadly, hopeless trance,
yet lies antique Adam who died sixty round centuries ago; how it is
that we still refuse to be comforted for those who we nevertheless
maintain are dwelling in unspeakable bliss; why all the living so strive
to hush all the dead; wherefore but the rumor of a knocking in a tomb
will terrify a whole city[?] (7: *41*)

"All these things," Ishmael suggestively concludes, "are not without
their meanings."

The "meanings" are, however, perplexing. The paragraph has ostensibly been developing the idea of death-as-annihilation, but "antique Adam" has *not* been annihilated. Instead, the phrasing suggests he is somehow *still alive* and *still aware*, frozen for "sixty round centuries" in some appalling kind of "unstirring paralysis" and "hopeless trance" which is "eternal." Except for Queequeg's Ramadan, twenty-four hours of immobility during which the savage seems to be practicing up for just such a trance-after-death, nothing in *Moby-Dick* is of direct help in explaining Ishmael's meaning concerning "antique Adam." We are therefore forced once again to seek in the extracetological evidence for clarification.

Melville himself, it turns out, entertained fears of a Godless nothingness beyond death in which, somehow, the individual might continue to exist. In *Clarel*, Rolfe suggests that atheism really solves no philosophical problems: "But though 'twere made / Demonstrable that God is not— / What then? it would not change this lot: / The ghost would haunt, nor could be laid."[10] This is the ghost of Things Still Possible. The reason it cannot be laid is simple: God may *not* be ultimate, and therefore His non-existence would have no effect on ultimate problems. It is suggestive that in his London *Journal* the only reference Melville makes to the theories of his companion on the journey, George Adler, is the notation that Adler "believes that there are things *out* of God and independent of him,—things which would have existed were there no God:—such as that two & two make four."[11] The idea of such an antedeific realm of predeific being is adumbrated in *Moby-Dick*. During his confrontation with the corpusants, which Ishmael pointedly calls a "tri-pointed trinity of flames" (119: *416*), Ahab affirms the existence of some "unsuffusing thing" which stands anterior to and therefore superior to deity, and in relation to which all deity's "eternity is but time, all [deity's] creativeness mechanical" (119: *417*). It was the possibility of a world presided over by this "unsuffusing thing," a world which might exist even if God did not, which terrified Melville. Sometime in April of 1862, a decade after the publication of *Moby-Dick*, he scored a passage in Madame de Stael's *Germany*: "Bayle has somewhere said, that *atheism does not shelter us from the fear of eternal suffering* [Melville's scoring]; it is a grand thought, and it offers to us a wide field for reflection." Then Melville scribbled a response to

Madame de Stael in the margin: "If we assume that the existence of God makes eternal suffering possible, *then* it may justly be said that Atheism furnishes no defences against the fear of it." [12] Man may live forever, even if God does not—even if God never lived—and if man may live forever, he may suffer forever. The horrifying implications of this idea are given a somewhat different thrust in *Mardi*. Babbalanja, in the course of his meditation on the ranked ancestors of Donjalolo in the House of the Afternoon (Chapter 68), draws out some of the implications of existence outside of time and in eternity. "But die we then living?" asks Babbalanja. "Yet if our dead fathers somewhere and somehow live, why not our unborn sons? For backward or forward, eternity is the same; *already have we been the nothing we dread to be*. Icy thought!" (italics mine). [13] Outside of time and in eternity, Babbalanja suggests, *we have always been*. Had we not always been in eternity, we could not now, for the moment, be in time. But this being in eternity, which brackets our temporal life is, if Babbalanja means what he says, a kind of being in nothingness. This is why we fear death, dreading to be once again the "nothing" we have already been—or perhaps more precisely, been *in*.

What this "icy thought" lacks in logical rigor it makes up for in sheer terror, a terror which is most unequivocally expressed in Melville's odd little tale, "The Happy Failure." The narrator's uncle has invented an "Hydraulic-Hydrostatic Apparatus," the purpose of which is "draining swamps and marshes, and converting them, at the rate of one acre the hour, into fields more fertile than those of the Genesee." The story has to do with man's persistent attempts to bring field out of swamp, order out of chaos, something out of nothing. The uncle's apparatus might be considered a sort of hydraulic-hydrostatic "chaos-reducer" or "nothing-eliminator." If this is the meaning, then there is immense significance in the uncle's reaction when the apparatus fails its first test. His nephew attempts to console him with the assertion that "While there is life there is hope." For this drearily conventional affirmation, the uncle has a terrible reply: "*While there is life hereafter there is despair,*" he howls (italics mine). [14] Melville shared this despair, and so does Ishmael. This is the meaning of his image of "antique Adam" who, denied the gift of oblivion and the nepenthe of annihilation, lies locked in an "eternal, unstirring paralysis, and deadly, hopeless trance," immured in nothingness forevermore. It also explains why "all the living so strive to hush all the dead," so that "but the rumor of a knocking in a tomb will terrify a whole city." It would be beyond bearing to have someone emerge from the grave only to confirm horribly what we all, in that dark region just beyond conscious formulation, already suspect.

But we have not yet reached the nadir of Ishmael's hypo concerning death. Eternal existence *without* God, the situation of "antique Adam," is Ishmael's penultimate death-hypo. Eternal existence *with* God is his ultimate one. This fact will not surprise the attentive reader. Hints concerning this supreme fear are scattered throughout *Moby-Dick*. If, as Ishmael asserts, "the invisible spheres were formed in fright" (42: *169*), then it follows inexorably that existence in those spheres would be frightful, and the presence of the Creator of them the ultimate fright. Ishmael cannot believe in the Beatific Vision. Given the nature of the "wolfish world," however, he finds it quite easy to believe in a Malefic Vision. Perhaps this is because he has already experienced it in oneiric form. When he awakens that Sunday morning in New Bedford to find the horrendous Queequeg embracing him, he tells us in what is probably the supreme piece of understatement in the novel, that "My sensations were strange." He then attempts an explanation of the strangeness he feels by recounting a childhood experience, when, because he was disobedient, his step-mother sent him to bed in broad daylight as punishment. "I lay there dismally calculating that sixteen entire hours must elapse before I could hope for a resurrection. Sixteen hours in bed!" And then, with daylight streaming into the room, he drifts into sleep:

> At last I must have fallen into a troubled nightmare of a doze; and slowly waking from it—half steeped in dreams—I opened my eyes, and the before sunlit room was now wrapped in outer darkness. Instantly I felt a shock running through all my frame; nothing was to be seen, and nothing was to be heard; but a supernatural hand seemed placed in mine. My arm hung over the counterpane, and the nameless, unimaginable, silent form or phantom, to which the hand belonged, seemed closely seated by my bed-side. For what seemed

ages piled on ages, I lay there, frozen with the most awful fears, not daring to drag away my hand; yet ever thinking that if I could but stir it one single inch, the horrid spell would be broken. (4: *33*)

The next thing he knows it is morning, and he is awake, returned to the temporal world, aware that the dream has some terrible significance: "I lost myself in confounding attempts to explain the mystery. Nay, to this very hour, I often puzzle myself with it."

The puzzle is not beyond resolution, even if Ishmael, perhaps in instinctive self-protection, has failed to solve it. His dream is a paradigm of life-after-death; his "horrid spell" is antique Adam's "deadly, hopeless trance"; his frozen inability to stir his hand "one single inch" is Adam's "eternal, unstirring paralysis"; his sense of interminable suffering, of "ages piled on ages" is equivalent to the "sixty round centuries" which Adam has endured (7: *41*; 4: *33*). The single difference is that undying Adam seems to be alone in his nothingness, whereas Ishmael, wrapped in stygian blackness, is in physical, immediate contact with a "nameless, unimaginable, silent form or phantom," an unknowable Malefic Presence. It does not force the textual evidence to suggest that this Presence is the God who formed the invisible spheres in fright, the God who made the whale, the squid, and the shark, the God whom Queequeg calls "one dam Ingin" (66: *257*). If this is what we will meet on the other side of death, then we can account for what Ishmael, in the supremely shrouded chapter on "The Whiteness of the Whale," calls that "one visible quality in the aspect of the dead which most appalls the gazer, ... the marble pallor lingering there." What the dead encounter in the next world, Ishmael suggests, causes them to turn pale with fright, "as if indeed that pallor were as much the badge of consternation in the other world, as of mortal trepidation here." Instinctively, perhaps subliminally, we know *why* the dead are pale, and give covert articulation to that fearful knowledge: "And from that pallor of the dead," Ishmael concludes, "we borrow the expressive hue of the shroud in which we wrap them" (42: *166*). Father Mapple, the voice of orthodox affirmation in *Moby-Dick*, promises ineffable delight—"top-gallant delight"—in the next world. If the next world is so delightful, Ishmael obliquely asks, why then this "badge of consternation" on the face of the dead?

The cenotaphs of the Whaleman's Chapel, however, are emblematic of more than Ishmael's hypo concerning death. Because they "cover no ashes," concealing only an emptiness, they give concrete expression to his second great hypo, a neurotic sense of nothingness behind phenomena and at the heart of noumena—a haunting fear of the *void*. This is a fear he shares with Ahab, who confesses in the quarter-deck scene that "Sometimes I think there's naught beyond" (36: *144*), and who later finds the hollow reverberation of the carpenter's mallet on Queequeg's coffin intolerable because he knows that "what in all things makes the sounding-board is this—there's naught beneath" (127: *432*). Naught beyond and naught beneath: it is this sense of an ontological vacancy beneath appearances which Ishmael develops most explicitly in the brilliant chapter on "The Whiteness of the Whale" (42: *163–70*). As with many chapters of *Moby-Dick*, it is the final paragraph which contains the quintessential meanings Ishmael is pursuing—in this instance, the color of white as a symbol of nothingness:

> Is it that by its indefiniteness it shadows forth the heartless voids and immensities of the universe, and thus stabs us from behind with the thought of annihilation, when beholding the white depths of the milky way? Or is it, that as in essence whiteness is not so much a color as the visible absence of color, and at the same time the concrete of all colors; is it for these reasons that there is such a dumb blankness, full of meaning, in a wide landscape of snows—a colorless, all-color of atheism from which we shrink? (42: *169*)

Even the life-giving sun, Ishmael will later assert in "The Try-Works" chapter, cannot mask from our sight the atheistical voids in and among which man must live his life: ". . . the sun hides not Virginia's Dismal Swamp, nor Rome's accursed Campagna, nor wide Sahara, nor all the millions of miles of deserts and of griefs beneath the moon." The very ocean through which the *Pequod* sails is a supreme instance of these "heartless voids and immensities" which constantly urge upon us that which we do not wish to know. "The sun hides not the ocean," Ishmael continues, "which is the dark side of this earth, and which is two thirds of this earth" (96: *354–55*).

Just as Ahab sneers at the sensuous "low, enjoying power," dis-

missing visible objects as "pasteboard masks," so does Ishmael, while
he remains under Ahab's influence, find it difficult to accept the
phenomenal world as anything more than a deceptive cover for the
voids which lie beneath:

> And when we consider that other theory of the natural philoso-
> phers, that all other earthly hues—every stately or lovely emblazon-
> ing—the sweet tinges of sunset skies and woods; yea, and the gilded
> velvets of butterflies, and the butterfly cheeks of young girls; all
> these are but subtile deceits, not actually inherent in substances, but
> only laid on from without; so that all deified Nature absolutely paints
> like the harlot, whose allurements cover nothing but the charnel-
> house within; . . . pondering all this, the palsied universe lies before us
> a leper; and . . . the wretched infidel gazes himself blind at the monu-
> mental white shroud that wraps all the prospect around him. (42:
> *169–70*)

Nature here, the sensuous manifold, is a universal cenotaph, covering nothing. Just as the summation of all colors is white, so also
the summation of all reality is the void. Human perception is a
subtly deceitful activity whereby an enshrouded albino cosmos is
endowed with a warm sensuousness, a reassuring beauty, a poly-
chromatic intensity, all of which encourage us in the belief that the
ultimate foundations of existence rest on something, instead of
nothing. Nature is thus the supreme harlot, bedecking herself with
overwhelming seductiveness, beguiling us into the fatuous conviction that that which is so beautiful must be as real, and as good,
as it is beautiful. It is this, the *aesthetic coherence* of the world, which
persuades us of the preponderant benignity of the cosmos—or, more
precisely, *almost* persuades us. For the whole burden of Ishmael's
dissertation on whiteness is that we are *not* persuaded, that even in
the most affirmative, mythically eloquent symbolism the human
race has devised, there lurk emblematic articulations of our doubts
and fears. With striking unanimity, men of all cultures and epochs
of history have chosen whiteness as the emblem of these misgivings,
for "there yet lurks an elusive something in the innermost idea of
this hue, which strikes more of panic to the soul than that redness
which affrights in blood."

A full appreciation of what Ishmael is saying can best be achieved
by reading this most crucial of chapters in a kind of backward

fashion, beginning at the end, with his assertion that whiteness is a "dumb blankness," a "colorless all-color of atheism" which, when fully understood, can only produce a "wretched infidel." When the innumerable instances of whiteness which he cites in the course of the chapter are interpreted from this "infidel" perspective, it becomes apparent that Ishmael's hypo is one which all men of all times have shared. If St. John, that raptly affirmative mystic, personified death as a pale rider on a pale horse, it is because St. John in his secret heart saw death as a plunge into the void. If phantoms and ghosts in all ages rise always in a "milk-white fog," it is because we secretly believe that they come to us from nothingness. Similarly, if we wrap the dead in white it is because we are covertly certain that they go only to nothingness. If "the Albino man so peculiarly repels and often shocks the eye" even though he has "no substantive deformity," it is because this "mere aspect of all-pervading whiteness" in human form makes overt our conviction that the void in nature is matched by a correlative void in man. "Appalling is the soul of a man!" exclaims the narrator of *Pierre*, using the pyramid-figure in precisely the sense that Ishmael uses the cenotaph-figure. "By vast pains we mine into the pyramid; by horrible gropings we come to the central room; with joy we espy the sarcophagus; but we lift the lid—and no body is there!—appallingly vacant as vast is the soul of a man!" [15]

But it is Ishmael's citations of whiteness in association with *deity* which are best calculated to produce the "wretched infidel." He points out that "in the higher mysteries of the most august religions [whiteness] has been made the symbol of the divine spotlessness and power." Jove incarnated himself in a "snow-white bull"; the Iroquois offered a sacred White Dog to the Great Spirit; the Christian priest wears a white alb over his black cassock; "in the Vision of St. John, white robes are given to the redeemed, and the four-and-twenty elders stand clothed in white before the great white throne, and the Holy One that sitteth there white like wool." Ishmael earnestly assures us that these uses of whiteness are intended to express "whatever is sweet, and honorable, and sublime." But it is obvious that he means, and thinks the Evangelist meant, something quite the reverse. In a long footnote on the white albatross, which with "vast archangel wings" seems to "embrace some holy ark," Ishmael protests that "I cannot tell, can only hint" what the manifestation of whiteness in celestial forms means to him. Nevertheless, he comes remarkably close to telling us in another footnote on the "intolerable hideousness" of the polar bear, a hideousness which "arises from the circumstance, that the irresponsible ferociousness of the creature stands invested in the fleece of celestial innocence and love." Whiteness, even when celestially rendered, may be but the mask for a malign reality beneath. It is no accident that Ishmael appended this footnote to the paragraph immediately following the one which treats of whiteness as an expression of the deific. It is only a page or two later, moreover, that he asserts that these many uses of whiteness are but expressions of that "instinct" which all sentient creatures have "of the knowledge of the demonism in the world." In his subterranean way, Ishmael is saying that the void at the heart of man, and the void at the heart of nature, may both find their source in a void at the heart of deity. The God of Revelation may be white, not because He is pure, but because He is not. In *Pierre* this idea of deific nullity is given ironic expression in a despairing play on the word "hollow." The narrator remarks that Pierre seemed to discern the "Finger of God" in the terrible things that Isabel has revealed to him. And then he says: "... Finger of God? But it is not merely the Finger, it is the whole outspread Hand of God; for doth not Scripture intimate, that He holdeth all of us in the hollow of His hand?—*a Hollow, truly!*" (italics mine).[16]

If this is the case, if (to phrase it crudely) God is hollow, then no ultimate affirmations can be made because no ultimates exist. Melville himself in a letter to Hawthorne probably written in April of 1851, suggested just such a conceptual void behind appearances. He tells Hawthorne of his desire to treat "with all Powers [of the cosmos] upon an equal basis. If any of those other Powers choose to withhold certain secrets, let them; that does not impair my sovereignty in myself; that does not make me tributary. *And perhaps, after all, there is no secret*" (italics mine).[17] Ishmael shares Melville's suspicion that the only secret is that there is no secret, and hence nothing to tell. This is why the primal forms of *Moby-Dick* are tongueless and voiceless. Ishmael notes that the "young Orient

World" in their "child-magian" wisdom made a god of the crocodile "because the crocodile is tongueless." Similarly, "the Sperm Whale has no tongue" and steadfastly maintains a "pyramidical silence" (79: *292*); he is a "vast dumb brute" which has "no voice" (81: *298*). Ahab complains of this silence, mistaking it for secretiveness. "Speak, thou vast and venerable head," he abjures the "black and hooded" presence lashed to the *Pequod's* side like a "Sphynx... in the desert." "... speak, mighty head, and tell us the secret thing that is in thee." But even though Leviathan, of all nature's creatures, has "dived the deepest," and "moved amid this world's foundations," he has nothing to say. "O head!" cries Ahab, "thou hast seen enough to split the planets and make an infidel of Abraham, and not one syllable is thine!" (70: *264*). It is this silence of the natural world which is, for both Melville and Ishmael, the definitive sign of an ultimate nullity beneath reality. "Silence," asserts the narrator of *Pierre* with covert irony, "is the only Voice of our God."[18]

In *Mardi*, written two years before *Moby-Dick*, Babbalanja, in what Mohi impatiently dismisses as a "tirade of nonsense," expatiates on the horribly predacious quality of much natural process in what he calls our "fighting world." "Spiders, vixens, and tigers all war with a relish," he asserts, "and on every side is heard the howls of hyenas, the throttlings of mastiffs, the din of belligerent beetles, the buzzing warfare of the insect battalions.... And all this existeth of necessity."[19] Babbalanja's "fighting world" is Ishmael's "wolfish world" (10: *53*), which in *Moby-Dick* finds symbolic expression in the sea and the sea's inhabitants. Together they articulate Ishmael's third corrosive hypo, a sense of cosmic *sharkishness*. Not only is the sea a "foe to man," says Ishmael, ready to "insult and murder him, and pulverize the stateliest, stiffest frigate he can make." The sea is also a "fiend to its own offspring; worse than the Persian host who murdered his own guests; sparing not the creatures which itself hath spawned":

> Consider the subtleness of the sea; how its most dreaded creatures glide under water, unapparent for the most part, and treacherously hidden beneath the loveliest tints of azure. Consider also the devilish brilliance and beauty of many of its most remorseless tribes, as the

dainty embellished shape of many species of sharks. Consider, once
more, the universal cannibalism of the sea; all whose creatures prey
upon each other, carrying on eternal war since the world began.
(58: *235–36*)

For Ishmael it is the "accursed shark" (58: *235*) which best expresses the "devilish" quality of the natural world in its animate and
sentient aspects. It is the shark, swarming the globe in such uncounted and ubiquitous numbers—Ishmael seeing "the whole round
sea [as] one huge cheese, and those sharks the maggots in it" (66:
256)—which nudges one into unbidden infidelities, hinting that the
visible as well as the invisible spheres may have been formed, not in
love, but in fright. The night-time spectacle of hordes of sharks
ravaging the body of dead Leviathan pushes the observer to atheism,
and from atheism to something much worse. There is "no conceivable time or occasion," Ishmael tells us in what must stand as the
despairing nadir of *Moby-Dick*, "when you will find [sharks] in
such countless numbers, and in gayer or more jovial spirits, than
around a dead sperm whale, moored by night to a whale-ship at sea.
If you have never seen that sight, then suspend your decision about
the propriety of devil-worship, and the expediency of conciliating
the devil" (64: *250*).

The loathing and terror with which Ishmael regards the rapacity
of the natural world are as nothing, however, to the emotions he
feels when he regards rapacious man. Melville asserts in *Mardi* that
"of all nature's animated kingdoms, fish are the most unchristian,
inhospitable, heartless, and cold-blooded of creatures." But men
are no better than fish. Consider the "head-hunting Dyaks of Bor-
neo, or the blood-bibbing Battas of Sumatra. And are these Dyaks
and Battas one whit better than tiger-sharks? Nay, are they so
good?"[20] Ishmael knows that *he* is not so good as a tiger-shark, and
the knowledge fills him with self-loathing. "I myself am a savage,"
he confesses, "owning no allegiance but to the King of the Cannibals; and ready at any moment to rebel against him." It is this sense
of his own sharkishness, and of the sharkishness of other men,
which drives him to the verge of suicide. As Ishmael is, so all men
are. The Christian whaler "is as much a savage as an Iroquois"; he
is the "white sailor-savage" (57: *232*). Nor is savagery confined to

those who live upon the blood of Leviathan. "For we are all killers, on land and on sea; Bonapartes and Sharks included" (32: *125*). As Bonaparte was a shark, so are even the most noble and civilized of men: Achilles, for Ishmael, is "the Greek savage," and Albert Dürer is "that fine old German savage" (57: *232*). Nations exhibit the predatory qualities of the citizens who comprise them; John Bull is simply a "harpooneer" with his lance in Ireland, while Brother Jonathan is an "apostolic lancer" busy harpooning Texas (89: *333*). Our savagery is our natural state, and can be attributed directly to God. "Long exile from Christendom and civilization," Ishmael remarks, "inevitably restores a man to that condition in which God placed him, *i.e.* what is called savagery" (57: *232*).

The entrance to Peter Coffin's Spouter-Inn furnishes, as early as Chapter 3, an expressive rendering of the fact that Christians are as cannibalistic as the cannibals. "The opposite wall of this entry was hung all over with a heathenish array of monstrous clubs and spears. Some were thickly set with glittering teeth resembling ivory saws; others were tufted with knots of human hair. . . . You shuddered as you gazed, and wondered what monstrous cannibal and savage could ever have gone a death-harvesting with such a hacking, horrifying implement." But the pagan savages of Pacific islands are not the only ones represented in Peter Coffin's collection. Christian viciousness is given equal and indiscriminate space. "Mixed with these were rusty old whaling lances and harpoons all broken and deformed" (3: *21*). Civilized man is as capable as savage man of what Melville, in an 1872 letter to Catherine Gansevoort, called "Hottentotishness."[21]

What Melville terms "Hottentotishness," Quaker Peleg calls "sharkishness." He complains irascibly that the diffident Ishmael "dost not talk shark a bit" (16: *69*), and is quick to intervene when Bildad tries to bring Queequeg within the softening influences of Christianity. "Avast there, avast there, Bildad, avast now spoiling our harpooneer," he roars at his partner. "Pious harpooneers never make good voyagers—it takes the shark out of 'em; no harpooneer is worth a straw who aint pretty sharkish" (18: *85*). Ishmael himself uses the word when he takes a sea-battle as emblematic of the fact that the butchers on deck are indistinguishable from the butchers over the side:

Though amid all the smoking horror and diabolism of a sea-fight, sharks will be seen longingly gazing up to the ship's decks, like hungry dogs round a table where red meat is being carved, ready to bolt down every killed man that is tossed to them; and though, while the valiant butchers over the deck-table are thus cannibally carving each other's live meat with carving-knives all gilded and tasselled, the sharks, also, with their jewel-hilted mouths, are quarrelsomely carving away under the table at the dead meat; ... were you to turn the whole affair upside down, it would still be pretty much the same thing, that is to say, a shocking sharkish business enough for all parties. (64: *249*)

But it is not the sharkishness of human *war* which most horrifies Ishmael. It is rather the sharkishness of *peace*, the rapacity of ordinary men pursuing their ordinary interests, a rapacity we do not see because it is all around us. "... no doubt the first man that ever murdered an ox was regarded as a murderer; perhaps he was hung; and if he had been put on his trial by oxen, he certainly would have been; and he certainly deserved it if any murderer does." We need not go to sea, or to war, to contemplate the terrible voraciousness of even the most gentle of human beings. We need only step out our front door:

> Go to the meat-market of a Saturday night and see the crowds of live bipeds staring up at the long rows of dead quadrupeds. Does not that sight take a tooth out of the cannibal's jaw? Cannibals? who is not a cannibal? I tell you it will be more tolerable for the Fejee that salted down a lean missionary in his cellar against a coming famine; it will be more tolerable for that provident Fejee, I say, in the day of judgment, than for thee, civilized and enlightened gourmand, who nailest geese to the ground and feastest on their bloated livers in thy paté-de-foie-gras. (65: *255–56*)

Our most altruistic efforts to meliorate this universal bloodbath founder in gore. Ishmael calls our attention to the fact that the "Secretary of the Society for the Suppression of Cruelty to Ganders" formerly indited his circulars with a goose quill, and has only just recently switched to steel pens.

Second-mate Stubb, essentially kindly and easy-going, nevertheless stands as the central expression of human sharkishness in *Moby-Dick*. With a huge Sperm Whale lashed to the *Pequod's* side, Stubb recalls that he has always found whale flesh "a flavorish thing to his palate." "A steak, a steak, ere I sleep!" he cries. "You, Daggoo! overboard you go, and cut me one from his small!" At midnight, "Stubb stoutly stood up to his spermaceti supper at the capstan-head, as if that capstan were a sideboard." Ishmael immediately makes his point: "Nor was Stubb the only banqueter on whale's flesh that night. Mingling their mumblings with his own mastications, thousands on thousands of sharks, swarming round the dead leviathan, smackingly feasted on its fatness." The sharks in the water are happy with their steaks, but the shark on deck is not. Stubb lodges a complaint with Fleece, the *Pequod's* black cook. "Cook," he grumbles, "don't you think this steak is rather overdone? You've been beating this steak too much, cook; it's too tender.... There are those sharks now over the side, don't you see they prefer it tough and rare?"

His sharkishness established, Stubb becomes a paradigm of the futility of our efforts to be other than the sharks we are. The uninhibited mastications of the sea-sharks disturb him. "Cook, go and talk to 'em; tell 'em they are welcome to help themselves civilly, and in moderation, but they must keep quiet." He gives Fleece a lantern and orders him to "preach to 'em!" The consequence is a "sermon" liberally salted with profanity. "Fellow-critters: I'se ordered here to say dat you must stop dat dam noise dare. You hear? Stop dat dam smackin' ob de lip! Massa Stubb say dat you can fill your dam bellies up to de hatchings, but by Gor! you must stop dat dam racket!" The use of "damn" four times in this brief homily shocks and enrages Stubb. "Cook! why, damn your eyes, you mustn't swear that way when you're preaching. That's no way to convert sinners, Cook!" This exchange must stand as the most expressive statement in *Moby-Dick* of man's inability to transcend absolutely his own sharkishness. The *Pequod's* cook is unable to deliver a sermon on moderation without using immoderate language. Similarly, Stubb is unable to object to the cook's profanity without using profanity himself. He complains of the cook's "damns" by damning the cook's eyes. In case we have missed the point, Fleece makes it for us as he retires. "Wish, by gor! whale eat [Stubb], 'stead of him eat whale. I'm bressed if he ain't more of shark dan Massa Shark hisself" (64: *249–54*).

It is against this background of sharkish sermonizing that Ishmael, two chapters later, shares with us the unbelievable spectacle of sharkishness devouring itself. The whale is still lashed to the side; the sharks still swarm by the thousands. Stages and lanterns are lowered; the cutting-spades are broken out, and Queequeg and a forecastle seaman initiate "an incessant murdering of the sharks, by striking the keen steel deep into their skulls, seemingly their only vital part":

> But in the foamy confusion of their mixed and struggling hosts, the marksmen could not always hit their mark; and this brought about new revelations of the incredible ferocity of the foe. They viciously snapped, not only at each other's disembowelments, but like flexible bows, bent round, and bit their own; till those entrails seemed swallowed over and over again by the same mouth, to be oppositely voided by the gaping wound. (66: *257*)

The theological implications of this diabolic vision are made explicit by Queequeg, who almost loses his hand to the mechanically snapping jaws of an already-dead shark. "Queequeg no care what god made him shark," says the cannibal, ". . . but de god wat made shark must be one dam Ingin" (66: *257*).

Though it has been little remarked, the Manxman raises this problem—of the sharkishness of God—early in the book, when Daggoo and a hot-blooded Spanish sailor get in a quarrel. When another sailor directs the rest of the crew to form a ring for them to fight in, the Manxman bitterly retorts that the ring for fighting is already formed by the "ringed horizon" itself, a natural arena within which "Cain struck Abel." And then the Manxman poses explicitly the question which is at the core of Ishmael's worst hypo: "Why then, God," he asks, "mad'st thou the ring?" (40: *154*).

It is Ishmael's hypos concerning death, the void, and a sharkish world which have driven him to sea as a substitute for pistol and ball. His experiences aboard the *Pequod* only confirm those corrosive insights of which he was already fully possessed *before* he abandoned his classroom for Cape Horn and the Pacific. When he comes under the spell of Captain Ahab he has already been, for an indeterminate length of time, profoundly depressed. Of all the crew, he is therefore the most susceptible to Ahab's hypnotic intensity:

I, Ishmael, was one of that crew; my shouts had gone up with the rest; my oath had been welded with theirs; and stronger I shouted, and more did I hammer and clinch my oath, because of the dread in my soul. A wild, mystical, sympathetical feeling was in me; Ahab's quenchless feud seemed mine. With greedy ears I learned the history of that murderous monster against whom I and all the others had taken our oaths of violence and revenge. (41: *155*)

It is important to stress Ishmael's depression, because he will change in the course of the novel. As the *Pequod* moves out of the frigidities of Christian New England and into the sensuous warmth of the pagan Pacific, Ishmael's malaise will gradually disperse, his hypos will slowly find resolution, and he will imperceptibly disentangle himself from Ahab's poisonous influence. Consequently, what Ishmael says on an early page must always be construed in the light of what he says on a later page. He speaks here, for example, of Leviathan as a "murderous monster." This is Ahab's version of Moby Dick. Ishmael at this point has never seen Moby Dick, and even more important, *never seen a whale*. Chapter 41, which develops rumor and myth concerning Moby Dick; Chapter 44, which details the movement of whales about the world; and especially Chapter 45, "The Affidavit," which retails the alleged destructiveness and viciousness of the Sperm Whale—all three are merely congeries of rumor and hearsay, presented to us by a man in the grip of a major neurosis who will not himself encounter veritable Leviathan in all his ponderous reality until Chapter 48, "The First Lowering." The moment Ishmael confronts his first *real* whale, his salvation begins— and it is to this redemptive process that we must now turn our attention.

VIII

LEVIATHANIC REVELATIONS
The Two Whales of *Moby-Dick*

AMONG THE YANKEE simplicities hidden beneath the convolute surface of *Moby-Dick*, none is more fundamental than the fact that the novel incorporates two versions of Leviathan. One is Ahab's whale. The other is Ishmael's whale. To confound them, to deal with the cetological data as if they constituted an homogenous expository continuum, is to confound the meaning of Melville's novel. *Moby-Dick*—and the criticism of it—will remain little more than a fascinating hodge-podge of "higgledy-piggledy whale statements" ("Extracts": 2) until the reader distinguishes Ahab's *transcendental* whale from Ishmael's *naturalistic* whale.[1]

Ahab's whale can be dealt with in brief compass. It is astonishing to discover what a small portion of Ahab's speaking lines are devoted to comment on Moby Dick, or even on whales in general.

Ahab has less to say about Leviathan than Shakespeare's Mercutio has to say about Queen Mab. In the quarter-deck scene, we learn only that Moby Dick is a "white-headed whale with a wrinkled brow and a crooked jaw, . . . with three holes punctured in his starboard fluke"; his back is full of harpoons, he has a spout "like a whole shock of wheat," and he "fan-tails" when he swims. Ahab is also exasperatingly minimal in explaining what the albino whale *means* to him. Of the forty lines of his "little lower layer" discussion, only five deal directly with Moby Dick. The world, he tells Starbuck, is an "unreasoning" pasteboard mask, an opaque perceptual wall behind which a "still reasoning thing" hides itself. "To me, the white whale is that wall, shoved near to me. . . . He tasks me; he heaps me; I see in him outrageous strength, with an inscrutable malice sinewing it. That inscrutable thing is chiefly what I hate; and be the white whale agent, or be the white whale principal, I will wreak that hate upon him" (36: *142–44*).*

In sum: Moby Dick is illimitably strong. Moby Dick is pervasively malicious. Moby Dick is inscrutably intelligent. Moby Dick is physically vulnerable, perceptually violable. Moby Dick, finally, has bitten off my leg. These five propositions, crudely simplistic as they are, cover virtually all that Ahab has to say about his archenemy in the 135 chapters of a very long novel.

Ishmael tries to fill the gaps in Ahab's perfunctory account of his motivations, but even Ishmael's garrulous tendencies are satisfied with a single paragraph. "Small reason was there to doubt," he begins, establishing the speculative nature of what follows,

> . . . that ever since that almost fatal encounter, Ahab had cherished a wild vindictiveness against the whale, all the more fell for that in his frantic morbidness he at last came to identify with him, not only all his bodily woes, but all his intellectual and spiritual exasperations. The White Whale swam before him as the monomaniac incarnation of all those malicious agencies which some deep men feel eating in them, till they are left living on with half a heart and half a lung. That in-

---

* The number before the colon in all parenthetical references in the text indicates chapter, which will be the same for most American editions of *Moby-Dick*; the italicized numbers after the colon indicate page in the Norton Critical Edition of *Moby-Dick*, edited by Harrison Hayford and Hershel Parker (New York: W. W. Norton & Company, 1967).

tangible malignity which has been from the beginning; to whose dominion even the modern Christians ascribe one-half of the world; which the ancient Ophites of the east reverenced in their statue devil; —Ahab did not fall down and worship it like them; but deliriously transferring its idea to the abhorred white whale, he pitted himself, all mutilated, against it. All that most maddens and torments; all that stirs up the lees of things; all truth with malice in it; all that cracks the sinews and cakes the brain; all the subtle demonisms of life and thought; all evil, to crazy Ahab, were visibly personified, and made practically assailable in Moby Dick. He piled upon the whale's white hump the sum of all the general rage and hate felt by his whole race from Adam down; and then, as if his chest had been a mortar, he burst his hot heart's shell upon it. (41: *160*)

Nevertheless, it would be a mistake to assume from all of this that Ahab's pursuit of the whale is similar to Ishmael's—conceptual, inquiring, broadly philosophical. It is not. It is as narrowly personal, as visceral, as the clenching of a fist. During that first, pre-literary encounter, Ahab, his three boats stove and splintered, "seizing the line-knife from his broken prow, had dashed at the whale, as an Arkansas duellist at his foe, blindly seeking with a six inch blade to reach the fathom-deep life of the whale" (41: *159*). Professionally this is equivalent—the reader will forgive a somewhat strained analogy—to a matador's suddenly flinging aside his cape and kicking the bull squarely in the ribs on his next pass. Ahab's petulant gesture with his six-inch knife reduces his confrontation with Moby Dick to a raw power-equation, an equation unable to bear the loading of meaning which Ishmael, endlessly inferential, gives it in the hints (42: *163*) of the "Moby Dick" chapter. Ahab translates *all* meanings of the whale into the unmodulated idiom of brute force and simple power. This is evident in his speech to the corpusants, which he sees as an appropriately trinitarian manifestation of what Moby Dick represents. He has called the dying whale a "trebly hooped and welded hip of power" (116: *409*). He now addresses invisible cosmic deity in the same terms, as "speechless, placeless power." Love, he says, is deity's "lowest form." Deity's "highest" form is "mere supernal power," the most characteristic expression of which is the grossly quantitative launching of "navies of full-freighted worlds" (119: *417*).

These launched flotillas of worlds, these endless galactic armadas, are redolent of post-Copernican man's exploding world-view, his dispiriting sense of incomprehensible stellar distances and illimitable cosmic voids. They furnish the terms which define Ahab's whale, and distinguish it from Ishmael's: gross size, gross power, gross mass. Alfred Kazin has remarked that "The greatest single metaphor in the book is bigness."[2] This is an oversimplification if the novel belongs (as it does) to Ishmael, but for Ahab it says all that needs saying. The *Pequod's* Captain and his whale stand as the best expression in American literature of what might be called the *empirical bogey*, technological man's resentful awareness of the steady erosion in stature which he has suffered ever since Galileo ground his first lens and Newton evolved his first principle. The pre-literary Ahab may have been a "mighty pageant creature," but the aging and mutilated Ahab of *Moby-Dick*, fronting an empirically conceived cosmos, is simply and pathetically *puny*. The "Leviathanism" (32: *127*) of the whale expresses that which for Ahab is *the* salient quality of both the cosmos he can see and the deity he cannot see: sheer, gross *size*.

The reductionism of this point of view accounts for the meagerness of Ahab's cetological exposition. Monolithic ideas such as size and power demand for their communication no more than that laconic handful of sentences which is all that Ahab has to say about the whale. Moby Dick struck Ahab; Ahab will strike back: thump and counter-thump. To subtilize this raw schemata is to distort the meaning of both Ahab and Ahab's whale. Paradoxically, it is the grossness of Ahab's conception which makes the Ahabian whale what it is: a quasi-mythic affirmation of a transcendental reality behind the visible cosmos. The twisted harpoon-irons embedded in Moby Dick's back may suggest to Ahab that his antagonist is "practically assailable." But so much size, so much outrageous strength, and so much malign intelligence place Ahab's whale above nature, beyond contingency, outside of space and time. The Ahabian whale may not be specifically Christian, but he is just the sort of whale a Christian—even a Quaker Christian—would conceive of. Ahab's whale is the whale of Father Mapple's sermon and, as principal or agent, the visible manifestation of an overkill, megaton God. Like

Mapple's whale, Ahab's whale is emblematic of nature, but he is not *part* of nature. Ahab's whale is transcendental, not naturalistic.

Ishmael's whale is as complex as Ahab's is simple. Part of this complexity has its source in the fact that Ishmael's whale comes in two distinct forms: the conceptual Leviathan, and the perceptual Leviathan. A useful oversimplification makes Chapter 61, "Stubb Kills a Whale," the line of demarcation between the two. Ishmael's conceptual whale is the whale of the "Moby Dick" and "Whiteness" chapters, the whale of "The Advocate," "The Affidavit," and "The Town-Ho's Story"—the whale *before* tyro Ishmael has actually seen a whale. This is the whale-as-conceived, "the overwhelming *idea* of the great whale himself" (1: *16*; italics mine). In a sense, Ishmael's conceptual whale is as starkly monolithic as Ahab's. Ahab sees Moby Dick as *size*; Ishmael sees Moby Dick as *white*. Ahab conceives of Moby Dick as cosmic *immensity*; Ishmael conceives of Moby Dick as cosmic *void*. "It was," he tells us, "the whiteness of the whale that above all things appalled me" (42: *163*).

But only *at times*. Perhaps the most overlooked qualification in *Moby-Dick* is the one which occurs twice in the first half-dozen lines of Chapter 42. "What the white whale was to Ahab, has been hinted," Ishmael begins; "what, *at times*, he was to me, as yet remains unsaid" (italics mine). A few lines later he speaks of a "vague, nameless horror" concerning Moby Dick "which *at times* by its intensity completely overpowered all the rest" (italics again mine). The meaning is clear: there were *other times* when Ishmael saw a different whale than the atheistically pallid and ontologically evacuated one developed in the "Whiteness" chapter. This other whale is Ishmael's perceptual whale, the whale as experienced rather than as conceived. The true narrative line of *Moby-Dick* is not the pursuit of the White Whale, but rather the transmutation which Ishmael's sensibility undergoes as that pursuit is prosecuted—and the essence of this transmutation is the gradual displacement of the conceptual whale by the perceptual whale.

In the actual text of *Moby-Dick*, of course, these distinctions tend to coalesce to produce a single all-encompassing symbol, *Leviathan*. It makes no difference whether we are dealing with Ahab's or Ishmael's whale, with Moby Dick in particular or whales in general—

the "affirmative fact" is Leviathan's "prodigious bulk and power" (80: *293–94*). The whale is for Ishmael, no matter how regarded, "the mightiest animated mass that has survived the flood; most monstrous and most mountainous! That Himmalehan, salt-sea Mastodon, clothed with such portentousness of unconscious power, that his very panics are more to be dreaded than his most fearless and malicious assaults!" (14: *62*). As percept or concept, Leviathan remains a "portentous and mysterious monster" of "island bulk" (1: *16*). Ishmael may see Moby Dick himself as the pale symbol of the void beneath appearances, but even from this attenuated perspective he remains wholly Leviathan, of "uncommon magnitude and malignity," of "great ferocity, cunning, and malice," a whale of "pre-eminent tremendousness," and of "earthly make and incontestable character" (41: *155, 157, 159*).

From the beginning, then, Ishmael gives Moby Dick his due as quintessential Leviathan. Nevertheless, even while he is still under Ahab's influence, Ishmael indicates his own skepticism concerning Moby Dick as supernal juggernaut. The attribution of "supernatural agencies" to the White Whale, the suggestion that he is both ubiquitous and immortal, as well as the many feats of maliciousness which Moby Dick is said to have performed are nothing but "wild rumors," "fabulous rumors," and "outblown rumors," finding their source in "morbid hints, and half-formed foetal suggestions" making the rounds of the whaling fleets. Such "unearthly conceit[s]" and "prodigies" concerning Moby Dick are, Ishmael suggests, the natural products of the "superstitious belief" of the sailor-mind, which regards any tale of any whale with "childish fire-side interest and awe" (41: *156–58*). As a consequence Ishmael is careful to attach a sly demurrer to nearly everything he says about Moby Dick. He speaks of "that unexampled, intelligent malignity which, *according to specific accounts,* [Moby Dick] had over and over again evinced in his assaults" (41: *159*; italics mine). In a clear instance of unobtrusive equivocation, he asserts that "such *seemed* the White Whale's infernal aforethought of ferocity, that every dismembering or death that he caused, was *not wholly regarded* as having been inflicted by an *un*intelligent agent" (41: *159*; italics mine). Ahab is overwhelmed by Leviathan. Ishmael is almost overwhelmed, but not quite. Even when dealing with Moby Dick, he nurtures a saving skepticism which leaves open the possibilty that the whale may be something other than the "murderous monster" (41: *155*) which Ahab has made him seem.

What makes it difficult for Ishmael to keep such a healthy skepticism alive, however, is the fact that the ordinary, garden-variety of whale is quite as terrifying as Moby Dick. It is difficult to get beyond that first impression of a vitality which, if not transcendental, is the next thing to it. The everyday whale is an "enormous creature of enormous power" (45: *178*), comprised of "tons of ponderosity" (81: *303*) which are not infrequently brought to bear in "wilful, deliberate designs of destruction to his pursuers" (45: *181*). Even if Moby Dick himself had never existed, therefore, the terror would be there: "The Sperm Whale is in some cases sufficiently powerful, knowing, and judiciously malicious, as with direct aforethought to stave in, utterly destroy, and sink a large ship; and what is more, the Sperm Whale *has* done it." And indeed he has: Ishmael cites the case of the *Essex*, which sank within ten minutes of a large whale's angrily dashing his forehead against her bow (45: *178*). Another everyday whale raised a large ship "three feet at least out of the water. The masts reeled, and the sails fell altogether." A ship in hundreds of fathoms of water suffered a "terrible shock," probably inflicted by a whale, the suddenness of which "made the guns leap in their carriages, and several of the men were shaken out of their hammocks." Another harpooned monster, when the whale-line was passed from the boat to the ship itself, turned tables on his pursuers, "the whale towing [the ship's] great hull through the water, as a horse walks off with a cart" (45: *180–81*). Philosophically the problem is the same whether one is dealing with Moby Dick or ordinary whales. The fact of incredible "concentrations of potency" is so suggestive of transcendental superiority that any other truth about Leviathan is nearly obliterated. "For unless you own the whale," Ishmael admonishes us, "you are but a provincial and sentimentalist in Truth" (76: *285–86*).

That part of Leviathan's vast anatomy most difficult for philosophical sentimentalists to own up to—because it expresses the insensate qualities of cosmic process—is the Sperm Whale's *head*. Ishmael, so long as he contemplates Moby Dick from Ahab's vantage-point, can "see naught in that brute but the deadliest ill" (41: *163*). It is the Sperm Whale's battering-ram head, "one broad firmament of a forehead, pleated with riddles; dumbly lowering with the doom of boats, and ships, and men" (79: *292*), which gives full expression to Leviathan as malign, as a "brute" of "deadliest ill." The skull of the Sperm Whale, which is only a small part of the entire head, will nevertheless "measure at least twenty feet in length," while above it rests the "enormous superincumbent mass of the junk and sperm," a "vast outworks" like the "amplified forti-fications of Quebec" (80: *293*). The result is an unbelievably mas-sive front of "battering-ram" power, the "compacted collectedness" of which makes a "dead, blind wall, without a single organ or tender prominence of any sort whatsoever." Like the pyramid of Stubb's dream, the whale's head exhibits an ontological perdurability un-matched in other sentient creatures. It is of a "boneless toughness, inestimable by any man who has not handled it. The severest pointed harpoon, the sharpest lance darted by the strongest human arm, impotently rebounds from it. It is as though the forehead of the Sperm Whale were paved with horses' hoofs. I do not think that any sensation lurks in it." Behind this "dead, impregnable, uninjur-able wall" lies a "mass of tremendous life, only to be adequately estimated as piled wood is—by the cord" (76: *284–85*). All whales —and not just Moby Dick—thus become expressions of what Ishmael calls the "universal thump" (1: *15*), the definitive articulation of juggernaut cosmic dynamism.

If Ishmael's whale were only this—a symbol for the universal thumpishness of the cosmos—it would differ merely in degree of dramatic development from Ahab's whale. But from the first low-ering on, Ishmael's whale carries an increasingly dualistic cluster of meanings. Like Babbalanja of *Mardi*, Ishmael knows that "there are things infinite in the finite; and dualities in unities."[3] The duality of Ishmael's whale reflects his growing realization that just as there is an inner man as well as an outer man, so also there is an *inner whale* as well as an *outer whale*. The outer reality is the reality of the battering-ram—the reality of brute power brutishly applied. But there is another reality secreted in the vast interiorities of Le-viathan, a reality Ahab's empirical and narrowly quantitative perceptions have never achieved, but which Ishmael begins to know as, the fascinated tyro, he watches a succession of whales butchered by the *Pequod's* crew.

This is not to say that Ishmael himself is not often empirically factual in his observation of Leviathan. It is a truism of Melville criticism that the cetological data of *Moby-Dick*—such as Ishmael's discussion of the Sperm Whale's brain and spinal cord (80: *293–94*), his examination of the spout, the spouting canal, and the canal's connection with the whale's mouth (85: *311–12*), and his description of the complex musculature of the tail (86: *314–15*)—all serve as dramatic "ballast," furnishing a stabilizing foundation for a romantically top-heavy tale. But the chapters devoted to cetacean physiology—the "cetological center," as Howard P. Vincent terms them—have a more subtle function. Ishmael's redemption depends on his breaking free of Ahab's version of Leviathan as deific correlate. Leviathan must be de-mythologized before he can be re-mythologized. The physiological facts of the whale serve this process of de-mythification. Much of the mystery and terror of Ishmael's "murderous monster" dissipates as he—and we—learn that alien Leviathan has a brain like our brain, lungs like our lungs, and an eye like our eye.

The crucial meanings to be found at the secret heart of Leviathan are, however, *qualitative* rather than quantitative. Ishmael's treatment of cetacean fact is poetic. It is no accident that this poetizing of inner Leviathan finds its locus in the whale's head. For the battering-ram forehead is only half the story, the half Ahab has acted upon. The other half begins to unfold as Ishmael remarks an anomaly of Sperm Whale physiology. As the *Pequod's* boats pursue the first whale which is actually killed and butchered, Ishmael says that "All alive to his jeopardy, he was going 'head out;' that part obliquely projecting from the mad yeast which he brewed." Reluctant to break into the action, but aware that the whale's ability to elevate his massive head clear of the water demands an explanation, Ishmael adds a footnote. "It will be seen in some other place of what a very light substance the entire interior of the sperm whale's enormous head consists. Though apparently the most massive, it is by far the most buoyant part about him. So that with ease he elevates it in the air, and invariably does so when going at his utmost speed" (61: *243n*).

This simple physiological paradox, that the part of the whale most "massive" is the part most "buoyant," furnishes the factual foundation for the dualistic connotations of Ishmael's whale. If the *outside* of the head is a "dead, blind wall" of "inestimable" toughness, the *inside*, "that mystic part" of the whale (80: *293*), is "the lightest and most corky part about him." This is because the head's interior is "tissued" and "infiltrated" (78: *290*) with "the most delicate oil" (76: *284*). This oil, running to as much as five hundred gallons in a large whale and, like all oil, lighter than water, makes the battering-ram as buoyant as it is ponderous. But these cetological facts are, of themselves, unimportant. What *is* important is the imaginative transmutation Ishmael accords them. Having gone to extraordinary lengths to render the outer whale as juggernaut mass, Ishmael now goes to equal lengths to render the inner whale as *fragility*, *delicacy*, *rarity*, and *preciousness*. The "upper and unctuous" part of the whale's head is more than simply the "case," which is the whaleman's technical term:

> The upper part, known as the Case, may be regarded as the great Heidelberg Tun of the Sperm Whale. And as that famous great tierce is mystically carved in front, so the whale's vast plaited forehead forms innumerable strange devices for the emblematical adornment of his wondrous tun. Moreover, as that of Heidelberg was always replenished with the most excellent of the wines of the Rhenish valleys, so the tun of the whale contains by far the most precious of all his oily vintages; namely, the highly-prized spermaceti, in its absolutely pure, limpid, and odoriferous state. (77: *286*)

The dualism is best expressed by the contrast between the inner and outer surfaces of the Tun. The outer surface is a "dense tendinous wall," a "double welded, hammered substance" (78: *290*). The inner surface—the ontological obverse—is very different. "I know not with what fine and costly material the Heidelberg Tun was coated within, but in superlative richness that coating could not possibly have compared with the silken pearl-colored membrane, like the lining of a fine pelisse, forming the inner surface of the

Sperm Whale's case" (77: *287*). Again and again, Ishmael cites that inner fragility and delicacy lying hidden beneath the gross ponderosity of outer Leviathan. "But the spermaceti itself," he rhapsodizes, "how bland and creamy that is; like the transparent, half-jellied, white meat of a cocoanut in the third month of its growth" (65: *255*). The mouth of the whale, which externally is an awe-inspiring "portcullis jaw" (81: *298*), internally exhibits the same fragility. "What a really beautiful and chaste-looking mouth!" Ishmael exclaims, "from floor to ceiling, lined, or rather papered with a glistening white membrane, glossy as bridal satins" (74: *280*).

The symbolic thrust of all this is unmistakable. Ishmael's cetological dive into the interior of the whale leads to the redemptive discovery that cosmic brawn is but the obverse of cosmic fragility, that nature's abrasive and adamantine exterior is but the ontological conjugate for nature's delicate and emollient interior. Ishmael stresses this dualism by pointing out the deep paradox the Sperm Whale's head represents. "Finally, though," he says, "as will soon be revealed, [the head's] contents partly comprise the most delicate oil; yet, you are now to be apprised of the nature of the substance which so impregnably invests all that apparent effeminacy." Not content with this bivalent figure, he goes on to speculate that the "mystical lung-celled honeycombs" comprising the "unique interior of the head" may "have some hitherto unknown and unsuspected connexion with the outer air." And then he renders the metaphysical duality which sets Ishmael's whale decisively apart from Ahab's: "If this be so," he concludes, "fancy the irresistibleness of that might, *to which the most impalpable and destructive of all elements contributes*" (76: *284–85;* italics mine).

It is in Chapter 94, "A Squeeze of the Hand," that the unguent assuasiveness of the inner whale is fully developed. Ishmael has already explained that the spermaceti of the Heidelberg Tun, "Though in life it remains perfectly fluid, yet, upon exposure to the air, after death, it soon begins to concrete; sending forth beautiful crystalline shoots, as when the first thin delicate ice is just forming in water" (77: *286*). This tendency to concretion makes necessary "squeezing case"—reducing the spermaceti to fluid by hand—to ready it for the try-works. Ishmael shares this task with other members of the crew. His arms plunged in spermaceti to the elbows, he finally achieves a full sense of that aspect of Leviathan which represents the sanative, rather than the destructive, capacities of nature and cosmic process. It is difficult to remember he is talking about the battering-ram when he describes squeezing case as a "sweet and unctuous duty! No wonder that in old times this sperm was such a favorite cosmetic. Such a clearer! such a sweetener! such a softener! such a delicious mollifier" (94: *348*).

But the sperm of Leviathan (Ishmael uses the term *spermaceti* only once in this chapter) is much more than a palliative for his exacerbated sensibilities. Squeezing case precipitates a change in attitude toward Ahab, Ahab's "quenchless feud," and Ishmael's part in that feud:

> As I sat there at my ease, cross-legged on the deck; after the bitter exertion at the windlass; under a blue tranquil sky; the ship under indolent sail, and gliding so serenely along; as I bathed my hands among those soft, gentle globules of infiltrated tissues, woven almost within the hour; as they richly broke to my fingers, and discharged all their opulence, like fully ripe grapes their wine; as I snuffed up that uncontaminated aroma,—literally and truly, like the smell of spring violets; I declare to you, that for the time I lived as in a musky meadow; *I forgot all about our horrible oath; in that inexpressible sperm, I washed my hands and my heart of it*; I almost began to credit the old Paracelsan superstition that sperm is of rare virtue in allaying the heat of anger: *while bathing in that bath, I felt divinely free from all ill-will, or petulance, or malice, of any sort whatsoever.* (94: *348*; italics mine)

It was that aspect of cosmic dynamism represented by Pyramidical Leviathan and the Battering-Ram Whale which caused Ishmael to identify with Ahab. In a crucial turnabout, it is that aspect of cosmic dynamism represented by Unguent Leviathan and the Oleaginous Whale which enables Ishmael to begin (washing in sperm is only a beginning) to liberate himself from Ahab's doomed cause and his own "horrible oath." The case-squeezing also initiates the revitalization in Ishmael of the "enjoying power" which Ahab sees as "low," and for which he has such contempt. The baroque luxuriance of Ishmael's language, the Levantine sensuousness of his imagery of wine and grapes, of violets and meadows, of softness and gentleness, of gliding indolence and blue tranquillity, suggest how Ishmael's sperm-bath precipitates a dissociation from Ahab's view of visible objects as mere "pasteboard," and his own view of the sensuous manifold as deceitful harlot color. Inner Leviathan, deliciously unguent, ontologically emollient, initiates Ishmael's reintegration with the luxuriously tropical world through which the *Pequod* sails.

Finally, inner Leviathan becomes a vigorous antidote for the alienation from others and separation from self which are the consequences of an astringent New England Puritanism and an Ahabian view of the world as antagonist:

> Squeeze! squeeze! squeeze! all the morning long; I squeezed that sperm till I myself almost melted into it; I squeezed that sperm till a strange sort of insanity came over me; and I found myself unwittingly squeezing my co-laborers' hands in it, mistaking their hands for the gentle globules. Such an abounding, affectionate, friendly, loving feeling did this avocation beget; that at last I was continually squeezing their hands, and looking up into their eyes sentimentally; as much as to say,—Oh! my dear fellow beings, why should we longer cherish any social acerbities, or know the slightest ill-humor or envy! Come; let us squeeze hands all round; nay, let us all squeeze ourselves into each other; let us squeeze ourselves universally into the very milk and sperm of kindness. (94: *348–49*)

It would be a mistake to assume that Ishmael intends that we take this apostrophe with entire seriousness. He himself terms the experience a "strange sort of insanity." He admits that his feelings for his crewmates were debilitated by sentimentality. He has already suggested that the emotions he felt were temporary, "for the time." Finally, the homosexuality of his imagery is so perfervid, so close to caricature, that one suspects he is pulling the reader's leg. Nevertheless, there is a core of moral validity. The reconceptualization of friendship and brotherhood in terms of frank sensuality represents a vast advance over the theoretical prescriptions concerning brother-love which were part of Ishmael's icy Calvinist heritage. Inner Leviathan validates that affective, immediate brotherliness toward which Ishmael is already tending, and of which Queequeg, that kindly cannibal, has been a master all along.

Thus, the epistemological penetration of the inner whale redresses the imbalance caused by Ishmael's obsessive concentration on the outer whale. His cetological explorations open avenues of apprehension which will make possible a sanely balanced view both of reality and of his place in it. These generalized effects are reinforced by a change in imaginative realization addressed directly to two of Ishmael's hypos, death and the void. The vehicle for this affective realignment is Tashtego's dive into the Heidelberg Tun in "Cistern and Buckets" (78: 287–90). Standing high above the decks on the upturned whale's head, the Gayhead Indian has been busy ramming a bucket deeper and deeper into the case so that the spermaceti can be lifted out. As the "eightieth or ninetieth bucket came suckingly up—my God! poor Tashtego—like the twin reciprocating bucket in a veritable well, dropped head-foremost down into this great Tun of Heidelberg, and with a horrible oily gurgling, went clean out of sight!" Catastrophe is compounded when the tackles part and the enormous mass of the head itself drops away, taking "poor, buried-alive Tashtego . . . utterly down to the bottom of the sea!" But Queequeg, boarding-sword in hand, dives to the rescue and, pursuing the slowly sinking head, scuttles a large hole in its side, retrieving Tashtego from certain death. Tashtego's dive—an analogue for the dive of Narcissus—is a plunge into the pallid world of noumenal reality. The Sperm Whale's satin-white mouth, the creamy spermaceti, the ivory membranes which line the case—these particulars suggest that under the skin *all* whales are as Moby Dick, primal forms made of the same essential stuff as the squid, the polar bear, the spirit-spout, the albatross, even the "ivory" *Pequod*. Tashtego's fall has immured him in the "colorless all-color of atheism" which terrifies Ishmael. It is, moreover, a dive into the ontological void which Ishmael fears. The partially drained head is as empty at the center as the Egyptian pyramids. Finally, it is a dive into death, into the realm lying on the other side of the cenotaph: Tashtego is, for horrified Ishmael, "poor, buried-alive Tashtego."

It is therefore an enormous break-through for Ishmael when Tashtego is born again out of the whale. He leaves no doubt that he has witnessed a birth. It was entirely due to "the courage and great skill in obstetrics of Queequeg, [that] the deliverance, or rather, delivery of Tashtego, was successfully accomplished." Not that it was an easy birth. Queequeg had to "thrust his long arm far inwards and upwards" into Leviathan in order to haul out "our

poor Tash by the head." Queequeg averred that "upon first thrusting in for him, a leg was presented; but well knowing that that was
not as it ought to be, and might occasion great trouble;—he had
thrust back the leg, and by a dexterous heave and toss, had wrought
a somerset upon the Indian; so that with the next trial, he came forth
in the good old way—head foremost." Caesarean sections and breech
births, however, exact their toll. "As for the great head itself," Ishmael concludes, "that was doing as well as could be expected" (78:
288–90).

This death-and-rebirth sequence marks a major turning-point.
Tashtego's accident makes Ishmael see that death and birth are but
the dualities of a unity, the two sides of a single coin. For the first
time, he is able to apprehend death as a beginning, rather than an
ending. Moreover, the sensuousness of inner Leviathan alters the
way Ishmael pictures death:

> Now, had Tashtego perished in that head, it had been a very
> precious perishing; smothered in the very whitest and daintiest of
> fragrant spermaceti; coffined, hearsed, and tombed in the secret inner
> chamber and sanctum sanctorum of the whale. Only one sweeter
> end can readily be recalled—the delicious death of an Ohio honey-
> hunter, who seeking honey in the crotch of a hollow tree, found
> such exceeding store of it, that leaning too far over, it sucked him in,
> so that he died embalmed. How many, think ye, have likewise fallen
> into Plato's honey head, and sweetly perished there? (78: *290*)

While the oblique reference to Platonic idealism adds an ambiguous note, the general thrust is clear. The terror-words of Ishmael's
death-hypo—*perish, smother, coffin, hearse, tomb*—are here con-
ceptualized in the idiom of fructosity. The result is sweet death, or
more precisely, honeyized death, a sensuously apprehended *mort de
sucre*. Whiteness ("whitest . . . spermaceti") and the void ("secret
inner chamber") are also subsumed under the same saccharous rubric. Tashtego's dive thus translates Ishmael's preoccupation with
death from the aridly conceptual to the richly affective regions of his
sensibility.

All of this, however, has to do with the inner reality of the *live*
whale. It is a measure of the protean capacities of Ishmael's imagination that he is able to bring the inner-whale motif to a climax with

the stinking carcass of a *dead* whale. Some twenty chapters after Tashtego's plunge, the *Pequod* gams with a French whaler, the *Bouton de Rose*, whose Captain—a novice in the fisheries—has, despite the violent remonstrances of his mates, tied up along side two "blasted" whales, a blasted whale being one "that has died unmolested on the sea, and so floated an unappropriated corpse." "It may well be conceived," Ishmael redundantly remarks, "what an unsavory odor such a mass must exhale; worse than an Assyrian city in the plague, when the living are incompetent to bury the departed." One of these Leviathanic rosebuds has been dead only a few weeks; the other, long dead, is "one of those problematical whales that seem to dry up and die with a sort of prodigious dyspepsia, or indigestion; leaving their defunct bodies almost entirely bankrupt of anything like oil." Crafty Stubb is nevertheless anxious to get his hands on this second corpse; he suspects the presence of ambergris in its reeking bowels. He convinces the *Rose-Bud's* gullible Captain that such blasted whales often carry the plague and, the Frenchman having hurriedly cast off and fled the vicinity, he initiates an excavation with his boat-spade in the gigantic corpse. "You would almost have thought he was digging a cellar there in the sea," Ishmael observes, "and when at length his spade struck against the gaunt ribs, it was like turning up old Roman tiles and pottery buried in fat English loam":

> And all the time numberless fowls were diving, and ducking, and screaming, and yelling, and fighting around them. Stubb was beginning to look disappointed, especially as the horrible nosegay increased, when suddenly from out the very heart of this plague, there stole a faint stream of perfume, which flowed through the tide of bad smells without being absorbed by it, as one river will flow into and then along with another, without at all blending with it for a time. (91: *337–42*)

Stubb drops his spade, plunges in his hands, and draws forth heaped handfuls of ambergris, looking like "ripe Windsor soap, or rich mottled old cheese; very unctuous and savory withal." Again, inner Leviathan provides images of delicacy and richness, of rarity and preciousness. Ambergris is "so highly fragrant and spicy, that it is largely used in perfumery, in pastilles, precious candles, hair-powders, and pomatum. The Turks use it in cooking, and also carry it to Mecca, for the same purpose that frankincense is carried to St. Peter's in Rome. Some wine merchants drop a few grains in claret, to flavor it." The appearance of this preciousness in the midst of death, a sweet essence out of "the inglorious bowels of a sick whale," has the same effect as Tashtego's death-and-rebirth. "Now that the incorruption of this most fragrant ambergris should be found in the heart of such decay; is this nothing? Bethink thee of that saying of St. Paul in Corinthians, about corruption and incorruption; how that we are sown in dishonor, but raised in glory" (91, 92: *342–43*).

This is the final lesson of the inner whale: at the core of all being, in the heart of all natural process—even those processes which seem to man repulsive or terrifyingly destructive—there is a sweetness, a vitality, a purity, an inherent preciousness which affirms the fundamental goodness of existence and the preponderant salubrity of cosmic activity. Ishmael will never again be able to view death simply as interruption, termination, annihilation, or decay. The shift in sensibility he has undergone is suggested by the labored analogy he constructs in this same chapter as he attempts to describe the odor of the Greenland whaler which, unlike the Pacific whalers of *Moby-Dick*, does not render the oil at sea, but rather stores the raw blubber in the hold. "The consequence is," Ishmael concludes, "that upon breaking into the hold, and unloading one of these whale cemeteries, in the Greenland dock, a savor is given forth *somewhat similar to that arising from excavating an old city grave-yard, for the foundations of a Lying-in Hospital*" (92: *343*; italics mine). The simile is unlikely, far-fetched, strained. Ishmael is reaching for his comparison. But this may be because he is signaling a new phase in his struggle with the pale specter on the pallid horse. There is a new note of health, a certain sane wholeness, implicit in his suggestion that a building devoted to the rites of birth be constructed on ground dedicated to the rites of death.

The preponderant inner-outer duality of Ishmael's whale is reinforced by a secondary duality aligned along a different conceptual axis: *head-tail*. The head of the Sperm Whale analogizes cosmic power in its unmodulated battering-ram manifestations. The tail analogizes cosmic power in its *aesthetic* manifestations. "Other poets have warbled the praises of the soft eye of the antelope, and the lovely plumage of the bird that never alights," Ishmael begins; "less celestial, I celebrate a tail" (86: *314*). There is not, he assures us, any diminution of power as one moves along the incredible ninety-foot distance from Leviathan's head to his tail. The vast flukes, comprising on their upper surface alone "an area of at least fifty square feet," and in the mature whale at least "twenty feet across," are "a dense webbed bed of welded sinews":

> But as if this vast local power in the tendinous tail were not enough, the whole bulk of the leviathan is knit over with a warp and woof of muscular fibres and filaments, which passing on either side of the loins and running down into the flukes, insensibly blend with them, and largely contribute to their might; so that in the tail the confluent measureless force of the whole whale seems concentrated to a point. Could annihilation occur to matter, this were the thing to do it. (86: *314–15*)

But Ishmael now sees *more* than simple power. The tail of the Sperm Whale teaches him that the immense vitality of natural processes is not merely brutish, not simply juggernaut activity. Although he remains fully cognizant of the "measureless crush and crash of the sperm whale's ponderous flukes, which in repeated instances have one after the other hurled entire boats with all their oars and crews into the air" (86: *317*), he is now able also to see that "In no living thing are the lines of beauty more exquisitely defined than in the crescentic borders of these flukes" (86: *314*). The consequence of this insight is the coalescence of *power with beauty*. Digressing into aesthetic theory, he even argues that power is an essential aspect of much beauty:

> Nor does this—[the tail's] amazing strength, at all tend to cripple the graceful flexion of its motions; where infantileness of ease undulates through a Titanism of power. On the contrary, those motions derive their most appalling beauty from it. Real strength never impairs beauty or harmony, but it often bestows it; and in everything imposingly beautiful, strength has much to do with the magic. Take away the tied tendons that all over seem bursting from the marble in the carved Hercules, and its charm would be gone. (86: *315*)

Ishmael has undergone a revolution in perception. Ahab, to the bitter end, sees the whale as a manifestation of *outrageous strength*.

Ishmael, absorbing the lesson offered by the tail, will henceforth see the whale as *beautiful strength*. In *Moby-Dick*, power is redeemed by beauty.

The tail of the whale helps Ishmael come to terms with cosmic *power*. The eye and ear of the whale help him to meet the issue of cosmic *size*. I have said that the Sperm Whale of *Moby-Dick* is the definitive expression of the empirical bogey, puny man's brooding awareness of the giantism of the cosmos. But in two significant particulars the whale is not. Both his eye and his ear are incredibly small for a ninety-foot monster of "island bulk." "Far back on the side of the head," Ishmael explains, "and low down, near the angle of . . . [the] whale's jaw, if you narrowly search, you will at last see a lashless eye, which you would fancy to be a young colt's eye; so out of all proportion is it to the magnitude of the head." The ear exhibits the same astonishing disproportion. "But the ear of the whale is full as curious as the eye. If you are an entire stranger to . . . [the] race, you might hunt . . . for hours, and never discover that organ. The ear has no external leaf whatever; and into the hole itself you can hardly insert a quill, so wondrously minute is it." This paradox of smallness-in-immensity leads Ishmael to ask—and answer—a crucial question:

> Is it not curious, that so vast a being as the whale should see the world through so small an eye, and hear the thunder through an ear which is smaller than a hare's? But if his eyes were broad as the lens of Herschel's great telescope; and his ears capacious as the porches of cathedrals; would that make him any longer of sight, or sharper of hearing? Not at all.—Why then do you try to "enlarge" your mind? Subtilize it. (74: *278–80*)

The fundamental metaphor has to do with the metaphysics of perception. If size were a significant datum, then, Ishmael argues, there would have to be some sort of proportion between the size of the thing perceived and the size of the perceiving apparatus. To cognize an Herschelian universe one would have to command an Herschelian eye. But this is not the case. Again, given two perceptual systems of differing size, the larger would somehow perceive *more* than the smaller. But neither is this the case. Perception is therefore not a function of the size of the thing perceived. Neither is it a function of the size of the perceiver. Perception is absolute. In short, *thought obliterates magnitude as a meaningful parameter.* To be overawed, as Ahab is, with either Leviathan or Leviathanism is to do battle with shadows.

Thus, as cosmic power is redeemed in *Moby-Dick* by beauty, so cosmic immensity is redeemed by thought. The cetological facts of Leviathan's tail, and of his eye and ear, rescue Ishmael from the *cul-de-sac* in which Ahab is trapped. This redemption is accomplished through a naturalistic whale naturalistically observed. Moreover, the empirical study of real whales instead of conceptual whales makes possible the gradual *humanizing* of alien Leviathan, and it is to this fascinating process that we now turn our attention.

IX

FRATERNAL CONGENERITY
The Humanizing of Leviathan

IN 1923, in the brilliant *Studies in Classic American Literature*, D. H. Lawrence asserted that the Leviathan of *Moby-Dick* is "warm-blooded and lovable, . . . a mammal. And hunted, hunted down."[1] Never given to explaining his oracularities, Lawrence did not develop his "lovable" whale, and subsequent criticism has been little influenced by it. Early readings of the Melville revival accepted Ahab's version of the whale as "evil." More recent interpretations have either mythologized the whale into pure idea and transcendent archetype, or made him neutral, indifferent, naturalistically unaware, at best distantly benign, akin to Emerson's "commodity" in his usefulness to man. Since Lawrence, it has seldom been suggested that Melville's alien monster is sufficiently *human* to be an appropriate object for affectionate regard—and yet that he is in fact both loving and lovable is the most significant of the "special leviathanic revelations" (32: *116*)* made to Ishmael in the course of *Moby-Dick*. While this humanizing often consists of almost imperceptible shifts in Ishmaelian apprehension, three encounters with Leviathan can be taken as typical of the entire process. Two of these have to do with a pair of whales actually killed and butchered by the *Pequod's* crew. The first is *Stubb's Whale*. The second is the *Gerontological* or *Medicare Whale*. The third is the *Social Whale* as he reveals himself in the massed thousands of that immense whale-pod, the Grand Armada.

The *Pequod's* first lowering for whales (Chapter 48), while it gives Melville the opportunity to liberate Fedallah and his boat-crew from the ship's hold, and explain the factual essentials of whale-pursuit, cannot be considered a true encounter with Leviathan. A "raw recruit" (48: *193*), Ishmael is too busy rowing to turn around for even a glimpse of the monster Starbuck's boat pursues, and no sooner is the harpoon darted than the boat is overtaken by a blinding squall and the whale lost. It is not until Chapter 61, "Stubb Kills a Whale," that Ishmael, standing his turn at the mast-head, starts abruptly from a brief doze to find the fabulous creature he has never seen, and which he has come so far to see, floating hardly an arm's length away. "And lo! close under our lee, not forty fathoms off, a gigantic Sperm Whale lay rolling in the water like the capsized hull of a frigate, his broad, glossy back, of an Ethiopian hue, glistening in the sun's rays like a mirror." Caught off his guard, one might expect that Ishmael would describe this frigate-sized and sudden Leviathan in the Ahabian terms of earlier chapters. Instead, his first spontaneous impression is one of ponderous and corpulent *placidity*. "But lazily undulating in the trough of the sea, and ever and anon tranquilly spouting his vapory jet, the whale looked like a portly burgher smoking his pipe of a warm afternoon" (61: *242*). With this anthropomorphic analogy, the humanizing of the whale begins.

* The number before the colon in all parenthetical references in the text indicates chapter, which will be the same for most American editions of *Moby-Dick*; the italicized numbers after the colon indicate page in the Norton Critical Edition of *Moby-Dick*, edited by Harrison Hayford and Hershel Parker (New York: W. W. Norton & Company, 1967).

It is the *pipe* this Leviathanic burgher smokes which expresses
the essential equivalence between man and whale. For Melville,
pipe-smoking is emblematic of the on-going life-processes which
unite all sentient beings. Babbalanja of *Mardi* asserts that "life itself
is a puff and a wheeze. Our lungs are two pipes which we constantly
smoke."[2] Ishmael uses the same figure when, in speculating on the
ultimate effects of the whaling industry, he asks "whether Leviathan
can long endure so wide a chase . . . ; whether . . . the last whale,
like the last man, [will] smoke his last pipe, and then himself
evaporate in the final puff" (105: *383*). The pipe also connotes
humanity and fraternal identity. It is as a consequence of Ishmael's
having proposed a "social smoke" that he and Queequeg become
friends. "If there yet lurked any ice of indifference towards me in
the Pagan's breast, this pleasant, genial smoke we had, soon thawed
it out, and left us cronies" (10: *53*). Ahab's inability to feel such
emotions is the reason he casts his pipe into the sea. "What business
have I with this pipe? This thing that is meant for sereneness, to send
up mild white vapors among mild white hairs, not among torn iron-
grey locks like mine. I'll smoke no more—" (30: *114*).

It is no accident, then, that Stubb, during the interval when the
whale sounds, lights a pipe to match the one of the "portly burgher"
he is pursuing. In the subsequent chase, Ishmael returns to Stubb's
pipe with repetitive frequency. The whale, his sounding out, rises
"in advance of the smoker's boat." When the whale tries to escape,
Stubb, "still puffing at his pipe, . . . cheered on his crew to the assault." "Start her, start her, my men!" he shouts, "spluttering out the
smoke as he spoke." As the boat comes within harpoon-range, he
encourages the men to even greater efforts, "all the while puffing
the smoke from his mouth." When the harpoon is thrown and the
whale dives, Stubb wraps the whale-line around the boat's logger-
head, "whence, by reason of its increased rapid circlings, a hempen
blue smoke now jetted up and mingled with the steady fumes from
his pipe." Ishmael clearly is after a meaning. What that meaning is
becomes clear as the whale, harpooned and lanced, fights for life.
"And all the while, jet after jet of white smoke was agonizingly
shot from the spiracle of the whale, and vehement puff after puff
from the mouth of the excited headsman." Stubb and his whale are
not totally alien antagonists. They are both pipe-smokers. The fact

that one is butchering the other cannot obliterate this symbolic identity. Finally, the whale goes into his flurry, "surging from side to side; spasmodically dilating and contracting his spout-hole, with sharp, cracking, agonized respirations. At last, gush after gush of clotted red gore . . . shot into the frighted air; and falling back again, ran dripping down his motionless flanks into the sea. His heart had burst!" At this climax, the tragic identity of pursuer and pursued is stated by Stubb himself who, here as elsewhere, is not nearly so unaware as he often pretends to be. "He's dead, Mr. Stubb," Tashtego announces. "Yes; both pipes smoked out!" Stubb responds, and, "withdrawing his own from his mouth, [he] scattered the dead ashes over the water; and, for a moment, stood thoughtfully eyeing the vast corpse he had made" (61: *241–45*).

The pipe-figure is important because it measures Ishmael's capacity for empathic identification. Ahab regards the whale as "prey," and pursues him "with tornado brow, and eyes of red murder, and foam-glued lips" (48: *193*), but Ishmael cannot. Leviathan may be the salt-sea mastodon, an utterly alien creature from those regions of the natural world least familiar to man. Nevertheless, as the butchery proceeds, Ishmael feels *with* the whale rather than *against* the whale. In a definitive instance of the moral power of the creative lamp-mind, he projects his own humanity out upon that alien *other*, that inconceivable and unimaginable *not-me* which is Leviathan. Indeed, Ishmael suffers nearly as much as the whale during this first confrontation. He is unable to muster the methodical and dispassionate distance of the professional butcher. Words like *horrible, agonizing,* and *unspeakable* suggest what he is feeling. "The red tide now poured from all sides of the monster like brooks down a hill. His tormented body rolled not in brine but in blood, which bubbled and seethed for furlongs behind in their wake. The slanting sun playing upon this crimson pond in the sea, sent back its reflection into every face, so that they all glowed to each other like red men." The nightmare comes to a climax as Stubb employs his lance with surgical deliberation:

> "Pull up—pull up!" he now cried to the bowsman, as the waning whale relaxed in his wrath. "Pull up!—close to!" and the boat ranged along the fish's flank. When reaching far over the bow, Stubb slowly churned his long sharp lance into the fish, and kept it there, carefully

churning and churning, as if cautiously seeking to feel after some
gold watch that the whale might have swallowed, and which he was
fearful of breaking ere he could hook it out. But that gold watch he
sought was the innermost life of the fish. And now it is struck; for,
starting from his trance into that unspeakable thing called his
"flurry," the monster horribly wallowed in his blood, overwrapped
himself in impenetrable, mad, boiling spray, so that the imperilled
craft, instantly dropping astern, had much ado blindly to struggle out
from that phrensied twilight into the clear air of the day. (61: *244–45*)

But Ishmael is not in the clear air of day. He is engulfed in horror,
a horror which initiates the redemptive process he must undergo.

Stubb's Whale, however, is Leviathan in his prime, the whale
in all his cetacean vigor. This first encounter proves that the whale
is vulnerable to man as for eons of time the deer, the buffalo, and the
bear have been vulnerable, suffering in the unique crisis of death as
man suffers. But there is little in the incident to suggest any further
identity. Had the voyage of the *Pequod* been terminated at this
point, the whale would have remained one of those raptly mythic
figures from the natural world with which man has for centuries
adorned his cave-walls, his hogans, and his domestic artifacts—wist-
ful images of an animalistic integrity, of an organically flawless
relationship with the external world, which sundered and distracted
man perpetually seeks and never finds. Many interpretations of
Moby-Dick develop Leviathan in just these terms—and thus miss one
of Melville's major meanings.

That Ishmael's Leviathan is much more than a conventionally
mythopoeic figure becomes clear twenty chapters after the slaughter
of the pipe-smoking burgher. As the *Pequod* gams with the German
whaler *Jungfrau*, whales are sighted simultaneously from both mast-
heads. The main pod of young and vigorous whales proves too swift
for the pursuing boats, but wallowing helplessly in their rear, unable to keep up with his juniors, is a bull whale whose condition
alters decisively Ishmael's perception of Leviathanic reality:

Full in [the] rapid wake [of the younger whales], and many
fathoms in the rear, swam a huge, humped old bull, which by his
comparatively slow progress, as well as by the unusual yellowish

incrustations over-growing him, seemed afflicted with the jaundice, or some other infirmity. . . . His spout was short, slow, and laborious; coming forth with a choking sort of gush, and spending itself in torn shreds, followed by strange subterranean commotions in him, which seemed to have egress at his other buried extremity, causing the waters behind him to upbubble.

"Who's got some paregoric?" said Stubb, "he has the stomach-ache, I'm afraid. Lord, think of having half an acre of stomach-ache! Adverse winds are holding mad Christmas in him, boys. It's the first foul wind I ever knew to blow from astern." (81: *296*)

Old and tired, dyspeptic and flatulent, jaundiced and short of breath: this is hardly the whale of mythic or archetypal affirmation, nor the Leviathan of transcendental indomitability. This ancient and infirm whale, feebly struggling to escape the *Pequod's* boats, brings Ishmael to the redemptive realization that the largest and most powerful creature on the face of the earth is, like man, subject to all the ills that flesh is heir to. That this is Melville's meaning becomes clear as the whale, in his frantic efforts to escape, rolls from one side to the other:

As an overladen Indiaman bearing down the Hindostan coast with a deck load of frightened horses, careens, buries, rolls, and wallows on her way; so did this old whale heave his aged bulk, and now and then partly turning over on his cumbrous rib-ends, expose the cause of his devious wake in the unnatural stump of his starboard fin. Whether he had lost that fin in battle, or had been born without it, it were hard to say.

"Only wait a bit, old chap, and I'll give ye a sling for that wounded arm," cried cruel Flask, pointing to the whale-line near him. (81: *296*)

The Medicare Whale thus joins that gallery of human characters in *Moby-Dick* who, having been thumped by natural process, carry forevermore as emblem of their affliction, a multilated extremity. Captain Ahab is missing a leg. Captain Boomer is missing an arm (100: *367*). And Perth, the *Pequod's* blacksmith, victim of alcoholism and frostbite, yaws his way through life bereft of the better part of both feet (112: *401*). And so the whale. One of the great ironies of *Moby-Dick* is that although Ahab here encounters a whale of hundred-barrel ponderosity who has been "dismasted" and "razeed" just as he has been (36: *143*), the *Pequod's* Captain is unable to detect the redemptive analogy or draw the saving parallel which the Medicare Whale represents.

What Ahab misses, however, Ishmael sees. As the *Pequod's* boats draw near, the tragic debility of so stupendous a creature generates a compassionate horror which marks decisively the beginning of Ishmael's separation from Ahab:

> It was a terrific, most pitiable, and maddening sight. The whale was now going head out, and sending his spout before him in a continual tormented jet; while his one poor fin beat his side in an agony of fright. Now to this hand, now to that, he yawed in his faltering flight, and still at every billow that he broke, he spasmodically sank in the sea, or sideways rolled towards the sky his one beating fin. So have I seen a bird with clipped wing, making affrighted broken circles in the air, vainly striving to escape the piratical hawks. But the bird has a voice, and with plaintive cries will make known her fear; but the fear of this vast dumb brute of the sea, was chained up and enchanted in him; he had no voice, save that choking respiration through his spiracle, and this made the sight of him unspeakably pitiable; while still, in his amazing bulk, portcullis jaw, and omnipotent tail, there was enough to appal the stoutest man who so pitied. (81: *298*)

The stress on the whale's "one poor fin" and "one beating fin" reinforces the covert affinity, deeply ironic, which Ishmael wishes to establish between Ahab and Leviathan. He has already told us that however much others may "thump and punch" him about, he nevertheless has "the satisfaction of knowing that it is all right; that everybody else is one way or other served in much the same way—either in a physical or metaphysical point of view, that is; and so the universal thump is passed round" (1: *15*). The Medicare Whale makes it clear that the "everybody else" Ishmael speaks of includes the great whale himself. As Ahab has been served, so is Leviathan served. It follows that Ahab's conception of the whale as transcendent and untrammeled power is false.

That the Medicare Whale initiates such a repudiation of the Ahabian version of Leviathan becomes apparent when the whale desperately sounds to escape his pursuers:

Not eight inches of perpendicular rope were visible at the bows. Seems it credible that by three such thin threads the great Leviathan was suspended like the big weight to an eight day clock. Suspended? and to what? To three bits of board. Is this the creature of whom it was once so triumphantly said—"Canst thou fill his skin with barbed irons? or his head with fish-spears? The sword of him that layeth at him cannot hold, the spear, the dart, nor the habergeon: he esteemeth iron as straw; the arrow cannot make him flee; darts are counted as stubble; he laugheth at the shaking of a spear!" [Job 41: 7, *26–29*]. This the creature? this he? Oh! that unfulfilments should follow the prophets. For with the strength of a thousand thighs in his tail, Leviathan had run his head under the mountains of the sea, to hide him from the Pequod's fish-spears! (81: *300*)

It is appropriate that Ishmael should quote from Job, since much more is being dismissed here than Ahab's whale. In a more general way, the triumphalism and arrogant transcendentalism of traditional Christian theism are also being repudiated. Ishmael here rejects not only the Leviathan of Job, of Jonah, and of Father Mapple; he also implicitly rejects the overkill, megaton God which all three presuppose. This is what he means when he speaks of the "unfulfilments" which "follow the prophets." The shift is crucial. Ishmael could never learn to love Omnipotent Leviathan, much less what Omnipotent Leviathan might represent. But he can learn to love— in the sense suggested by D. H. Lawrence—a Leviathan as humanly vulnerable as he is himself. And if Ishmael can learn to love the whale, he can learn to love the immense cosmos of which the whale is symbol.

For Ishmael, pity and compassion are the beginnings of such a pan-naturalistic love. The Medicare Whale, finally forced to return to the surface for air, provides an ample field for both humanizing emotions:

As the boats now more closely surrounded him, the whole upper part of his form, with much of it that is ordinarily submerged, was plainly revealed. His eyes, or rather the places where his eyes had been, were beheld. As strange misgrown masses gather in the knot-holes of the noblest oaks when prostrate, so from the points which the whale's eyes had once occupied, now protruded blind bulbs, horribly pitiable to see. But pity there was none. For all his old age, and his one arm, and his blind eyes, he must die the death and be murdered, in order to light the gay bridals and other merry-makings of men, and also to illuminate the solemn churches that preach unconditional inoffensiveness by all to all. (81: *301*)

To age, to dyspepsia and flatulence, to jaundice and emphysema, and to the crippling loss of an "arm," must now be added blindness. But Melville is not yet done. Nothing could better express the tragic vulnerability of great Leviathan than the ulcerated growth which the struggles of the Medicare Whale reveal. "Still rolling in his blood, at last he partially disclosed a strangely discolored bunch or protuberance, the size of a bushel, low down on the flank." Insensitive Flask cannot resist: "A nice spot," he exclaims; "just let me prick him there once." Starbuck tries to intervene: "Avast!" he cries, "there's no need of that!":

> But humane Starbuck was too late. At the instant of the dart an ulcerous jet shot from this cruel wound, and goaded by it into more than sufferable anguish, the whale now spouting thick blood, with swift fury blindly darted at the craft, bespattering them and their glorying crews all over with showers of gore, capsizing Flask's boat and marring the bows. It was his death stroke. For, by this time, so spent was he by loss of blood, that he helplessly rolled away from the wreck he had made; lay panting on his side, impotently flapped with his stumped fin, then over and over slowly revolved like a waning world; turned up the white secrets of his belly; lay like a log, and died. It was most piteous, that last expiring spout. (81: *301–02*)

Thus does the Medicare Whale become a symbol of the tragic condition of all sentient beings, and of the universal suffering which can—or should—draw all sentient beings together in brotherhood. This final meaning of Ishmael's second whale is amplified by the two artifacts which are discovered to be embedded in its ancient flesh. One is a modern harpoon-head, badly corroded but intact, found in the bushel-sized ulceration which Flask punctures. The other is very different: "But still more curious was the fact of a lance-head of stone being found in him, not far from the buried iron, the flesh perfectly firm about it. Who had darted that stone lance? And when? It might have been darted by some Nor' West Indian long before America was discovered" (81: *302*). Both artifacts, steel and stone, express a universal vulnerability, a tragic capacity,

which is as indifferent to mere time as it is to mere size. The Medicare Whale suffers and dies in Ishmael's nineteenth century. But
the aboriginal stone lance-head suggests that he was equally vulnerable, and might just as well have died a violent death, in some
neolithically distant epoch when both he and the world were
young.

The killing of the Medicare Whale provides an opportunity to
attend to the problem—so far ignored—of whether Melville intended
to write a cetological *epic*. The question is important because the
answer to it will determine the light in which the reader regards
the killing of the various whales the *Pequod* encounters, as well as
the attack on Moby Dick himself. At first glance, there would seem
to be considerable sanction for an epic-heroic reading. Chapter 82,
"The Honor and Glory of Whaling," which immediately follows
the killing of the Medicare Whale, appears to develop the epic
qualities of the fisheries:

> The more I dive into this matter of whaling, and push my re-
> searches up to the very spring-head of it, so much the more am I
> impressed with its great honorableness and antiquity; and especially
> when I find so many great demi-gods and heroes, prophets of all sorts,
> who one way or other have shed distinction upon it, I am transported
> with the reflection that I myself belong, though but subordinately,
> to so emblazoned a fraternity. (82: *304*)

Ishmael leads off his fraternity roster with the intrepid Perseus, who
rescued Andromeda from a coastal rock just as Leviathan was about
to carry her off. "It was an admirable artistic exploit," he dryly
observes, "rarely achieved by the best harpooneers of the present
day; inasmuch as this Leviathan was slain at the very first dart."
With a similar air of droll earnestness, he cites the story of St.
George and the Dragon, "which dragon I maintain to have been a
whale":

> Let not the modern paintings of this scene mislead us; for though
> the creature encountered by that valiant whaleman of old is vaguely
> represented of a griffin-like shape, and though the battle is depicted
> on land and the saint on horseback, yet considering the great igno-
> rance of those times, when the true form of the whale was unknown to
> artists; and considering that as in Perseus' case, St. George's whale

might have crawled up out of the sea on the beach; and considering that the animal ridden by St. George might have been only a large seal, or sea-horse; bearing all this in mind, it will not appear altogether incompatible with the sacred legend . . . to hold this so-called dragon no other than the great Leviathan himself. (82: *305*)

The dragon a whale; the whale an amphibian; the horse a seal; and the sea the land: is sly Ishmael once again pulling the reader's leg? Such a possibility becomes a probability when Hercules is added to the epic roster because he was "swallowed down and thrown up by a whale." Ishmael admits that this is not the usual way one becomes a whaleman, or an epic hero for that matter. "Nevertheless, [Hercules] may be deemed a sort of involuntary whaleman; at any rate the whale caught him, if he did not the whale. I claim him for one of our clan." Ishmael's final examples are Jonah and Vishnoo, the second of whom became incarnate in the whale and plunged to the bottom of the sea to rescue the sacred Vedas. "Was not this Vishnoo a whaleman, then?" Ishmael rhetorically asks, "even as a man who rides a horse is called a horseman?" He concludes: "Perseus, St. George, Hercules, Jonah, and Vishnoo! there's a member-roll for you! What club but the whaleman's can head off like that?" (82: *304–06*).

It is distressing to discover that this arrant Ishmaelian nonsense has been used as the foundation for readings of *Moby-Dick* almost certainly at odds with what Melville actually intended. Alfred Kazin, for example, regards *Moby-Dick* as "an epic, a long poem on a heroic theme," and Warner Berthoff characterizes the novel as "a meditative-heroic poem on the honor and glory, and practical enterprise, of whaling."[3] There is no way to disprove categorically such readings, but certain facts should give us pause. It is striking, for example, that Ishmael juxtaposes the Homeric simile with the brutal butchery of the Medicare Whale. Five times in seven pages he resorts to this formalistic and hyperliterary device, with all its epic and heroic associations. The five instances are worth listing in sequence:

As an overladen Indiaman bearing down the Hindostan coast with a deck load of frightened horses, careens, buries, rolls, and wallows on her way; so did this old whale heave his aged bulk, and now and then partly turning over on his cumbrous rib-ends, expose the cause of his devious wake in the unnatural stump of his starboard fin. (81: *296*)

And the second:

> Now to this hand, now to that, he yawed in his faltering flight, and
> still at every billow that he broke, he spasmodically sank in the sea,
> or sideways rolled towards the sky his one beating fin. So have I
> seen a bird with clipped wing, making affrighted broken circles in the
> air, vainly striving to escape the piratical hawks. (81: *298*)

And the third:

> Yet so vast is the quantity of blood in [the whale], and so distant and
> numerous its interior fountains, that he will keep thus bleeding and
> bleeding for a considerable period; even as in a drought a river will
> flow, whose source is in the well-springs of far-off and undiscernible
> hills. (81: *301*)

And the fourth:

> As strange misgrown masses gather in the knot-holes of the noblest
> oaks when prostrate, so from the points which the whale's eyes had
> once occupied, now protruded blind bulbs, horribly pitiable to see.
> (81: *301*)

And the fifth:

> As when by unseen hands the water is gradually drawn off from some
> mighty fountain, and with half-stifled melancholy gurglings the
> spray-column lowers and lowers to the ground—so the last long
> dying spout of the whale. (81: *302*)

Once again, Ishmael is after a meaning. He employs the Homeric
simile to express, not the epic aspects of whaling, but rather the
counter-epic aspects. There is immense irony in the fact that the
"antagonist" of Chapter 81 is not a many-headed hydra breathing
fire and destruction, nor a cyclops able to tear up trees by the roots.
It is not even Fabulous Leviathan in all the vast brawn of his cetacean
prime. It is instead the Medicare Whale, wheezing, flatulent, and
terrified. Where Ishmael launches into Homeric simile, the matter
of comparison is not the indomitable might of Leviathan, but rather
his age, his helplessness, his blindness, his tragic blood-vulnerability.
In Chapter 81, the crew of the *Pequod* attacks and kills a helpless
cripple. No amount of critical transmogrification can elevate this
brutal encounter into the epic mode. Moreover, to do so would be
to distort the ultimate meanings of *Moby-Dick*. The redemption of

Ishmael and the resolution of his hypos depend upon his learning to *love Leviathan*, the alien, the cosmic, other. The epic frame of mind can only retard this redemptive process. The one universal emotion which has no place in the epic idiom is *love* for the antagonist which the hero must encounter and conquer by feats of derring-do. Beowulf, to put the matter another way, could rest in a heroism much less exalted than that to which Ishmael is called. He had only to *kill* Grendel. He did not have to *love* him.

Apparently Ishmael was fearful that some readers might miss these ironic reversals and counter-epic insinuations. So he embedded two clues in the text as to his real meaning. One involves chapter-juxtaposition: Ishmael has the sly habit of saying one thing in one chapter, and precisely the opposite thing in the next. Thus, the butchery of the Medicare Whale in Chapter 81, and in particular Flask's sadistic puncturing of the ulcerated wound in the old whale's flank, must stand as direct moral commentary on Chapter 82 in which Ishmael, tongue-in-cheek, pretends to claim an epic sanction for the bloody business in which the *Pequod* is engaged. The heroic habit of mind, he seems to be saying, is only a cover for, and a shabby rationalization of, a vicious hankering after the brutal and sanguine in sharkish man. Indeed, at the instant when cruel Flask plunges his lance into the bushel-sized ulceration, Ishmael introduces a second and decisive clue. It is the word *glory*, or more precisely, *glorying*. The context bears repeating: "At the instant of [Flask's] dart an ulcerous jet shot from this cruel wound, and goaded by it into more than sufferable anguish, the whale now spouting thick blood, with swift fury blindly darted at the craft, bespattering them and their *glorying* crews all over with showers of gore" (81: *301*; italics mine). Ishmael's disgust could hardly be made clearer. It is in the light of this calculated use of *glory* that the title and substance of the succeeding chapter, "The Honor and Glory of Whaling," must be read.

This pair of chapters, and especially the droll "emblazoned fraternity" of heroes which Ishmael owlishly assembles—Perseus, St. George, Hercules, Jonah, and Vishnoo—is a specimen of the invincible taste for sly japes which afflicts Ishmael, and which makes the reading of *Moby-Dick* such a tricky business. He is too polite ever to say so, but Ishmael clearly harbors a thorough contempt for the superficial or naive reader. He cannot resist waylaying such literary innocents by playing upon established prejudice or habitual response. The conventional translation of butchery into heroism and murder into epic is such a conventional response. What Melville and Ishmael feel about it is best expressed by the narrator of *White Jacket*, who has his own definition of *glory*. "How were these officers to gain glory?" he asks. "How but by a distinguished slaughtering of their fellow-men. How were they to be promoted? How but over the buried heads of killed comrades and mess-mates." It is sentiments such as these, applied not to man, but to the suffering world for which Leviathan is the symbol, which make *Moby-Dick* the anti-heroic and counter-epic document that it is.[4]

Stubb's Whale and the Medicare Whale are, however, only prelusive to the encounter of Ishmael with the Social Whale of Chapter 87, "The Grand Armada." Sailing through the Straits of Sunda, the *Pequod* overtakes and pursues an "immense caravan" consisting of "thousands on thousands" of Sperm Whales. As they emerge upon the China Seas, three keels are lowered and the chase continued by oar for several hours, when suddenly and inexplicably the entire herd *gallies*, which Ishmael defines as "to confound with fright" (87: *322n*):

> The compact martial columns in which they had been hitherto rapidly and steadily swimming, were now broken up in one measureless rout; and like King Porus' elephants in the Indian battle with Alexander, they seemed going mad with consternation. In all directions expanding in vast irregular circles, and aimlessly swimming hither and thither, by their short thick spoutings, they plainly betrayed their distraction of panic. This was still more strangely evinced by those of their number, who, completely paralysed as it were, helplessly floated like water-logged dismantled ships on the sea. (87: *322*)

That these thousands of the great Sperm Whale should gally, victims of blind panic, vitiates further the Ahabian and Biblical version of "indomitable" Leviathan. The point is not lost on Ishmael. "Had these leviathans been but a flock of simple sheep," he dryly observes, "pursued over the pasture by three fierce wolves, they could not possibly have evinced such excessive dismay." But whales are, after all, only "herding creatures," and like all such animals, given to "occasional timidity." Such timidity is touchingly human, and especially so when it appears in so vast an animal; the tragic vulnerability of Stubb's portly burgher and the Medicare Whale is not diminished by mere numbers.

Ishmael's initiation into the secret life of Leviathan begins when Queequeg harpoons a lone whale on the outskirts of the shoal, whereupon "the stricken fish darted blinding spray in our faces, and then running away with us like light, steered straight for the heart of the herd." At precisely the right moment, the harpoon pulls free, and the translation—it is really an epistemological voyage covering immense conceptual distances—is complete: ". . . we glided between two whales into the innermost heart of the shoal, as if from some mountain torrent we had slid into a serene valley lake." It is a movement from active pursuit to contemplative stasis: "Here the storms in the roaring glens between the outermost whales, were heard but not felt." In a culminating instance of the metaphor of reflective transparency, Ishmael, like Narcissus, is presented with a water-mirror he can both gaze at and gaze through: "In this central expanse the sea presented that smooth satin-like surface, called a sleek, produced by the subtle moisture thrown off by the whale in his more quiet moods." He thus enters a magic realm. "Yes, we were now in that enchanted calm which they say lurks at the heart of every commotion." The whales in this "innermost fold" inhabit a "wondrous world"; floating in their "enchanted pond," they seem to be "entranced," "becharmed," under a "spell." Ishmael is now immured in Leviathanism, swallowed up by the Sperm Whale herd just as Jonah was swallowed by a single whale. "We must watch for a breach in the living wall that hemmed us in," he remarks, betraying an initial consternation; "the wall that had only admitted us in order to shut us up."

What Ishmael has been brought here to see is the Social Whale, secretly leading a domestic life much like man's.[5] The first significant consequence is a change in Ishmael's perception of the whale as sheer size, overweening bulk, untrammeled power. This shift is accomplished by a re-articulation of Leviathanism—the cosmically constitutive aspects of the whale—in feminine and infantile modes. Ishmael perceives that the "cows and calves" of the herd "had been purposely locked up in this innermost fold." He immediately humanizes them. They are "the women and children of this routed host," placed at the protected center because they are "so young, unsophisticated, and every way innocent and inexperienced." Viewed from another vantage-point, great Leviathan becomes not very different from the domestic cat purring on the hearth-stone, or the dog nuzzling our hand, importunate to be patted and spoken to:

> ... these smaller whales—now and then visiting our becalmed boat from the margin of the lake—evinced a wondrous fearlessness and confidence, or else a still, becharmed panic which it was impossible not to marvel at. Like household dogs they came snuffling round us, right up to our gunwales, and touching them; till it almost seemed that some spell had suddenly domesticated them. Queequeg patted their foreheads; Starbuck scratched their backs with his lance. (87: *324–25*)

The profoundly human process underlying this perceptual and conceptual shift is identical with that which shapes other pages of *Moby-Dick*. Following Tashtego's plunge into the Heidelberg Tun, death was *honeyized* in the analogue of the Ohio honey-hunter (78: *290*). Similarly, the annihilative power of the Sperm Whale's tail was *aestheticized* in crescentic "lines of beauty" (86: *314*). So now, the vastness of Leviathan is *femininized* and *infantilized*. The change is most clearly seen in the young whales snuffling around Ishmael's boat. A baby whale is inevitably more baby than whale. While having a care for the lethally unconscious power of such a junior juggernaut, the redemptively human impulse is to do what Starbuck and Queequeg do: pat his head or scratch his back. Once you have done this, Ishmael seems to suggest, once you have so touched Leviathan, you can never again return to the excoriated sterilities of the Ahabian world-view.

So far, however, Ishmael has dealt only with the surface of this "wondrous world." In a consummate elaboration of the protometaphor which shapes all of *Moby-Dick*, he is now permitted a glimpse of the most intimate interiorities of Leviathanic life. "But far beneath this wondrous world upon the surface," he continues, "another and still stranger world met our eyes as we gazed over the side." Beneath the perceptual interface, in that pallidly noumenal world which up to this point has been populated only with terrifying primal forms such as the shark and the squid, another and quite opposite aspect of natural process is revealed. "Some of the subtlest secrets of the seas," Ishmael raptly observes, "seemed divulged to us in this enchanted pond." This is the second time that Ishmael has used the word *subtle* in connection with the sea. The first occurred in the "Brit" chapter when, in an ecstasy of horror, he asked his readers to "Consider the subtleness of the sea," a subtleness which he saw in the "devilish brilliance and beauty" of the sea's most "remorseless tribes," and the "dainty embellished shape" of even the most vicious of sharks (58: *235*). Now, however, the subtlety of the sea is re-articulated in terms totally benign. Ishmael has been haunted by the fear that the surface of nature was a deceitful array of harlot colors, and that were he ever permitted to pierce the phenomenal derma, he would find a ghastly "charnel-house" of noumenal horror (42: *170*). In "The Grand Armada" he is permitted such a perceptual dive. What greets his eyes is not a charnel-house, but rather a house of life, a fecund and proliferant realm of "submarine bridal chambers and nurseries":

> For, suspended in those watery vaults, floated the forms of the nursing mothers of the whales, and those that by their enormous girth seemed shortly to become mothers. The lake ... was to a considerable depth exceedingly transparent; and as human infants while suckling will calmly and fixedly gaze away from the breast, as if leading two different lives at the [same] time; and while yet drawing mortal nourishment, be still spiritually feasting upon some unearthly reminiscence;—even so did the young of these whales seem looking up towards us, but not at us, as if we were but a bit of Gulf-weed in their new-born sight. (87: *325*)

Cetacean infants and human infants: they are strikingly similar, one as much as the other trailing clouds of glory. The scene is redolent with a vast maternal placidity: "Floating on their sides, the mothers also seemed quietly eyeing us." Utterly fascinated, Ishmael returns to the paradox which infantile Leviathanism represents:

> One of these little infants, that from certain queer tokens seemed hardly a day old, might have measured some fourteen feet in length, and some six feet in girth. He was a little frisky; though as yet his body seemed scarce yet recovered from that irksome position it had

so lately occupied in the maternal reticule; where, tail to head, and all ready for the final spring, the unborn whale lies bent like a Tartar's bow. The delicate side-fins, and the palms of his flukes, still freshly retained the plaited crumpled appearance of a baby's ears newly arrived from foreign parts. (87: *325*)

Ishmael, one recalls, was arrested by the fact that the eye of a creature so vast as the whale should be no larger than a colt's eye, hardly larger than a human's. It was this cetological consideration which led him to conclude that size was a meaningless philosophical parameter, and that human perception and human thought could encompass anything. "Why then," he asked, "do you try to 'enlarge' your mind? Subtilize it" (74: *280*). This day-old whale-pup, frisking at the heart of the Grand Armada, represents that process of subtilization precisely. Ishmael describes him empirically: he is fourteen feet long and six feet around. One wishes that Ishmael had added that datum which so concerns human mothers: the baby's probable weight. Surely we have here an infant tipping the scales at over a ton.[6] If this is the case, the baby whale might stand as a supreme example of what I have called the "empirical bogey," that dispiriting sense of the vast *size*, the outrageous *extension*, of most aspects of the cosmos in relation to puny man. But Ishmael is not dispirited by this incredible specimen of infantile ponderosity. Rather, he is charmed, fascinated, delighted. The reason has that simplicity which characterizes all metaphysical subtleties. This baby Leviathan is not, for Ishmael, a ton of whale. Rather, he is a *ton of baby*. As a consequence, the humane and humanizing emotions which all babies naturally generate have, simply, a much more ample field in which to play. For the first time in *Moby-Dick*, Ishmael achieves a mode of apprehension forever closed to Ahab: he is able to take delight in immensity, pleasure in size. The baby whale is much more than a sentimental diversion. He is ontologically significant, representing for Ishmael the definitive obliteration of the empirical bogey.

It is characteristic of the Ishmaelian sensibility that this humanizing of the Grand Armada should reach its fullest development in a series of sexual analogues. As Ishmael proceeds with his description of Leviathan's secret life, it becomes apparent that he labors under a difficulty. Addressing a nineteenth-century American audience, he cannot be as explicit as he would. His discomfort becomes obvious when he irrelevantly terminates a paragraph devoted to the Leviathanic umbilical cord with a sentence which has nothing to do with the topic at hand. "We saw young Leviathan amours in the deep," he blurts out, and then, chafing under the constraints of conventional expression, he drops into the relative inconspicuousness of a footnote:

> The sperm whale, as with all other species of the Leviathan, but unlike most other fish, breeds indifferently at all seasons; after a gestation which may probably be set down at nine months, producing but one at a time; though in some few known instances giving birth to an Esau and Jacob:—a contingency provided for in suckling by two teats, curiously situated, one on each side of the anus; but the breasts themselves extend upwards from that. When by chance these precious parts in a nursing whale are cut by the hunter's lance, the mother's pouring milk and blood rivalingly discolor the sea for rods. The milk is very sweet and rich; it has been tasted by man; it might do well with strawberries. When overflowing with mutual esteem, the whales salute *more hominum*. (87: *326n*)

Year-round sexual activity; a nine-month gestation period; occasional twins and teats to match; mother's milk worthy of human consumption; and—here Ishmael drops into Latin to further mask what he is saying—an ability to copulate and a way of going about it, both of which are distinctly human, differentiating the whale not only from other fish, which do not copulate, but also from mere quadrupedal mammals, which do. Such analogues derived from cetacean sexuality round out the humanizing similarities between man and this most alien of sea-creatures. That such humanizing is Ishmael's conscious intention is suggested by his selection of nine months as the probable gestation period of *Physeter catodon*. Writing in 1850, he cannot and does not know that nine months is more probable than eight, or ten—or even twenty. But nine months is the figure which makes Leviathan most human.[7]

In Chapter 58, "Brit," Ishmael assured us that "you can hardly regard any creature of the deep with the same feelings that you do those of the shore." Historically, he added, "the native inhabitants of the seas have ever been regarded with emotions unspeakably unsocial and repelling" (58: *234–35*). These assertions concerning the intractably alien nature of all sea-creatures occur just three chapters before Ishmael's catalyzing encounter with the pipe-smoking Leviathan of "Stubb Kills a Whale" (61: *241–45*), and long before his observation of the Medicare Whale (81: *295–304*) and the Grand Armada (87: *318–28*). Through a crucial span of thirty chapters, in short, Ishmael changes his mind. He discovers that Leviathan is *not* like other sea-creatures, is indeed like man, and must stand as a redemptive exception to his own rule. It is this pivotal shift in Ishmaelian perception which provides the dramatic justification for the accumulations of factual data on cetacean physiology and behavior scattered through *Moby-Dick*. The humanizing of the whale, while imaginative in thrust and effect, is solidly scientific in basis. Ishmael discovers, or comes to realize, that vast Leviathan is, like man, a placental mammal. This makes him a congener of man, with all the manifold and intimate identities such a scientific relationship implies.[8] The consequence is that growing feeling of *fraternal congenerity* regarding the whale which Ishmael exhibits, and which leads in turn to more subtle feelings of tragic affinity and metaphysical consanguinity with this unbelievably vast taxonomic relative. Leviathan is not, after all, an alien. Rather, and in literal scientific fact, he is a brother.

Ishmael prepares for this change in perception of Leviathanic reality between Chapters 58 and 87 by rejecting all exaggerated and fabulous versions of the whale. In Chapter 55, "Of the Monstrous Pictures of Whales," he cannot too much deprecate illustrations in which Leviathan is represented with a "distended tusked mouth into which the billows are rolling," or where "whales, like great rafts of logs, are represented lying among ice-isles, with white bears running over their living backs." Equally reprehensible are those prints which endow the whale with an eye like a "bow-window some five feet long," or which depict the whale as a fabulous "hippogriff" resembling, Ishmael thinks, nothing so much as an "amputated sow." Worst of all, however, are those wildly exaggerated whales encountered in any American city:

As for the sign-painters' whales seen in the streets hanging over the shops of oil-dealers, what shall be said of them? They are generally Richard III. whales, with dromedary humps, and very savage; breakfasting on three or four sailor tarts, that is whaleboats full of mariners: their deformities floundering in seas of blood and blue paint. (55: *225–27*)

Such deprecation of Fabulous Leviathan is important for two reasons. First, Ahab's whale is very much a Richard III whale. Implicit in Chapter 55 is a repudiation of Ahab's version of Moby Dick as a creature of "outrageous strength" and "inscrutable malice," a veritable breakfaster on sailor tarts. Second, Ishmael's rejection of Fabulous Leviathan is helpful in arriving at a proper perspective on *Moby-Dick* as a whole. Almost without exception, commentators on the novel have been unable to resist the temptation to mythologize (and in the process, dehumanize) Leviathan. It is difficult to reconcile such an approach with Ishmael's persistent efforts, from Chapter 55 on, at *de*mythification.

Such demythification is necessary because Fabulous Leviathan cannot at the same time be Brotherly Leviathan. The two are irreconcilable. So Ishmael sets to work, using cetology as his tool, to minimize the strange and maximize the familiar in the whale.[9] It is only twelve chapters after his rejection of monstrous whales that he makes overt his growing sense of identity. He is describing the warm overcoat of blubber, some twelve or fifteen inches thick, which sets the whale apart from other fish:

It is by reason of this cosy blanketing of his body, that the whale is enabled to keep himself comfortable in all weathers, in all seas, times, and tides. What would become of a Greenland whale, say, in those shuddering, icy seas of the North, if unsupplied with his cosy surtout? True, other fish are found exceedingly brisk in those Hyperborean waters; but these, be it observed, are your cold-blooded, lungless fish, whose very bellies are refrigerators; creatures, that warm themselves under the lee of an iceberg ... *whereas, like man, the whale has lungs and warm blood.* Freeze his blood, and he dies. How wonderful is it then ... that this great monster, *to whom corporeal warmth is as indispensable as it is to man*; how wonderful that he should be found at home, immersed to his lips for life in those Arctic waters! (68: *261*; italics mine)

Some twenty chapters later Ishmael returns to this cetological fact, that the whale has "regular lungs, like a human being's" (85: *310*). He notes that the whale cannot remain under the surface indefinitely as a gilled fish can. Instead, at hourly intervals he must return to the upper air and oxygenate his blood through his spout-hole. Nor is this process susceptible of variation: he must "have his spoutings out," achieving full aeration before returning to the bottom. This fact gives the whale-hunter his advantage. "For not by hook or by net could this vast leviathan be caught, when sailing a thousand fathoms beneath the sunlight. *Not so much thy skill, then, O hunter, as the great necessities, that strike the victory to thee!*" (85: *311*; italics mine). Fabulous Leviathan could not, in the nature of things, be subject to the "great necessities" of life, and still be fabulous. Mythic and transcendental figures are not necessitarian figures. But flesh-and-blood Leviathan, tragically subject to ineluctable necessity, thus achieves identity with man on philosophical as well as physiological grounds.

The consequence of such philosophical cetology is a persistent humanizing of the whale not only in set scenes such as those dealing with the Medicare Whale and the Grand Armada, but in isolated paragraphs and passing references scattered through the latter half of *Moby-Dick*. There are young whales, for example, "in the highest health, and swelling with noble aspirations, . . . in the warm flush and May of life, with all their panting lard about them[,] . . . brawny, buoyant heroes." There are old whales, "broken-hearted creatures, their pads of lard diminished and all their bones heavy and rheumatic" (81: *303*). Forty-barrel bulls are "Like a mob of young collegians, . . . full of fight, fun, and wickedness, tumbling round the world at such a reckless, rollicking rate, that no prudent underwriter would insure them any more than he would a riotous lad at Yale or Harvard" (88: *330*). Like man, Leviathan has his unbuttoned moments: "Stealing unawares upon the whale in the fancied security of the middle of solitary seas, you find him unbent from the vast corpulence of his dignity, and kitten-like, he plays on the ocean as if it were a hearth" (86: *316*). Brother Whale even progresses through something very like the seven ages of man. Ishmael remarks that a pod of female whales is almost always accompanied by a "Grand Turk" or "Bashaw." "In truth, this gentleman is a luxurious Ottoman, swimming about over the watery world, surroundingly accompanied by all the solaces and endearments of the harem." Master and maids travel the globe "Like fashionables" who in their "indolent ramblings" are "in leisurely search of variety." But such "omnivorous roving lovers" come to a very human end:

> In good time, ... as the ardor of youth declines; as years and dumps increase; as reflection lends her solemn pauses; in short, as a general lassitude overtakes the sated Turk; then a love of ease and virtue supplants the love for maidens; our Ottoman enters upon the impotent, repentant, admonitory stage of life, forswears, disbands the harem, and grown to an exemplary, sulky old soul, goes about all alone among the meridians and parallels saying his prayers, and warning each young Leviathan from his amorous errors. (88: *328–30*)

It is in precisely these terms that Captain Boomer of the *Samuel Enderby*, who has lost an arm to Moby Dick, perceives the great White Whale. Moby Dick is to him, not a monster, but simply "this old great-grandfather" (100: *365*). Such capacity for humanizing vision makes it possible for Captain Boomer to survive, his sense of humor intact, that same experience which destroys Captain Ahab.

Among the various Yankee simplicities which lie at the heart of *Moby-Dick*, one of the most important is that insight toward which the humanizing of Leviathan tends: Ishmael's realization that even the great whale, the mightiest creature of the living earth, is part of a tragic continuum from which *nothing* is free. He makes this point as the whitened corpse of Stubb's Whale, peeled of its blubber and cast loose from the ship, floats away to the horizon:

> There's a most doleful and most mocking funeral! The sea-vultures all in pious mourning, the air-sharks all punctiliously in black or speckled. In life but few of them would have helped the whale, I ween, if peradventure he had needed it; but upon the banquet of his funeral they most piously do pounce. *Oh, horrible vulturism of earth! from which not the mightiest whale is free.* (69: *262*; italics mine)

Melville apparently found the point totally compelling; he returns to it in *Clarel*:

A Thug, the sword-fish roams the sea—
The falcon's pirate in the air;
Betwixt the twain, where shalt thou flee,
Poor flying-fish? whither repair?
What other element for thee?
Whales, mighty whales have felt the wound—
Plunged bleeding through the blue profound.[10]

Absolute freedom, a power essentially transcendental, does not exist. The universal thump is just that: universal. *All* nature suffers. This is an insight forever denied to Ahab. His pervasively Christian outlook, his deicidal envy, and his consequent sense of nature as antagonist, make it inevitable that he will detect an element of transcendental indomitability in natural process. Ishmael, through the humanizing of the whale, avoids this tragic mistake. As a result, Leviathan, which began as a focus of terror and despair for Ishmael, becomes in the end a source of hope. In Chapters 42 and 51, "The Whiteness of the Whale" and "The Spirit-Spout," the whale and his spout became emblematic of the noumenal world which Ishmael believed lay hidden under the chromatic richness of sensuous nature. Both were albescent forms suggestive of a "colorless all-color of atheism." Now, in a crucial turnabout, the whale—and his spout—are suddenly integrated with the *rainbow*, that prismatic color-array which Ishmael has explicitly associated with "hope and solace" (42: *168*):

And how nobly it raises our conceit of the mighty, misty monster, to behold him solemnly sailing through a calm tropical sea; his vast, mild head overhung by a canopy of vapor . . . and that vapor . . . glorified by a rainbow, as if Heaven itself had put its seal upon his thoughts. For, d'ye see, rainbows do not visit the clear air; they only irradiate vapor. And so, through all the thick mists of the dim doubts in my mind, divine intuitions now and then shoot, enkindling my fog with a heavenly ray. And for this I thank God; for all have doubts; many deny; but doubts or denials, few along with them, have intuitions. Doubts of all things earthly, and intuitions of some things heavenly; this combination makes neither believer nor infidel, but makes a man who regards them both with equal eye. (85: *314*)

The rainbow imagery of this passage—a compelling instance of the metaphor of illumination—gives us for the first time a whale endowed with *philosophical chromaticity*. Such a Rainbow Leviathan, such a Tingent Whale, suggests that Ishmael, having plunged in despair to the antipodes of the anteperceptual realm, is now on his way back to the polychrome world of sensuous apprehension—and is bringing his newly-found cetacean brother with him. Ishmael here stands poised on a knife-edge. If he is not a believer, neither is he now the "wretched infidel" of the "Whiteness" chapter, nor the haunted man insinuating the possible "propriety of devil-worship" during Stubb's supper. Rainbow intuitions of "things heavenly," brought to him by the whale and the whale's irradiated spout, have acted as counterpoise. For the first time viewing all things with "equal eye," Ishmael is now ready for—indeed, is already involved in—a series of insights which will profoundly alter his despairing view of cosmic reality.

 X

GREEN SKULLS
Ahab's Entropism and Ishmael's Cyclicism

FROM BEGINNING to end, *Moby-Dick* is dominated by the shark's saw-pit of mouth and charnel of maw. Into that gaping, apparently bottomless rictal void everything must go. All things are, finally, *consumed*. It is this sense of both cosmic activity and life process as a hideously predacious, devouring kind of business, that makes *Moby-Dick* the supremely horrible book that it is. Moreover, Ishmael's increasing identification with the whale, while it meliorates certain of his hypos, exacerbates this one. It is not entirely consoling to realize that one's fraternal congenerity with alien Leviathan rests in part on a shared susceptibility to life's cormorant rapacity. "Oh, horrible vulturism of earth!" Ishmael exclaims, "from which not

the mightiest whale is free" (69: *262*).* It is in the figure of *self-*
consumption, however, that Ishmael's hypos achieve their agonized
climax. Certainly the most frightful passage in a frightful novel is
Ishmael's description of sharks, disemboweled by random thrusts of
the cutting-spades, ravenously devouring their own entrails (66:
257). These are, however, relatively obvious matters. What is not
so obvious is that the auto-cannibalism of the sharks finds its parallel
in the *Pequod's* Captain. If, on a physical level, sharks in their frenzy
devour themselves, on a congruent metaphysical level Ahab in his
frenzy devours himself. The point is important because the self-
consumption of Ahab—who at one point even refers to himself as
"cannibal old me" (132: *444*)—provides him with a paradigm of
natural process which is radically different from the one which Ishmael gradually develops. There is a subterranean connection between the sharkishness of the *Pequod's* world and the differing
cosmologies of Ahab and Ishmael.

The motif of auto-consumption extends to the whale himself.
When the try-works fires are first lighted, they are fed only for a
short time with precious wood. After a certain point the residue
of the rendering process, the "crisp, shrivelled blubber, now called
scraps or fritters," is sufficient to sustain the flames without the
addition of other fuel. Ishmael cannot resist the obvious analogy:
"Like a plethoric burning martyr, or a self-consuming misanthrope,
once ignited, the whale supplies his own fuel and burns by his own
body" (96: *352–53*). The reference to misanthropic Ahab is obvious and inevitable, and Ishmael has already exploited it. "For a
long time, now," he observed just before the *Pequod's* encounter
with the Grand Armada, "the circus-running sun has raced within his
fiery ring, and needs no sustenance but what's in himself. So Ahab"
(87: *319*). Such images of combustive self-expenditure are repeatedly associated with Ahab. The *Pequod's* Captain is a man "consumed with the hot fire of his purpose" (46: *182*). Ahab himself
asserts that the fire by which he lives represents an irreversible ex-

* The number before the colon in all parenthetical references in the
text indicates chapter, which will be the same for most American editions
of *Moby-Dick*; the italicized numbers after the colon indicate page in the
Norton Critical Edition of *Moby-Dick*, edited by Harrison Hayford and
Hershel Parker (New York: W. W. Norton & Company, 1967).

penditure of self. The crew-members are "so many ant-hills of powder," and he must be, to achieve his purpose, their igniting match. "Oh, hard!" he bitterly exclaims, "that to fire others, the match itself must needs be wasting!" (37: *147*). Life for Ahab is not a process of regeneration or renewal or rebirth. It is instead a steady declension into nothingness and annihilation. Starbuck makes this point near the end of the novel: "I have sat before the dense coal fire and watched it all aglow, full of its tormented flaming life; and I have seen it wane at last, down, down, to dumbest dust. Old man of oceans! of all this fiery life of thine, what will at length remain but one little heap of ashes!" (118: *412*).

It is, however, the images of auto-cannibalism, rather than of auto-combustion, which relate rapacious Ahab most precisely to the self-devouring shark and the cosmic processes of which the shark is symbol. Ahab is, Ishmael tells us, the victim of "all those malicious agencies which some deep men feel eating in them, till they are left living on with half a heart and half a lung" (41: *160*). Of his own insane choice, Ahab is "Gnawed within . . . with the infixed, unrelenting fangs of some incurable idea" (41: *162*). He is like the hibernating bear whose winter-life is based on self-consumption: "And as when Spring and Summer had departed, that wild Logan of the woods, burying himself in the hollow of a tree, lived out the winter there, sucking his own paws; so, in his inclement, howling old age, Ahab's soul, shut up in the caved trunk of his body, there fed upon the sullen paws of its gloom!" (34: *134*). "God help thee, old man," Ishmael exclaims, "thy thoughts have created a creature in thee; and he whose intense thinking thus makes him a Prometheus; a vulture feeds upon that heart for ever; that vulture the very creature he creates" (44: *175*). The "horrible vulturism" which so appalls Ishmael is not confined to external nature. Ahab's internal self also embodies it.

But there is more to the self-consumption of Ahab than a simple pattern of imagery. A fundamental concept of certain cosmologies is *entropy*, which articulates the hypothesis that all motion and activity simply reflect an inexorable downhill process, the steady degradation of matter and energy to a state of inert uniformity. Inevitably, entropy predicts, the last temperature gradient will disappear, the last star will blink out, the last world cease to spin, the primal darkness and the primordial frigidity once again enveloping everything. Entropy thus proposes a view of microcosmic and macrocosmic activity as irreversible *expenditure*. The concept is useful here because it furnishes an analogue for Ahab's sense of his own life-process, a kind of ontological entropism. This is the philosophical thrust of the imagery of self-consumption, and this is what he means when, Starbuck having reported to him a leak in some buried oil-cask deep in the *Pequod's* hold, he flatly rejects the request to "up Burtons and break out." "Begone!" he tells the first mate, "Let it leak! I'm all aleak myself. Aye! leaks in leaks! ... Yet I don't stop to plug my leak; for who can find it in the deep-loaded hull; or how hope to plug it, even if found, in this life's howling gale?" (109: *393*).

Such a sense of ontological "leak" makes the life-process degenerative rather than regenerative; Ahab's living is only dying. What seems to have brought him to this pervasive pessimism was not the loss of his leg to Moby Dick, but rather the consequent injury to his groin, his regenerative faculty, which occurred when he fell and was "stake-wise smitten" by his new ivory leg (106: *385*). It is well to remember that Ahab, as Peleg tells Ishmael, "has a wife—not three voyages wedded—a sweet, resigned girl" (16: 77). M. O. Percival touches on the general significance of this "agonizing wound": "In this incident we find that Moby Dick—present in the ivory stake—had bitten into the very center of [Ahab's] being, leaving a wound that was to prove incurable."[1]

Ahab regards the groin injury as the "direct issue" of the mutilation inflicted by the White Whale. This sense of *consequence* leads him to speculate on the preponderance of woe over joy. Evil, he at first thinks, regenerates itself equally with good: "the most poisonous reptile of the marsh perpetuates his kind as inevitably as the sweetest songster of the grove; so, equally with every felicity, all miserable events do naturally beget their like." Such a formulation is *not* entropic; it suggests rather an even-handed balance of light and dark in life. But Ishmael, who is once again—as in the "Surmises" chapter—imaginatively inferring Ahab's thoughts, immediately cancels this equivalence:

> Yea, more than equally, thought Ahab; since both the ancestry and posterity of Grief go further than the ancestry and posterity of joy.

> For, not to hint of this: that it is an inference from certain canonic teachings, that while some natural enjoyments here shall have no children born to them for the other world, but, on the contrary, shall be followed by the joy-childlessness of all hell's despair; whereas, some guilty mortal miseries shall still fertilely beget to themselves an eternally progressive progeny of griefs beyond the grave; not at all to hint of this, there still seems *an inequality* in the deeper analysis of the thing. (106: *385–86*; italics mine)

Ahab has moved now from ontological entropism to a much more immediate psychological and moral entropism. Grief, in the nature of things, preponderates over and will finally annihilate Joy; the "inequality" is inescapable. But there is more. Entropic inequality touches not only the whole cosmos, but ultimately whatever divinity stands behind the cosmos: "To trail the genealogies of these high mortal miseries, carries us at last among the sourceless primogenitures of the gods; so that, in the face of all the glad, hay-making suns, and soft-cymballing, round harvest-moons, we must needs give in to this: *that the gods themselves are not for ever glad*" (106: *386*; italics mine). Ahab thus arrives at the ultimate formulation: *theological entropism*. Even the beatitude and joy of divine being, which we mortals know by their reflection in the ecstatic beauty of the natural world, are forms of deific expenditure which, like all other active principles, must be terminal by nature. The death of the cosmos will be the death of God.

When Ishmael speaks of "dark Ahab" (47: *187*; 48: *189*), then, he means Entropic Ahab. "So far gone am I in the dark side of earth," the *Pequod's* Captain confesses, "that its other side, the theoretic bright one, seems but uncertain twilight to me" (127: *433*). For Ahab, death is more fundamental than life, dark more fundamental than light, stasis more fundamental than any activity. He expresses this entropic despair when, the day after the *Pequod* gams with the *Bachelor*, four whales are slain just before sunset, one of them by Ahab. Once again, as in the "Sunset" chapter (37: *146–47*), Ahab contemplates the "lovely sunset sea and sky," and watches as "sun and whale both stilly died together," noting that "strange spectacle observable in all sperm whales dying—the turning sunwards of the head, and so expiring" (116: *409*). "He turns and turns him to it," Ahab exclaims, "how slowly, but how steadfastly, his homage-rendering and invoking brow, with his last dying motions. He too worships fire; most faithful, broad, baronial vassal of the sun!" But the whale's sun-faith is, Ahab thinks, futile: "see!" he ponders, "no sooner dead, than death whirls round the corpse, and it heads some other way." The final motion of the whale is entropic, toward dark rather than light:

> Oh, thou dark Hindoo half of nature [Ahab exclaims], who of drowned bones hast builded thy separate throne somewhere in the heart of these unverdured seas; thou art an infidel, thou queen, and too truly speakest to me in the wide-slaughtering Typhoon, and the hushed burial of its after calm. Nor has this thy whale sunwards turned his dying head, and then gone round again, without a lesson to me. (116: *409*)

The lesson is that all life is subject to irreversible entropic decay. The sun, which appears to be a life-source, and is so worshipped by the whale, is really a death-source, since the bringing forth of life but augments the ultimate quantum of cosmic death, of which, for Ahab, the "unverdured" sea itself is the macrosymbol:

> Oh, trebly hooped and welded hip of power! Oh, high aspiring, rainbowed jet!—that one striveth, this one jetteth all in vain! In vain, oh whale, dost thou seek intercedings with yon all-quickening sun, that only calls forth life, but gives it not again. Yet dost thou, darker half, rock me with a prouder, if a darker faith. All thy unnamable imminglings float beneath me here; I am buoyed by breaths of once living things, exhaled as air, but water now. (116: *409*)

It is no accident that in the next chapter but one, Ahab at high noon smashes the quadrant in a gesture symbolic of his rejection of natural fire, natural guidance, and natural life, nor that, in the very next chapter, we find him defying the unnatural fire of the corpusants. Even at the moment of his death he sustains this rejection. In the closing chapter, as the *Pequod* starts to sink and Ahab realizes that all is lost, he makes, like the dying whale, a last gesture of entropic despair: "I turn my body from the sun," he exclaims (135: *468*).

This analysis makes possible a more precise reading of Ahab's confrontation with the corpusants than might otherwise be possible. At the height of the typhoon, in the blackness of night, "God's burning finger" is suddenly laid upon the *Pequod*. "All the yard-arms were tipped with a pallid fire; and touched at each tri-pointed lightning-rod-end with three tapering white flames, each of the three tall masts was silently burning in that sulphurous air, like three gigantic wax tapers before an altar" (119: *415*). This trinitarian manifestation Ahab addresses as "thou clear spirit of clear fire." He acknowledges its "speechless, placeless power," but asserts that the "right worship" of such a deific phenomenon is "defiance." Ahab can risk such defiance, he thinks, because the worst the fire can do is kill, "and *all* are killed" (italics mine). Ahab, it becomes evident, includes God Himself in this "all" which will be killed. "There is," he tells the fire, "some *unsuffusing* thing beyond thee, thou clear spirit, to whom all thy eternity is but time, all thy creativeness mechanical" (italics mine). This is unmistakably entropic: the fiery deity which Ahab addresses is "suffusive," an active principle and creative force which, by virtue of that active creativity, must eventually suffer termination. This is to say that there must be an inactive, non-creative, hence "unsuffusing" principle anterior to God and therefore superior to God, an entity which will outlast God Himself. Ahab recognizes that God exists in eternity, and this would appear to imply the impossibility of termination. But as Ahab— chopping his logic with condensed subtlety—uses the term, eternity is nothing more than infinite time, and time is process, and process must end. Hence eternity is not eternal, nor the God of eternity timeless. Behind both stands something even more fundamental, absolute timelessness and total stasis. This is the "unsuffusing thing" superior to creative deity: the Final Darkness. "Light though thou be," Ahab tells his fiery Trinity, "thou leapest out of darkness; but I am darkness leaping out of light, leaping out of thee!" Such a dark-light-dark sequence renders the entropic paradigm: light coming out of darkness, doomed to return to darkness. Because "dark Ahab" is "darkness leaping out of light," he is—and this is the ultimate statement of his rampant egotism in all of *Moby-Dick*—superior to God. This is the demonic consequence of his entropic theology. This is also what is meant when the barbed tip of Ahab's own harpoon is suddenly invested with the same "levelled flame of pale, forked fire" which burns upon the masts. Ahab seizes the harpoon, brandishes its burning tip over the heads of the importunate Starbuck and the terrified crew, and then "with one blast of his breath he extinguished the

flame" (119: *418*). This is the supreme entropic gesture: defiant
Ahab snuffs out, like a mere candle, the suffusive God of Light.

There is, however, an unresolved element in all of this. Ahab's
dark faith has answered all his questions but one. Concerning the
genealogy of God there is for Ahab no problem: God is, must be,
the deified child of the Final Darkness. Because entropic stasis is the
ultimate nothingness, and that which is nothing cannot be known,
God cannot know his own source. "Thou knowest not how came
ye," Ahab tauntingly tells the corpusants, "hence callest thyself un-
begotten; certainly knowest not thy beginning, hence callest thyself
unbegun." In this respect too Ahab thinks himself superior to God;
he knows *his* paternity. "I am darkness . . . leaping out of thee!" But
this, he thinks, is only half the story. If the trinitarian God is his
Father—and all Ahab's Quaker and Biblical background reinforces
such a concept—*then he must also have a mother.* "But thou art but
my fiery father," he says to the corpusants; "my sweet mother, I
know not. Oh, cruel! what has thou done with her? *There lies my
puzzle*" (119: *417*; italics mine). In terms of the final meanings of
Moby-Dick, this is a crucial admission. Despite Ahab's subtlety and
demonic brilliance, one essential element remains beyond his ken,
unaccounted for. It is this single crack in the otherwise seamless
monolith of his dark denial, which suggests that Ahab's reading of
cosmic process may not be the final reading, either for Ishmael or
for Melville himself.[2]

It is only six chapters—some eight or ten pages—after Ahab tells
the corpusants that "thou canst but kill; and all are killed" (119:
417), that he is confronted with the startling possibility that death
may not be the entropically terminal entity he thinks it is. Steering
south-eastward on the White Whale's own grounds, a man is lost
overboard. When the life-buoy—an iron-bound wooden cask which
hangs at the *Pequod's* stern—is dropped, it proves so badly weath-
ered that it follows the doomed sailor to the bottom. There is no
time to fashion another cask; Queequeg therefore suggests that the
coffin which the carpenter had made for him and of which, as it
turned out, he had no need, be used as a replacement. "A life-buoy
of a coffin!" cries Starbuck, starting. "Rather queer, that, I should
say," observes Stubb. Queer though it is, Starbuck orders the task

accomplished. The carpenter reluctantly obeys: "Some supersti- tious old carpenters, now," he grumbles, "would be tied up in the rigging, ere they would do the job." Yet he perceives, if only dimly, that the change from coffin to life-buoy is not a *conversion*, but only an *obversion*, an alteration in aspect but not in essence: "It's like turning an old coat; going to bring the flesh on the other side now" (126: *429–31*). While he is busy nailing down the lid and calking the seams, Ahab appears, demanding to know what he is about. "Aye, sir; I patched up this thing here as a coffin for Queequeg; but they've set me now to turning it into something else." Ahab, perceiving a signification which in these penultimate hours he can ill afford to contemplate, reacts violently: "Then tell me; art thou not an arrant, all-grasping, inter-meddling, monopolizing, heathenish old scamp, to be one day making legs, and the next day coffins to clap them in, and yet again life-buoys out of those same coffins? Thou art as un- principled as the gods, and as much of a jack-of-all-trades" (127: *432*). This is the irritable petulance of the puzzled, secretly uncer- tain man confronting a possibility which threatens everything for which he stands. Deeply shaken, Ahab demands that the carpenter "get these traps out of my sight," but just for a moment he is ar- rested by the possibility that his entropic despair is without founda- tion, and that death may have a meaning he does not grasp:

> There's a sight! There's a sound! ... Here now's the very dreaded symbol of grim death, by a mere hap, made the expressive sign of the help and hope of most endangered life. A life-buoy of a coffin! Does it go further? Can it be that in some spiritual sense the coffin is, after all, but an immortality-preserver! I'll think of that. But no. So far gone am I in the dark side of earth, that its other side, the theoretic bright one, seems but uncertain twilight to me. (127: *432– 33*)

But although Ahab cannot accept the concept of immortality, much less the idea of death as something which "preserves" im- mortality, *Moby-Dick* is nevertheless full of just this idea. Para- doxically, it is the shark himself who suggests the existence of a vitality, a dynamism, which is *not* terminated by death. When, during the shark massacre, one brain-spaded monster was hoisted to the *Pequod's* deck for the sake of his skin, he "almost took poor

Queequeg's hand off, when he tried to shut down the dead lid of his murderous jaw." Ishmael offers a brief but important explanation for this apparent manifestation of life after death: "A sort of generic or Pantheistic vitality seemed to lurk in [the shark's] very joints and bones, *after what might be called the individual life had departed*" (66: *257*; italics mine). The shark, in other words, suggests the possibility of a dynamistic residue which exists independently of, and transcends the death of, the individual. As the dead shark epitomizes this dynamism in the animal world, Ahab is made to epitomize it in the human world. For although Ahab yet lives, a major part of him has already died. One leg, presumably, has suffered dissolution in the belly of Moby Dick. But that dead leg nonetheless lives. At one point, the carpenter is busy making a new whalebone leg to replace the one which Ahab accidentally splintered in his haste to leave the congenial decks of the *Samuel Enderby*. "Well, then," Ahab asks the long-suffering old man, "will it speak thoroughly well for thy work, if, when I come to mount this leg thou makest, I shall nevertheless feel another leg in the same identical place with it; that is, carpenter, my old lost leg; the flesh and blood one, I mean."

> "Truly, sir [the carpenter replies], I begin to understand somewhat now. Yes, I have heard something curious on that score, sir; how that a dismasted man never entirely loses the feeling of his old spar, but it will be still pricking him at times. May I humbly ask if it be really so, sir?"
> "It is, man. Look, put thy live leg here in the place where mine once was; so, now, here is only one distinct leg to the eye, yet two to the soul. Where thou feelest tingling life; there, exactly there, there to a hair, do I." (108: *391*)

Ahab thus experiences in a uniquely personal way—though its significance escapes him—that same phenomenon which Queequeg encountered in the dead shark. There is, apparently, a dynamistic element at work behind life-process which is not and cannot be accounted for by entropic Ahab's dark faith. "Is't a riddle?" Ahab asks the carpenter.

It *is* a riddle, the key to which lies in the carpenter's hint that the coffin-to-life-buoy sequence is an obversion rather than a conversion. For obversion suggests, as conversion cannot, a single entity, a unitary phenomenon, which is seen *alternately*, first under one aspect, and then under another. The obversive viewpoint, in other words, is best articulated by an essentially alternative, *cyclic* conceptual framework. Such a cyclic way of seeing the world shapes almost every page of *Moby-Dick*. Back-and-forth images, to-and-fro images, up-and-down images, images of circularity, are the cornerstone of an idiom which gradually brings into focus a dynamistic Ishmaelian cosmology radically different from Ahab's entropic world-view. In its most rudimentary form, this cosmic dynamism is rendered as a simple to-and-fro rocking motion. A turn at the mast-head, Ishmael asserts, puts one in mystic consonance with the languorous rhythms of the entire universe. "There you stand," he tells us, "lost in the infinite series of the sea, with nothing ruffled but the waves. The tranced ship indolently rolls; the drowsy trade winds blow; everything resolves you into languor." These rhythms then interpenetrate the spiritual rhythms of thought so that man and nature become one. As a consequence, "lulled into such an opium-like listlessness of vacant, unconscious reverie . . . by the blending cadence of waves with thoughts, . . . at last [the mast-head stander] loses his identity; [and] takes the mystic ocean at his feet for the visible image of that deep, blue, bottomless soul, pervading mankind and nature" (35: *136–37, 140*). Ishmael endows this cyclic dynamic with cosmic breadth, extending without interruption from the barnacled hull of the *Pequod* to the very throne of deity: "There is," he continues, "no life in thee, now, except that rocking life imparted by a gently rolling ship; by her, borrowed from the sea; by the sea, from the inscrutable tides of God" (35: *140*). Such imagery occurs in *Moby-Dick* with repetitive emphasis:

> It was my turn to stand at the foremast-head [says Ishmael on another occasion]; and with my shoulders leaning against the slackened royal shrouds, to and fro I idly swayed in what seemed an enchanted air. No resolution could withstand it; in that dreamy mood losing all consciousness, at last my soul went out of my body; though my body still continued to sway as a pendulum will, long after the power which first moved it is withdrawn. (61: *241*)

The other two sailors at the other two mast-heads are similarly overcome by the systole and diastole of cosmic activity, "So that at last
all three of us lifelessly swung from the spars, and for every swing
that we made there was a nod from below from the slumbering
helmsman. The waves, too, nodded their indolent crests; and across
the wide trance of the sea, east nodded to west, and the sun over
all" (61: *242*). It is this natural vibration which soothes Queequeg
toward the death which he only at the last moment rejects. The
imperturbable savage "quietly lay in his swaying hammock, and the
rolling sea seemed gently rocking him to his final rest, and the
ocean's invisible flood-tide lifted him higher and higher towards his
destined heaven" (110: *396*).

But that toward which Queequeg moves, urged by the to-and-fro
movement of universal cycle, is *not* a death in the terminal sense that
Ahab would recognize. For there is that in Queequeg, Ishmael asserts, something in his luminous eyes, which constitutes a "wondrous
testimony to that immortal health in him which could not die, or
be weakened." As a consequence, Queequeg's approaching death is
for Ishmael, not an end, but rather an *"endless end"* (110: *395*;
italics mine). It is this simple oxymoron which furnishes the requisite clue to the significance of the cyclic imagery in *Moby-Dick*.
Ahab's entropic view of cosmic activity is declensive, retrograde,
and intractably terminal. Conversely, the cyclic view of cosmic
process—Ishmael's view—is regenerative, autovitalistic, and non-
terminal. In the ebb and flood of cosmic cycle, at the completion of
each isochrone, at both the nadir and zenith of natural activity, an
obversion rather than a termination occurs: flex becomes reflex,
death becomes life, dark becomes light, stasis becomes movement.
All of this stands as a direct repudiation of Ahab's entropic despair.
No end is terminal. All ends are really endless. The cyclic structure
of universal activity endows all being—and that activity itself—with
immortality. "Oh! the metempsychosis!" exclaims Ishmael, "Oh!
Pythagoras, that in bright Greece, two thousand years ago, did die,
so good, so wise, so mild; I sailed with thee along the Peruvian coast
last voyage—and, foolish as I am, taught thee, a green simple boy,
how to splice a rope!" (98: *358*).

The clearest expression of Ishmael's "endless end" occurs in the
cycle become specifically circular, returning always upon itself.[3] In

that same passage where Ishmael describes how the sea rocks dying Queequeg, he also remarks a symbolic circularity in the cannibal's fading expression: "And like circles on the water, which, as they grow fainter, expand; so his eyes seemed rounding and rounding, like the rings of Eternity" (110: *395*). Repeatedly, key ideas in *Moby-Dick* are expressed in such circular terms. The ship itself stands as symbol for such activity. She is, for Ishmael, the "circumnavigating Pequod" (87: *319*). Ahab shouts to the *Goney* that "This is the Pequod, bound round the world!" (52: *203*), and reiterates this idea at the conclusion of the gam: "Up helm! Keep her off round the world!" Ishmael makes the obvious point: "Round the world! There is much in that sound to inspire proud feelings; but whereto does all that circumnavigation conduct? Only through numberless perils to the very point whence we started, where those that we left behind secure, were all the time before us" (52: *204*).

These conventional uses of circularity fade into insignificance, however, in comparison to the gradual evolution of the vortex image in *Moby-Dick*. For both Ishmael and Melville, the vortex is a void surrounded by a cycle. Through the vortex, and through the Cartesian cosmology associated with it,[4] Ishmael achieves a brilliant fusion of cosmic activity and cosmic stasis, of the universal *something* and the universal *nothing*, and of the way in which matter and the void stand in a relation of reciprocal definition. Initially, the concentration is not on the substance and activity of the cosmos, but on the frightening metaphysical vacuity which that substance and its activity articulate. While standing a mast-head watch and being gently rocked into ontological somnolence by the cosmic tides, one is in mortal danger: "But while this sleep, this dream is on ye, move your foot or hand an inch; slip your hold at all; and your identity comes back in horror. Over Descartian vortices you hover. And perhaps, at mid-day, in the fairest weather, with one half-throttled shriek you drop through that transparent air into the summer sea, no more to rise for ever. Heed it well, ye Pantheists!" (35: *140*). It is this sense of the vortex-as-void which Melville uses for humorous effect in *Pierre*, in speaking of the impoverished "Apostles." "Their mental tendencies," he remarks, ". . . are still very fine and spiritual . . . since the vacuity of their exchequers leads them to reject the coarse materialism of Hobbes, and incline to the airy ex-

altations of the Berkeleyan philosophy. Often groping in vain in
their pockets, they can not but give in to the Descartian vortices."⁵
Nullity is, for both Ishmael and Melville, the *primary* signification
of the vortex.

But in *Moby-Dick* the vortex is redeemed—as so many things
are redeemed—by great Leviathan. During the *Pequod's* encounter
with the Grand Armada (87: *318–28*), Ishmael stresses the fact
that the gallied whales form an incredible Leviathanic vortex. "In
all directions expanding in vast irregular circles, and aimlessly
swimming hither and thither, by their short thick spoutings, [the
whales] plainly betrayed their distraction of panic." As the whale
dragging Ishmael's boat penetrates the herd, he notes that "as we
went still further and further from the circumference of commotion, the direful disorders seemed waning." Finally they reach the
quiet center: "And still in the distracted distance we beheld the
tumults of the outer concentric circles, and saw successive pods of
whales, eight or ten in each, swiftly going round and round, like
multiplied spans of horses in a ring; and so closely shoulder to shoulder, that a Titanic circus-rider might easily have over-arched the
middle ones, and so have gone round on their backs." The Armada
is a tremendous system of outer "revolving circles" and the "contracting orbits [of] the whales in the more central circles." But
Ishmael does not find at the center of this Leviathanic vortex that
ontological nullity which he perceived behind the cenotaphs of the
Whaleman's Chapel, and which the Cartesian vortex gives visual
rendering. In *this* vortex, at its very heart, Ishmael finds peace and
life rather than terror and death:

> And thus [he concludes], though surrounded by circle upon circle
> of consternations and affrights, did these inscrutable creatures at the
> centre freely and fearlessly indulge in all peaceful concernments; yea,
> serenely revelled in dalliance and delight. But even so, amid the
> tornadoed Atlantic of my being, do I myself still for ever centrally
> disport in mute calm; and while ponderous planets of unwaning woe
> revolve round me, deep down and deep inland there I still bathe me
> in eternal mildness of joy. (87: *322–26*)

The Grand Armada is a partial, essentially cetological resolution for
Ishmael's hypo concerning the void.

In the "Epilogue" of *Moby-Dick*, the cyclic vortex again appears. Ishmael, tossed from Ahab's boat, witnesses the destruction of the *Pequod* and the death of Ahab and his entire crew:

> So, floating on the margin of the ensuing scene, and in full sight of it, when the half-spent suction of the sunk ship reached me, I was then, but slowly, drawn towards the closing vortex. When I reached it, it had subsided to a creamy pool. Round and round, then, and ever contracting towards the button-like black bubble at the axis of that slowly wheeling circle, like another Ixion I did revolve. Till, gaining that vital centre, the black bubble upward burst; and now, liberated by reason of its cunning spring, and, owing to its great buoyancy, rising with great force, the coffin life-buoy shot lengthwise from the sea, fell over, and floated by my side. Buoyed up by that coffin, for almost one whole day and night, I floated on a soft and dirge-like main. (*470*)

At the heart of this final vortex, Ishmael once more finds, not the void, but rather life in the guise of death, rebirth in an "immortality preserver." The "Epilogue" is the ultimate statement of the redemptive cyclicism of *Moby-Dick*, and the final repudiation of Ahab's entropism.

Other cyclic metaphors also assist in this resolution. Particularly important are images of *weaving*, the idea of natural process as a back-and-forth, vibrational activity. Chapter 47, "The Mat-Maker," is the most obvious example. Here, in a synthesis which equals the vortex in imaginative brilliance, Ishmael integrates the three philosophical imponderables of necessity, chance, and free will. He and Queequeg are "mildly employed" in weaving a sword-mat for their boat:

> I was the attendant or page of Queequeg, while busy at the mat. As I kept passing and repassing the filling or woof of marline between the long yarns of the warp, using my own hand for the shuttle, and as Queequeg, standing sideways, ever and anon slid his heavy oaken sword between the threads, and idly looking off upon the water, carelessly and unthinkingly drove home every yarn: I say so strange a dreaminess did there then reign all over the ship and all over the sea, only broken by the intermitting dull sound of the sword, that it seemed as if this were the Loom of Time, and I my-

self were a shuttle mechanically weaving and weaving away at the Fates. (47: *185*)

Time itself here becomes a cycle, and necessity, free will, and chance become epicycles, concatenating to produce the final fabric of events:

> There lay the fixed threads of the warp subject to but one single, ever returning, unchanging vibration, and that vibration merely enough to admit of the crosswise interblending of other threads with its own. This warp seemed necessity; and here, thought I, with my own hand I ply my own shuttle and weave my own destiny into these unalterable threads. Meantime, Queequeg's impulsive, indifferent sword, sometimes hitting the woof slantingly, or crookedly, or strongly, or weakly, as the case might be; and by this difference in the concluding blow producing a corresponding contrast in the final aspect of the completed fabric; this savage's sword, thought I, which thus finally shapes and fashions both warp and woof; this easy, indifferent sword must be chance—aye, chance, free will, and necessity —no wise incompatible—all interweavingly working together. The straight warp of necessity, not to be swerved from its ultimate course —its every alternating vibration, indeed, only tending to that; free will still free to ply her shuttle between given threads; and chance, though restrained in its play within the right lines of necessity, and sideways in its motions modified by free will, though thus prescribed to by both, chance by turns rules either, and has the last featuring blow at events. (47: *185*)

This cyclic interplay affirms the *equality* of all three elements. Free will has as much importance in shaping the final event as either necessity or chance. Moreover, the mechanics of the paradigm suggest that necessity is *not* an inhibiting force, circumscribing free will. Rather, it is a liberating and enabling element. The shuttle of free will must act upon a medium—cannot, of itself, produce anything. The "right lines of necessity" provide that medium, which is to say that the *free agent can find freedom only within a necessitarian structure*.

Such an analysis controverts the idea that free will does not operate in the world of *Moby-Dick*. Stubb's off-hand assertion, that the "unfailing comfort is, it's all predestinated" (39: *149*) is wrong: *one-third* is predestinated, the other two thirds being left respectively to free will and chance. Ishmael himself, in the opening pages, asserts that it is a "delusion" to think that his decision to embark on a whaling voyage "was a choice resulting from my own unbiased free will and discriminating judgment" (1: *16*). But this is not, as he now sees, a delusion; it is rather a metaphorical "third" of the entire truth. Free will did indeed play a part in Ishmael's decision—as did necessity and chance. It is, however, Ahab's constant assertion of his helplessness before fate and necessity which the mat-maker paradigm specifically repudiates. "Here some one thrusts these cards into these old hands of mine," he mutters at one point; "swears that I must play them, and no others" (118: *413*). "What is it," he asks Starbuck, ". . . what cozening, hidden lord and master . . . commands me; that against all natural lovings and longings, I so keep . . . jamming myself on all the time. . . . Is Ahab, Ahab? Is it I, God, or who, that lifts this arm?" (132: *444–45*). These are, as I have already pointed out, the desperate rationalizations of a man who, of his own free will, has destroyed his own free will. Ahab, in the pre-literary limbo, has freely chosen his monomania, and the consequences of that free choice freely operate through every page of *Moby-Dick*. Ahab's *lack* of free will is in no way inconsonant with the play of free will postulated in "The Mat-Maker." But the crucial point is the fact that the operation of free will throughout *Moby-Dick*, and the consequent moral significance of the novel, are both dependent upon the *cyclic dynamic* through which these philosophical considerations are adumbrated. It is the "vibration" of the necessitarian imperatives, the active rather than static quality of the predestinative aspects of natural process, which provide the avenues along which free will can freely act. It is this necessitarian cyclicism which makes freedom possible.[6]

Ishmael's cyclic conceptualizations are further developed by the weaving imagery of Chapter 102, "A Bower in the Arsacides." The reader is prepared for this chapter by Pip's symbolic plunge to the bottom of the sea in Chapter 93, "The Castaway." Having leapt from Stubb's boat during a whale-chase, Pip's soul is "carried down alive to wondrous depths." There, "among the joyous, heartless, ever-juvenile eternities, Pip saw the multitudinous, God-omnipresent, coral insects, that out of the firmament of waters heaved the colossal orbs. He saw God's foot upon the treadle of the loom, and spoke it; and therefore his shipmates called him mad" (93: 347). The "Loom of Time" of "The Mat-Maker" chapter here becomes the Loom of Cosmic Process. The "multitudinous, God-omnipresent, coral insects" express in atomized form that same immanent cosmic dynamism of which the formless squid, much earlier in the book, is the symbol, and which Queequeg encountered as "generic or Pantheistic vitality" in the dead shark. The "loom" propelled by "God's foot" reaffirms the cyclic nature of these coral-insect processes, and consequently their non-entropic immortality, as "joyous, heartless, ever-juvenile eternities."

These consolidations of the imagery of cosmic dynamism set the stage for "A Bower in the Arsacides." It was while he was a crew-member of the trading ship *Dey of Algiers*, Ishmael tells us, that he was invited by "my late royal friend Tranquo, king of Tranque," to spend the Arsacidean holidays at Tranquo's "retired palm villa at Pupella." The king is an avid collector of barbaric vertu and natural wonders, chief among the latter being the skeleton of a huge Sperm Whale which, transported from the sea-side to a palm-bower, now serves as a chapel: "... in the skull, the priests kept up an unextinguished aromatic flame, so that the mystic head again sent forth its vapory spout" (102: 373–74). This astonishing sight causes Ishmael to launch into an examination of natural process centered on a weaving metaphor:

> It was a wondrous sight. The wood was green as mosses of the Icy Glen; the trees stood high and haughty, feeling their living sap; the industrious earth beneath was as a weaver's loom, with a gorgeous carpet on it, whereof the ground-vine tendrils formed the warp and woof, and the living flowers the figures. All the trees, with all their laden branches; all the shrubs, and ferns, and grasses; the message-carrying air; all these unceasingly were active. Through the lacings of the leaves, the great sun seemed a flying shuttle weaving the unwearied verdure. (102: 374)

This magnificent vegetable tapestry synthesizes two of the major preoccupations of *Moby-Dick*. First, the "gorgeous carpet" of the Arsacidean bower is the ultimate expression of the chromatically lovely world of sense perception through which Ishmael moves, and which I have called the phenomenal derma, the first term of the protometaphor of *color: interface: non-color.* Here, in the figures of the carpet, is Ishmael's lovely ocean, an endless vista of "long-drawn virgin vales [and] mild blue hill-sides" (114: *405*). Here too is the tropical weather through which the *Pequod* sails, a perpetual Quito spring of "warmly cool, clear, ringing, perfumed, overflowing, redundant days, . . . [like] crystal goblets of Persian sherbet" (29: *111*). Here also the "lovely light" of Ahab's sunset, making "the warm waves blush like wine" (37: *147*), and here the beauty of the Japanese sea, where "the days in summer are as freshets of effulgences" (118: *411*). The Arsacidean carpet brings to a climax Ishmael's epistemological preoccupation with all "earthly hues—every stately or lovely emblazoning—the sweet tinges of sunset skies and woods; yea, and the gilded velvets of butterflies, and the butterfly cheeks of young girls" (42: *169-70*).

Second, the "industrious earth" of the bower, the "unwearied verdure" of the trees, shrubs, ferns, and grasses, all "unceasingly . . . active" and knit together by the "flying shuttle" of the sun—all this is a kind of vegetative, botanical re-articulation of that "generic or Pantheistic vitality" which was exhibited by Queequeg's shark. The Arsacidean carpet is the cosmic dynamism of Pip's abyssal vision, the "multitudinous, God-omnipresent, coral insects" re-formulated in terms of the cyclic metaphor of the loom. Ishmael now broadens the metaphor by personifying this immanent dynamism as weaver:

> Oh, busy weaver! unseen weaver!—pause!—one word!—whither flows the fabric? what palace may it deck? wherefore all these ceaseless toilings? Speak, weaver!—stay thy hand!—but one single word with thee! Nay—the shuttle flies—the figures float from forth the loom; the freshet-rushing carpet for ever slides away. The weaver-god, he weaves; and by that weaving is he deafened, that he hears no mortal voice; and by that humming, we, too, who look on the loom are deafened; and only when we escape it shall we hear the thousand voices that speak through it. (102: *374*)

Having thus raised once again the issue of the possibility of an *agent* behind cosmic activity and natural process, Ishmael now resolves that issue once and for all. If there is a weaver-god, then He is to be found within the whale-chapel of Tranquo's bower. Indeed, the

priests claim, as priests have always claimed, that the smoke arising
from the jet-hole of the skeleton signifies a real presence within. So
Ishmael, like Theseus in the Cretan labyrinth, ball of twine in hand,
goes in search of the weaver-god:

> Now, when with royal Tranquo I visited this wondrous whale,
> and saw the skull and altar, and the artificial smoke ascending from
> where the real jet had issued, . . . I marvelled that the priests should
> swear that smoky jet of his was genuine. To and fro I paced before
> this skeleton—brushed the vines aside—broke through the ribs—and
> with a ball of Arsacidean twine, wandered, eddied long amid its
> many winding, shaded colonnades and arbors. (102: 375)

This plunge into the subterranean caverns of Leviathan is a venture
in theological speleology. Its outcome is unequivocally negative.
"But soon my line was out," spelunking Ishmael reports, "and following [the twine] back, I emerged from the opening where I en-
tered. *I saw no living thing within; naught was there but bones*"
(102: 375; italics mine). This, in Melville's nineteenth-century
America, is as close as Ishmael dare come to an overt denial of the
existence of an intelligent and personal God, and consequently to a
direct controversion of Captain Ahab's agentistic thesis.[7]
But if there is no agent behind the dynamism of the cosmos,
nevertheless Ishmael's visit to the Arsacidean bower is not without
positive consequences. The whale-skeleton may be only a bone-
engirdled void but, in a crucial turn in the symbolism, that skeleton
itself suddenly becomes the weaver:

> Now, amid the green, life-restless loom of that Arsacidean wood,
> the great, white, worshipped skeleton lay lounging—a gigantic idler!
> Yet, as the ever-woven verdant warp and woof intermixed and
> hummed around him, the mighty idler seemed the cunning weaver;
> himself all woven over with the vines; every month assuming green-
> er, fresher verdure; but himself a skeleton. *Life folded Death; Death
> trellised Life; the grim god wived with youthful Life, and begat him
> curly-headed glories.* (102: 375; italics mine)

The significance of this shift of the whale-skeleton from "idler" to
"weaver" can hardly be overstressed: it represents the conversion
of death from a static to a dynamic entity. Ishmael here realizes that
active death is the essential support or "trellis" of life, and that ob-
versely, life's vitality is more than sufficient to encompass or "fold"

death. This insight he expresses sexually, as a *marriage* of two vitalistic antitheses: "the grim god wived with youthful Life, and begat
him curly-headed glories." Just as life is the source of death, so now
death is the source of life. "A Bower in the Arsacides" gives, before
the fact, an answer to the "puzzle" of which Ahab will speak in
Chapter 119, "The Candles." "But thou art but my fiery father," he
tells the pallid flames, "my sweet mother, I know not" (119: *417*).
In the course of sixteen chapters the sexual designations of the metaphor become reversed, but this anomaly does not vitiate the point
being made. Ahab's "mother," the counterpart of the suffusive fire-
life of the corpusants, is death itself. Melville expresses this idea
elsewhere: ". . . the most mighty of nature's laws is this," asserts the
narrator of *Pierre*, "that out of Death she brings Life." But Ahab
can never understand this: his entropic cosmology makes comprehension impossible. Death, for Ahab, *must* be terminal, the doorway
to the Final Darkness, and so he goes to his own death with his dark
puzzle unresolved.[8]

For Ishmael, the tranquilizing insights of Tranquo's bower remove the neurotic fascination with death which drove him, a
crypto-suicide, to sea. A vitalistic death is one with which he can
come to terms. That he has achieved a partial resolution of his
death-hypo becomes apparent when, some ten chapters after his
Arsacidean recollection, the *Pequod* emerges upon the South Sea,
"a thousand leagues of blue." For bedeviled Ishmael the Pacific is
the sea of seas, the primordial ocean; reaching it answers the long
supplication of his youth. "It rolls the midmost waters of the
world," he tells us ecstatically, "the Indian ocean and Atlantic being
but its arms." Thus the Pacific "zones the whole world's bulk about;
makes all coasts one bay to it; seems the tide-beating heart of earth."[9]
In one of the loveliest paragraphs in the novel, Ishmael suggests that
in some mysterious manner his "divine" Pacific contains and sustains
the uncounted billions of deaths which have occurred in the long
course of natural process. The great South Sea becomes a kind of
vitalistic broth, a mystic medium in which all those things which
have died will never die, but only sleep:

> There is, one knows not what sweet mystery about this sea, whose
> gently awful stirrings seem to speak of some hidden soul beneath;
> like those fabled undulations of the Ephesian sod over the buried

Evangelist St. John. And meet it is, that over these sea-pastures, wide-rolling watery prairies and Potters' Fields of all four continents, the waves should rise and fall, and ebb and flow unceasingly; for here, millions of mixed shades and shadows, drowned dreams, somnambulisms, reveries; all that we call lives and souls, lie dreaming, dreaming still; tossing like slumberers in their beds; the ever-rolling waves but made so by their restlessness. (111: *399–400*)

Thus the primary macrosymbol of *Moby-Dick*, the ocean itself, becomes emblematic of dynamistic continuity—and Ishmael, in achieving such a sea has found, not mortality, but immortality. The Pacific's eternal activity assures him that no slightest movement of the cosmic medium, no least vibration of the cyclic continuum, no life, no thought, no dream, no impulse, is ever lost; all things remain in being, in restless slumber until, in some far turn of the ever-rolling waves, they may come back again.

The optimistic nature of Ishmael's cyclic cosmology is confirmed by the extracetological evidence. Melville would reject Ahab's world-view and embrace Ishmael's. In the late poem "Pontoosuce," a meditation on Autumn, the "best of seasons bland," the poet realizes that it merely "foreruns the blast / Shall sweep these live leaves to the dead leaves past." In an unmistakable echo of Ahab's despairing "all are killed" (119: *417*), the phrase "All dies!" becomes the refrain of the poem. But an unidentified "she"—obviously personified nature—sings to the desponding poet. What "she" has to say stands as clear controversion of Ahab's entropism and equally clear validation of Ishmael's cyclicism:

> Dies, all dies!
> The grass it dies, but in vernal rain
> Up it springs and it lives again;
> Over and over, again and again
> It lives, it dies and it lives again.
> Who sighs that all dies?
> Summer and winter, and pleasure and pain
> And everything everywhere in God's reign,
> They end, and anon they begin again:
> Wane and wax, wax and wane:
> Over and over and over amain

> End, ever end, and begin again—
> End, ever end, and forever and ever begin again! [10]

The same idea is expressed by Clarel, pondering on "Kedron's gulf":

> Returns each thing that may withdraw?
> The schools of blue-fish years desert
> Our sounds and shores—but they revert;
> The ship returns on her long tack:
> The bones of Theseus are brought back:
> A comet shall resume its path
> Though three millenniums go.

Rolfe, too, using the familiar loom metaphor, says much the same thing: "The flood weaves out—the ebb / Weaves back; the incessant shuttle shifts / And flies, and wears and tears the web." [11]

But the most enlightening reference to the cosmic cycle occurs early in *Mardi*, before that strange book begins to take on metaphysical and mystical colorations. The narrator's ship becomes locked in an intense calm: not a breath of air stirs, not a single wave is to be seen. "To a landsman," he tells us, "a calm is no joke. It . . . unsettles his mind; tempts him to recant his belief in the eternal fitness of things; in short, almost makes an infidel of him," one who in his feelings of "utter helplessness" becomes "madly skeptical." In such a Coleridgean trance of frozen immobility, "existence itself seems suspended. [The landsman] shakes himself in his coat, to see whether it be empty or no. He closes his eyes, to test the reality of the glassy expanse." In the end he begins to suffer "horrible doubts" as to the Captain's competence: "The ignoramus must have lost his way, and drifted into the *outer confines of creation, the region of the everlasting lull, introductory to a positive vacuity*" (italics mine). [12] What is missing are the usual evidences of the cyclic vibration of the cosmos: the heaving of the sea, the rocking of the ship, those reassuring tokens of an immanent dynamism which Ishmael mentions so often. Instead, the cosmic activity seems terrifyingly in abeyance. But that suspension is more than the onset of mere stasis. The very being of being seems threatened; lacking the cyclic rhythms, one is brought to the verge of metaphysical annihilation. The vast cycles of natural process are more than merely inherent in the nature of being. They are the very basis of being.

For death-obsessed Ishmael, Leviathan himself becomes the definitive expression of that generic or Pantheistic immortality which the endlessness of cyclic activity guarantees. Babbalanja asserts that "Through all her provinces, nature seems to promise immortality to life, but destruction to beings,"[13] and Ishmael applies precisely this argument to Leviathan:

> Wherefore, . . . we account the whale immortal in his species, however perishable in his individuality. He swam the seas before the continents broke water; he once swam over the site of the Tuileries, and Windsor Castle, and the Kremlin. In Noah's flood he despised Noah's Ark; and if ever the world is to be again flooded, like the Netherlands, to kill off its rats, then the eternal whale will still survive, and rearing upon the topmost crest of the equatorial flood, spout his frothed defiance to the skies. (105: *384–85*)

The limited optimism which such a concept of immortality makes possible is lost on entropic Ahab. On the third day of the chase of Moby Dick, just before his boat is lowered for the last time, Ahab apostrophizes the *Pequod's* ancient mast-head: "But good bye, good bye, old mast-head! What's this? green?—aye, tiny mosses in these warped cracks. No such green weather stains on Ahab's head! . . . By heaven this dead wood has the better of my live flesh every way. I can't compare with it" (135: *462*). Dark Ahab misses the meaning of that most universal of all nature's "stately or lovely emblazonings" —the color green. But its significance is not lost on Ishmael. He has already suggested that the most terrifying aspect of Lima, the city that "has taken the white veil," is that the pallor of her ruins "admits not the cheerful greenness of complete decay" (42: *168*). This is not the first time death and greenness have been associated in *Moby-Dick*. During the frolic of the *Pequod's* crew on the forecastle, the old Manx sailor, watching his juniors dance to Pip's tambourine, says: "I wonder whether those jolly lads bethink them of what they are dancing over. . . . O Christ! to think of the green navies and the green-skulled crews!" (40: *151*). The Manxman thus furnishes an apt figure—the green skull—for the partial resolution of Ishmael's death-hypo which his cyclic cosmology affords.[14] But the resolution is *only* partial. Full melioration of his death-hypo depends upon cannibal Queequeg, and it is to this amiable savage that we must now give our attention.

XI

QUEEQUEG
The Well-Governed Shark

THE ASSUMPTION which has given shape to almost all criticism of *Moby-Dick* since Raymond Weaver initiated the Melville revival a half-century ago is that the novel provides no answers to the questions it raises—perhaps because there are no answers. "*Moby-Dick* is an elaborate pattern of countercommentaries," asserts R. W. B. Lewis, "the supreme instance of the dialectical novel—a novel of tension without resolution."[1] It is Mr. Lewis' correct sense of the obsessive ambiguity of Melville's creative sensibility which leads him to deny the existence of thematic resolutions in *Moby-Dick—* but such a position overlooks the fact that the defining sensibility of the novel is *not* Melville's. It is, rather, Ishmael's—and Ishmael is too haunted, too driven by his hypos, ever to settle for mere dialectical tension. Ishmael not only seeks for resolutions to what he calls "the problem of the universe" (35: *139*)*—it can be demonstrated that he finds them. But the resolutions which seem to satisfy Ishmael did not, ultimately, satisfy Melville. The neurotic intensity, the near-psychotic darkness of the world of *Pierre*, into which the exhausted Melville plunged almost before the ink of *Moby-Dick* had time to dry, prove that Ishmael is no Melville, nor Ishmael's resolutions Melville's resolutions.

Whatever Melville's final position, Ishmael nevertheless postulates the possibility of resolution in the first chapter. "Not ignoring what is good," he says, "I am quick to perceive a horror, and could still be social with it—would they let me—since it is but well to be on friendly terms with all the inmates of the place one lodges in" (1: *16*). It seems obvious that to be "social" and "friendly" with the horrors of existence is to come to terms with them, to meet and somehow resolve them. And in fact it is difficult to see how one can emerge from a close examination of *Moby-Dick* and still maintain that resolutions do not occur. On the textually explicit level, for example, Ishmael's despairing certainty that the "great principle of light" only serves to produce a chromatic world of deceitful "harlot" colors (42: *170*) represents a tension, to which his later affirmation, that the "golden, glad sun" is the "only true lamp" (96: *354*) stands as resolution. Similarly, Ishmael's neurotic sense of a void behind phenomena and at the center of natural process, which he expresses in the cenotaphs and the Cartesian vortex, represents a tension for which the sexually conceived life-energies of the vortexical Grand Armada stand as partial resolution. On a less explicit level, the aestheticizing of the Sperm Whale's massive tail, the inner-outer dualizing of his battering-ram head, and the persistent humanizing of both his physiology and his behavior, all help to resolve Ishmael's early and Ahabian view of Leviathan as cosmic symbol of brute power and inscrutable malice. The "murderous monster" of Chapter 41 (*155*) becomes the "grand god" of Chapter 133 (*448*)

---

* The number before the colon in all parenthetical references in the text indicates chapter, which will be the same for most American editions of *Moby-Dick*; the italicized numbers after the colon indicate page in the Norton Critical Edition of *Moby-Dick*, edited by Harrison Hayford and Hershel Parker (New York: W. W. Norton & Company, 1967).

—a metamorphosis representing the definitive resolution of the novel.

But no resolution is so clear, and undertaken so early in *Moby-Dick*, as the one for which cannibal Queequeg is the catalyst. The essential outline is clear enough: the death-obsessed young schoolmaster who pauses before coffin warehouses and follows every chance funeral procession ends up, before the third chapter is finished, *in bed with* the very figure and image of death. For Queequeg is, in literal fact, a walking horror. His face is a ghastly nightmare mask, of a "dark, purplish, yellow color, here and there stuck over with large, blackish looking squares." When this "head-peddling purple rascal," preparatory to leaping into bed, removes his hat, Ishmael almost screams out with fright: "There was no hair on his head—none to speak of at least—nothing but a small scalp-knot twisted up on his forehead." In the crypt-like obscurity of a single dim candle, Ishmael suddenly finds himself face to face with the incarnation of all he fears most: "His bald purplish head . . . looked for all the world like a mildewed skull" (3: *28–29*). It is a total confrontation. The bed-relation, as Ishmael has already remarked, "is an intimate and confidential one in the highest degree" (3: *26*). The mere thought of entering into such intimacy with such an apparition from the charnel-house plunges necrophobic Ishmael into abject terror: "I confess I was . . . as much afraid of him as if it was the devil himself who had thus broken into my room at the dead of night" (3: *29*). But when Queequeg, Ishmael having fled the bed, with charity and civility invites him back—"You gettee in"—Ishmael abruptly reconsiders:

> I stood looking at him a moment. For all his tattooings he was on the whole a clean, comely looking cannibal. What's all this fuss I have been making about, thought I to myself—the man's a human being just as I am: he has just as much reason to fear me, as I have to be afraid of him. Better sleep with a sober cannibal than a drunken Christian. (3: *31*)

"I turned in," he tells us, "and never slept better in my life."

The next morning he awakens to find himself locked in the embrace of this figure of death: "I found Queequeg's arm thrown over me in the most loving and affectionate manner." Ishmael, admitting that "My sensations were strange," recalls a childhood nightmare in which a "nameless, unimaginable, silent form or phantom" had "seemed closely seated at my bed-side," holding his flesh-and-blood hand in its ghostly one. His present situation, in the "bridegroom clasp" of another death-figure, generates similar feelings, but with one crucial difference. "Now, *take away the awful fear*, and my sensations at feeling the supernatural hand in mine were very similar, in their strangeness, to those which I experienced on waking up and seeing Queequeg's pagan arm thrown round me" (4: *33*; italics mine). Such a shift in response represents the first small step on the long road to Ishmael's spiritual recovery. Thanks to outlandish Queequeg, he is now able to contemplate the unspeakable strangeness, the unutterably alien quality of death, but without the heretofore concomitant *fear*. Moreover, having once bedded down with death, Ishmael within a few more pages finds himself, in Queequeg's phrase, "married" to him, a union celebrated in the giving of an obviously symbolic gift. The cannibal, Ishmael tells us, "made me a present of his embalmed head" (10: *53*). The happy couple spend their last evening in New Bedford in bed together on their "hearts' honeymoon"—the very picture of a "cosy, loving pair" (10: *54*). Ishmael, as he prophetically suggested in the first chapter, has indeed become "social" with a veritable horror. He is not yet reconciled to death, nor does he yet understand it—these resolutions do not occur until he visits Tranquo's Arsacidean bower—but he is now, as a beginning, on "friendly terms" with death, in the person of Queequeg. It is thus that this kindly cannibal accomplishes the first resolution of *Moby-Dick*.

But Queequeg is not only death in human form. He is also the shark in human form. He is one of that carnivorous community of "Feegeeans, Tongatabooans, Erromanggoans, Pannangians, and Brighggians," most of them "savages outright," to be seen strolling the daylight Christian streets of any American whaling-port. Many of these exotics "yet carry on their bones unholy flesh" (6: *37*). Queequeg, with his "filed and pointed teeth" (13: *60*), belongs to this frightful fraternity. Ishmael, unspeakably repelled by that "cannibal propensity [Queequeg] nourished in his untutored youth" (12: *56*), prevents this amiable connoisseur of long pig from ever finishing a ghastly anecdote, casually begun, concerning a "feast given by his father the king, on the gaining of a great battle wherein fifty of the enemy had been killed by about two o'clock in the afternoon, and all cooked and eaten that very evening" (17: *82*). Queequeg is the anthropomorphic correlate of the "horrible vulturism of earth" (69: *262*) and the "universal cannibalism of the sea" (58: *235*). Stubb, avidly devouring rare whale-steak at the *Pequod's* capstan, is a shark only figuratively. File-toothed Queequeg is a shark almost literally. He is the internal and hidden sharkishness of all men made external and visible. His tattooed hide and nightmare visage delineate the heart of darkness, shadow forth all that is terrible and strange in man, and all that is horrible and demonic in what man does.

The full meaning of this frightful sharkishness in Ishmael's "bosom friend" does not come clear, however, until almost halfway through *Moby-Dick* when Fleece, the *Pequod's* black cook, delivers his homily to the sharks. This second sermon, in many respects contrapuntal to Father Mapple's sermon on Jonah, establishes the philosophical and moral parameters requisite for a true understanding of Queequeg's significance. When, at midnight, Stubb's whale-steak supper is disturbed by the mastications of thousands upon thousands of sharks swarming about the dead whale lashed to the ship's side, the petulant second mate orders old Fleece to "preach to 'em!" in the hope that decorum will be restored. Opening on an appropriately pastoral note, Fleece addresses the sharks as "Belubed fellow-critters":

> Dough you is all sharks, and by natur wery woracious, yet I zay to you, fellow-critters, dat dat woraciousness—'top dat dam slappin' ob de tail! How you tink to hear, 'spose you keep up such a dam slappin' and bitin' dare? [Here a profane remonstrance from Stubb on profanity, and then the sermon continues.] Your woraciousness, fellow-critters, I don't blame ye so much for; dat is natur, and can't be helped; but to gobern dat wicked natur, dat is de pint. You is sharks, sartin; but if you gobern de shark in you, why den you be angel; for all angel is not'ing more dan de shark well goberned. Now, look here, bred'ren, just try wonst to be cibil, a helping yourselbs from dat whale. Don't be tearin' de blubber out your neighbour's

mout, I say. Is not one shark dood right as toder to dat whale? And, by Gor, none on you has de right to dat whale; dat whale belong to some one else. I know some o' you has berry brig mout, brigger dan oders; but den de brig mouts sometimes has de small bellies; so dat the brigness ob de mout is not to swallar wid, but to bite off de blubber for de small fry ob sharks, dat can't get into de scrouge to help demselves. (64: *250–51*)

Over a century after Melville wrote these lines, one can only feel embarrassment at such evidence—pervasive in nineteenth-century American literature from Fenimore Cooper on—that possession of moral sensitivity and high creative gifts does not necessarily arm one against the prejudices and stereotypical thinking of one's culture. Melville's conception of the black personality in *Moby-Dick*—and most especially in Pip and Fleece—must be a source of chagrin to all twentieth-century readers. But revulsion at this tasteless attempt to draw on the crude traditions of "darky" humor should not prevent us from seeing that Melville is being crude with a purpose. For the fact is that the black pseudo-dialect of Fleece's sermon is a deliberate mask. All one has to do is rewrite the sermon in "straight" English to see that we are in actuality dealing with someone other than a sleepy ship's cook.

The tip-off is the word *voracious*, masked as *woracious*. Every other character in *Moby-Dick* speaks according to his station and background. Ahab has been to college as well as among the cannibals; Ishmael is a bookish ex-schoolmaster; Starbuck is deeply read in the Bible—and all three speak in a manner commensurate with these facts. Stubb and Flask speak the rough-and-ready idiom one expects from subordinate ship's officers. Queequeg, Tashtego, and Daggoo likewise express themselves in locutions reflecting their wild vitality. But this correlation breaks down with Fleece. Not only does the old man employ bookish adjectives such as *voracious* and *civil*, and learned verbs such as *to govern*. He also manages, in the compass of some twenty lines, to touch upon the issues of the *nature of life*, the place of *government*, the need for *civility*, the question of *inherent rights*, the sanctity of *private property*, the demands of *charity*, the problem of *equality*, the source and nature of *good and evil*, and the moral relationship of the *strong to the weak*. This is an astonishing midnight performance for a half-awake cook on a lowly American whaler. Fleece, it seems clear, is mouthing somebody else's words. It is equally clear that the "somebody else" is Melville himself. The old cook's sermon is perhaps the only place in *Moby-Dick* where, for a certainty, the mind of Melville himself can be detected moving beneath the dense web of the textual surface. Fleece's synthetic dialect represents a not-very-successful attempt to construct a verbal screen of maximum opacity, a diversionary mask to hide the sudden and unprecedented presence of the author in the fictional world he has created. Such an analysis prevents us from dismissing Fleece, as Warner Berthoff does, as a mere "figure of fun."[2] Fleece represents instead a unique instance of auctorial intrusion into an otherwise hermetic fictional world. As such, his sermon demands that close attention reserved for unique literary events.

The importance of what Fleece has to say lies in the differing reactions which Ishmael and the *Pequod's* cook exhibit when confronted with the fact of sharkishness. When Ishmael gazes over the side at the thousands of sharks insensately tearing head-sized chunks of blubber out of Stubb's whale, he speaks despairingly of *devils*. When, less than a page later, Fleece lowers a lantern and contemplates the same scene, he speaks of *angels*. This shift from devil to angel schematizes a major resolution in *Moby-Dick*. But the precise nature of that resolution cannot be established until another and quite distinct level of meaning is disentangled from Fleece's rambling monologue. This is the level on which Fleece's sermon can be read as a commentary on Father Mapple's. Jonah's story is a tale of "the sin, hard-heartedness, suddenly awakened fears, the swift punishment, repentance, prayers, and finally the deliverance and joy of Jonah." The prophet's sin is "wilful disobedience of the command of God." "And if we obey God," Father Mapple asserts, "we must disobey ourselves; and it is in this disobeying ourselves, wherein the hardness of obeying God consists" (9: 45). Self-disobedience, then, is the norm of Father Mapple's Christian universe. Jonah is not persuaded to do God's bidding. Rather, he is forced to—forced, that is, to disobey himself. Overwhelmed by the "hard hand of God," he becomes "aghast Jonah," reduced to "cringing attitudes" (9: 48). As with Jonah, so with the ship's crew. When they pity him, refusing to cast him overboard, "seek[ing] by other means to save the ship," God simply increases the intensity of the storm until the crew disobey their charitable instincts and throw Jonah over the side (9: *49*). Father Mapple's version of the Christian message demands, in short, that we go against our own natures and deny our own humanity. It is Augustinian and Calvinist Christianity, that same Stylitic tradition which, over the centuries, has persuaded some men to suppress their sexuality, some to abort their natural talents, others to withdraw into monastic isolation, and still others to flagellate their living flesh.

Put in these terms—man's relationship to his own human nature—the connection between Father Mapple's sermon and Fleece's sermon becomes immediately apparent. Fleece deals explicitly with the *nature* of the living, responding creature. He begins by reminding the blood-lusting rabble over the *Pequod's* side that "you is all sharks, and by natur wery woracious." Interrupted by Stubb, he resumes by making the same point again. "Your woraciousness, fellow-critters, I don't blame ye so much for; dat is natur, and can't be helped." Having twice asserted the intractability of "natur," Fleece then proves his thesis by urging the principal imperatives of Christian civilization upon his congregation. They should, for example, try to be civil, learning to love one another: "Now, look here, bred'ren, just try wonst to be cibil.... Don't be tearin' de blubber out your neighbour's mout, I say." He urges them to be sensitive to each other's rights: "Is not one shark dood right as toder [as good a right as another] to dat whale?" The sharks should also recognize the prior rights of possession and private ownership: "And, by Gor, none on you has de right to dat whale; dat whale belong to someone else." Above all, Fleece pleads for charity and the golden rule, especially as these apply to the strong and the gifted: "I know some o' you has berry brig mout, brigger dan oders; ... de brigness ob de mout is not to swallar wid, but to bite off de blubber for de small fry ob sharks." In short, in an unmistakable parody of Father Mapple's view of man, Fleece asks the sharks to "disobey themselves," to go against their own sharkish natures. He asks them to suppress, or more precisely, *extirpate* their own sharkishness. He asks them to *stop being sharks*. Lest we miss the point, Stubb makes it explicit. "Well done, old Fleece!" he exclaims, "that's Christianity" (64: *251*). But Fleece's homily is, on this level, an exercise in futility:

> No use goin' on; de dam willains will keep a scrougin' and slap-pin' each oder, Massa Stubb; dey don't hear one word; no use a-preachin' to such dam g'uttons as you call 'em, till dare bellies is full, and dare bellies is bottomless; and when dey do get 'em full, dey wont hear you den; for den dey sink in de sea, go fast to sleep on de coral, and can't hear not'ing at all, no more, for eber and eber. (64: *251–52*)

The meaning is clear: it is utterly hopeless to urge sharks to stop being sharks—or men to stop being men. Moral and ethical impera-tives which demand the suppression, the distortion, or (most espe-cially) the *extirpation* of essential nature can lead only to alienation from self and hypocrisy toward others.

But Fleece delivers his sermon not only to the finny and aqueous sharks over the *Pequod's* side. Standing at his shoulder to hear the exhortation is Stubb, a human shark who likes his steak blood-rare, but who in this respect is no different from Queequeg and Peleg and Bildad and Ahab, and indeed the entire crew of the *Pequod* —all of them, as Starbuck has it, "Whelped somewhere by the shark-ish sea" (38: *148*). What Fleece has to say applies even to ex-schoolmaster Ishmael, who despite his bookish mildness, admits that "I myself am a savage, owning no allegiance but to the King of the Cannibals; and ready at any moment to rebel against him" (57: *232*). For these bipedal and terrestrial sharks, Fleece introduces the idea of control, of *government*. This level of the sermon is signaled by the old man's addressing his congregation as "Belubed fellow-critters," and, a little later, as "bred'ren." Fleece speaks thus to Brother Shark because he knows that Stubb, and all of us, share with these most insensately vicious monsters of the deep a hankering taste for the carnivorous and the ensanguined. The whole sermon is on this level deeply ironic, darkly tinged with an inverted and demonic Franciscanism. For the oceanic sharks any degree of self-government is obviously out of the question. The failure of the sermon to produce the quiet and decorum which Stubb demands is proof enough of that. But Fleece's *human* "fellow-critters" are another matter. "Your woraciousness, fellow-critters, . . . is natur, and can't be helped; but to gobern dat wicked natur, dat is de pint. You is sharks, sartin; but if you gobern de shark in you, why den you be angel; for all angel is not'ing more dan de shark well goberned" (64: *251*).

Nothing could be more startling than this abrupt introduction of the idea of the *angelic* into Fleece's dark expostulation. Contemplating the same bloody scene only a page earlier, Ishmael spoke, not of the angelic, but of the demonic. "If you have never seen [this] sight," he despairingly admonished us, "then suspend your decision about the propriety of devil-worship, and the expediency of concilating the devil" (64: *250*). The contrast is too sharp to be accidental; Melville, once again, is after a meaning. The key to that meaning lies in the differing responses which Ishmael and Fleece bring to the idea of essential and intractable nature. Ishmael, at this point in *Moby-Dick*, is intellectually and emotionally incapable of accepting the fact that sharks are sharks. Evidently, nothing less than the absolute extirpation of the sharks' very nature would satisfy him. His residual Christianity makes him feel that only by ceasing to be sharks, only by disobeying themselves, could the sharks transcend the "diabolism" (64: *249*) which he sees them as representing. Since such a solution is impossible, Ishmael despairs, preparing to acknowledge the malign and bow to the demonic in life.

Fleece, in sharp contrast, imperturbably accepts essential nature. Voraciousness, in sharks and in humans, "is natur, and can't be helped." Then, in a crucial turn of thought, Fleece postulates the idea, not of self-disobedience, not of extirpation, but of *government*: ". . . but to gobern dat wicked natur, dat is de pint." The old man makes it clear that "government" is not the source of good, but rather only the *means* by which good is brought into being. In contrast to the radical dualism implicit in Ishmael's response to the feasting sharks, Fleece reveals himself as a monist, asserting that good and evil do *not* spring from distinct sources or from discrete vitalities, but rather from the same source and the same vitality. "You is sharks, sartin," he tells his congregation; "but if you gobern de shark in you, why den you be angel; *for all angel is not'ing more dan de shark well goberned*" (italics mine). It is, to say the least, disconcerting to conceive of the angelic choirs as consisting of rank upon rank of seraphic predators and cherubic carnivores. It is even more disconcerting to conceive of the God of Hosts as a Benign Shark, a Deific Cannibal. But this is precisely what old Fleece means. He is postulating sharkishness, the ineluctably rapacious life-dynamism of the self-sustaining individual, as the bedrock of animate creation, the raw stuff from which moral vitality—either Ahabian or Ishmaelian—must be made if it is to be made at all. He is saying that *both* good and evil spring from one source: sharkishness. He is explicitly rejecting Father Mapple's Christian idea of extirpation—the obsessive and foredoomed effort to eliminate absolutely the vicious, the nasty, or the simply unpleasant aspects of essential nature. Fleece knows that the extirpation of sharkishness would be the extirpation of good. Just as, to Ishmael, Queequeg is "George Washington cannibalistically developed" (10: 52), so the angel is the shark morally developed. The good man is simply the good shark. This is the burden of Fleece's sermon.[3]

The connection between Fleece's homily and Queequeg now becomes obvious. Queequeg is supremely the *good man*—the "angel" —of *Moby-Dick*. He is Fleece's well-governed shark. He is a horror—but he is an immensely hopeful horror. As such, he is Melville's portrait and Ishmael's paradigm of what man must remain, on the one hand, and what he can become, on the other. But an understanding of his significance requires a total reversal of the conventional conception of human goodness. Queequeg is not good *in spite of* his sharkishness. Rather, he is good *because of* his sharkishness: that is the source of his moral power. His tattooed visage, his shaved head, his scalp-lock, his filed teeth, his interest in beefsteaks done rare, his ubiquitous harpoon—all these are morally emblematic, functioning in *Moby-Dick* in a manner somewhat analogous to the picture of Dorian Gray, but with a meaning just the opposite of Wilde's. Queequeg's appearance signals, not inner degeneration, but rather inner integrity, an intact and undebased predacious vitality. Queequeg has achieved what few men ever achieve: he has learned to govern himself without disobeying himself. In contrast to the hypocritical, spiritually sundered, morally debilitated Christians of *Moby-Dick*, he has never engaged in the extirpation of the essential self. He was born a shark and he remains a shark. As such, he is an utterly realistic portrayal of what Reinhold Niebuhr has called that "entrenched predatory self-interest" which even the benevolent exhibit, and which only the fatuously idealistic would attempt to ignore. Queequeg thus stands as the only person in *Moby-Dick* who has been entirely true to himself. Ishmael remarks of such well-governed savages that "At first they are overawing; their calm self-collectedness of simplicity seems a Socratic wisdom":

> I had noticed . . . that Queequeg never consorted at all, or but very little, with the other seamen in the inn. He made no advances whatever; appeared to have no desire to enlarge the circle of his acquaintances. All this struck me as mighty singular; yet, upon second thoughts, there was something almost sublime in it. Here was a man some twenty thousand miles from home, . . . thrown among people as strange to him as though he were in the planet Jupiter; and yet he seemed entirely at his ease; preserving the utmost serenity; content with his own companionship; always equal to himself. Surely this was a touch of fine philosophy; though no doubt he had never heard that there was such a thing as that. But, perhaps, to be true philosophers, we mortals should not be conscious of so living or so striving. (10: 52)

Queequeg is "content with his own companionship" and "equal to himself" because—unlike the dichotomized Christians with whom he now associates—he has never been told that the self is an enemy. Comfortable in his cannibalism, reconciled to the horror of which he is the expression, always obeying himself, Queequeg obeys nature, and thus achieves a noble self-sufficiency.

The most expressive symbol of Queequeg's angelic sharkishness is his tomahawk-pipe. It is neither simply a tomahawk which can be used as a pipe, nor conversely is it a pipe which on occasion can be used as a tomahawk. Rather, it is fully pipe and fully tomahawk, and both at once. Terrified Ishmael first sees it as a tomahawk, full of burning tobacco, being brandished in the darkness over his head in the most incendiary way when Queequeg discovers him in his bed at the Spouter-Inn. "Who-e debel you?" the savage demands, "you no speak-e, dam-me, I kill-e." We underestimate Queequeg, or make him something he is not, if we regard this as an idle threat. Queequeg is perfectly capable of murder, and of using his pipe as a "hacking, horrifying implement" (3: *21*), despite Peter Coffin's grinning assurances to Ishmael, that he "wouldn't harm a hair of your head" (3: *31*). But this tomahawk which threatens Ishmael's life is also that pipe which, used for a "social smoke," makes him and Queequeg "cronies" and "bosom friends," "married" as Ishmael explains, in the sense that Queequeg "would gladly die for me, if need should be" (10: *53*). Shortly, the tomahawk-pipe becomes the focus of the most gentle and domestic of emotions:

> Be it said, that though I had felt such a strong repugnance to his smoking in the bed the night before, yet see how elastic our stiff prejudices grow when love once comes to bend them. For now I liked nothing better than to have Queequeg smoking by me, even in bed, because he seemed to be full of such serene household joy then. I no more felt unduly concerned for the landlord's policy of insurance. I was only alive to the condensed confidential comfortableness of sharing a pipe and a blanket with a real friend. (11: *55*)

Queequeg enjoys full "government"—in Fleece's sense of the term —of his tomahawk-pipe. It can be turned to the purposes of murder, or of love, as need be.[4]

Just as the murderous and loving are one in Queequeg's tomahawk-pipe, so are they also one—inextricably the same—in Queequeg himself. The pipe specifically, and Queequeg more generally, thus become the central expression of that curious, middling philosophical blend—more than naturalistic but less than transcendental —which I have termed the truncated transcendentalism or metanaturalism of *Moby-Dick*. The bloody and warlike aspects of the tomahawk-pipe testify to the inescapable immersion of Queequeg— and all men—in the sharkish life-processes of a sharkish world. But Queequeg is no Polynesian McTeague, no Kokovokoan Clyde Griffiths. Fleece urged his congregation to be "cibil" toward one another —an adjuration wasted on the sharks over the *Pequod's* side. But sharkish Queequeg is different. Ishmael twice uses Fleece's very word in connection with his new-found friend: Queequeg invites him back to bed on the night of their meeting in "not only a civil but a really kind and charitable way" (3: *31*), and the next morning has the "civility and consideration" to dress first and leave the room to Ishmael (4: *34*). This civility testifies to the fact that Queequeg, shark though he is, is *not* the helpless creature of natural process or or mere animal impulse. His capacity for self-government has made it possible for him to achieve a *limited* transcendence:

> Savage though he was, and hideously marred about the face—at least to my taste—his countenance yet had a something in it which was by no means disagreeable. You cannot hide the soul. Through all his unearthly tattooings, I thought I saw the traces of a simple honest heart; and in his large, deep eyes, fiery black and bold, there seemed tokens of a spirit that would dare a thousand devils. And besides all this, there was a certain lofty bearing about the Pagan, which even his uncouthness could not altogether maim. He looked like a man who had never cringed and never had had a creditor. (10: *51–52*)

This honest heart, this lofty bearing, this dare-devil spirit—these are "higher" than sharkishness, but they are not independent of sharkishness. If Queequeg were not a shark, if he did not command the almost unlimited vitality of a shark, he could not be these things. The transcendental view of man—exemplified in *Moby-Dick* by extirpative Christianity—implies an escape from, a "rising above" the "low," the impulsive and instinctual, the animal and insensate. Queequeg has not in this traditional sense *risen above*. Rather, he has *risen out of*. He thus conforms in the most perfect way to that carefully qualified image of man which Ishmael develops later in *Moby-Dick*, and which I have analyzed in the constitutive metaphor of the ocean-island. In the pivotal "Brit" chapter, Ishmael asks us to consider the "universal cannibalism" of the sea, the way in which the ocean is, and always will be, to "the crack of doom," both "foe to man" and "fiend to its own offspring":

> Consider all this; and then turn to this green, gentle, and most docile earth; consider them both, the sea and the land; and do you not find a strange analogy to something in yourself? For as this appalling ocean surrounds the verdant land, so in the soul of man there lies one insular Tahiti, full of peace and joy, but encompassed by all the horrors of the half known life. (58: *236*)

A similar image of insular elevation and isolation occurs as Ishmael contemplates the serene center of the Grand Armada:

> And thus, though surrounded by circle upon circle of consternations and affrights, did these inscrutable creatures at the centre freely and fearlessly indulge in all peaceful concernments; yea, serenely rev-

elled in dalliance and delight. But even so, amid the tornadoed Atlantic of my being, do I myself still for ever centrally disport in mute calm; and while ponderous planets of unwaning woe revolve round me, deep down and deep inland there I still bathe me in eternal mildness of joy. (87: *326*)

Neither of these passages suggests the possibility of an unqualified transcendence. The "tornadoed Atlantic of my being" cannot be escaped, is never left behind. The sharkish sea always and forever surrounds the ocean-island. We live and die "encompassed by all the horrors of the half-known life." But the "insular Tahiti" of our inner awareness, while forever rooted in a naturalistic world, nevertheless rises a limited distance above the dead level of the sharkish ocean, is of sufficient extent so that we can retreat "deep down and deep inland" to a place of psychological calm and spiritual quietude. Cannibal Queequeg exemplifies this metanaturalistic elevation of self. Rooted in sharkishness, part of nature, he is nevertheless more than shark. He governs his sharkishness—and he is able to do this because, unlike his oceanic "bred'ren," he commands an insular Tahiti.

Queequeg's metanaturalism is most evident in his relationship to death, that fact of natural life which generates such terror in Ishmael. To Ishmael, death means not so much dissolution or annihilation as *stasis*, or more precisely stasis-with-consciousness, a horrified and frozen awareness without escape or termination, for ever and ever. This is what he means when he describes his childhood nightmare of a "silent form or phantom" seated at his midnight bedside. "For what seemed ages piled on ages, I lay there, frozen with the most awful fears, not daring to drag away my hand; yet ever thinking that if I could but stir it one single inch, the horrid spell would be broken" (4: *33*). This, too, is what he means when, in a crescendo of neurotic horror triggered by the cenotaphs of the Whaleman's Chapel, he speaks of the "eternal, unstirring paralysis, and deadly, hopeless trance" of "antique Adam who died sixty round centuries ago" (7: *41*). Given a necrophobia of such hallucinatory intensity, it is little wonder that Ishmael reacts so violently to Queequeg's "Ramadan" during their stay at the Try-Pots Inn. Returning from his first interview with Captains Peleg and Bildad, and finding that

Queequeg will not unlock the door to their room, nor respond in any way to his persistent knocking, Ishmael throws his shoulder against the door with all his strength. "With a prodigious noise the door flew open, and the knob slamming against the wall, sent the plaster to the ceiling; and there, good heavens! there sat Queequeg, altogether cool and self-collected; right in the middle of the room; squatting on his hams, and holding Yojo on top of his head. He looked neither one way nor the other way, but sat like a carved image with scarce a sign of active life."

Nothing that either Ishmael or Mrs. Hussey can do causes Queequeg to alter his position by so much as a hair. "But all we said, not a word could we drag out of him; I almost felt like pushing him over, so as to change his position, for it was almost intolerable, it seemed so painfully and unnaturally constrained; especially, as in all probability he had been sitting so for upwards of eight or ten hours, going too without his regular meals." Finding the whole business so "intolerable," Ishmael goes to supper alone, and remains in the bar-room until nearly eleven o'clock, only to find that Queequeg "had not stirred an inch" in the interval.

> Despairing of him, therefore, I determined to go to bed and to sleep.... For some time, do all I would, I could not get into the faintest doze. I had blown out the candle; and the mere thought of Queequeg—not four feet off—sitting there in that uneasy position, stark alone in the cold and dark; this made me really wretched. Think of it; sleeping all night in the same room with a wide awake pagan on his hams in this dreary, unaccountable Ramadan! (17: *80–81*)

This situation is a repetition in real life of Ishmael's childhood nightmare. Then it was an "unimaginable ... phantom" seated in the darkness at his bedside; now it is the invisible, immovable Queequeg. Once again Ishmael, enveloped in darkness, is in the presence of personified death.

For this is the meaning of the Ramadan: Queequeg, while still in life, is *practicing death* as some men practice the piano. Squatting in the middle of the room for twenty-four hours "as if he had been screwed down to the floor," he is as good as dead, dead symbolically. His model is wooden Yojo, emblematic of the immovable and pyramidical serenity of the non-sentient world. During the Ramadan, Queequeg places himself under the aegis of cosmic inanimation; this is why he holds the little pagan idol on top of his head. Queequeg is his own *memento mori*. Sitting in darkness, conscious but immobile like antique Adam, he is also a *memento mori* for death-haunted Ishmael. It is the latter's fear of the grave which we glimpse in his "really wretched" sense of how Queequeg, though "not four feet off" from the bed, is nevertheless "stark alone in the cold and dark." The Ramadan thus typifies as nothing else could Queequeg's superb metanaturalism. We speak habitually of men "dying," but we do not usually intend this locution to be taken in an active sense. Death, in the ordinary view, is something inflicted on men, a visitation in which they take no active part, and indeed resist with all their strength. In this traditional sense, though he may be violently killed, Queequeg will never die. Instead, he will only, as during his yearly Ramadan, become dead. In the meantime, by ritualistically being that which he will eventually become, Queequeg triumphs over death. Unlike Ishmael, he is not now death's creature, nor will he ever be death's victim. Moreover, since he is in *Moby-Dick* the supreme death-figure, the apocalyptic imago with a head like a "mildewed skull," in prosecuting his Ramadan Queequeg simply becomes himself—and becoming oneself is, self-evidently, the most natural and inevitable of processes. All men, as the truism has it, carry their death about with them—but very few are, like Queequeg, entirely comfortable with the burden.

The metanaturalistic health which Queequeg represents—nature engaging in the natural conquest of itself—means little to Ishmael, however, until Queequeg, much later in *Moby-Dick*, undertakes to die. A leak in the bottom-most oil-casks forces the *Pequod's* crew to hoist Burtons and break out. The cannibal, crawling about in the dampness and slime of the hold, catches a chill "which lapsed into a fever; and at last, after some days' suffering, laid him in his hammock, close to the very sill of the door of death." Ishmael thus has an opportunity to be intimately "social" with yet another "horror." Queequeg's illness affords him a near view of dying, just as the voyage itself has already afforded him a near view of Leviathan. Ishmael's language in this crisis makes it clear that dying, or at least Queequeg's way of going about it, is more beautiful than terrible:

How he wasted and wasted away in those few long-lingering days, till there seemed but little left of him but his frame and tattooing. But as all else in him thinned, and his cheekbones grew sharper, his eyes, nevertheless, seemed growing fuller and fuller; they became of a strange softness of lustre; and mildly but deeply looked out at you there from his sickness, a wondrous testimony to that immortal health in him which could not die, or be weakened. . . . An awe that cannot be named would steal over you as you sat by the side of this waning savage, and saw as strange things in his face, as any beheld who were bystanders when Zoroaster died. . . . And the drawing near of Death, which alike levels all, alike impresses all with a last revelation, which only an author from the dead could adequately tell. So that . . . no dying Chaldee or Greek had higher and holier thoughts than those, whose mysterious shades you saw creeping over the face of poor Queequeg. (110: *394–96*)

Not by the merest phrase does Ishmael betray here the fear or revulsion that characterized his wintry contemplation of the cenotaphs of the Whaleman's Chapel. There are here no despairing references to "deadly voids and unbidden infidelities," no brooding hints that those who die in remote oceans, as Queequeg must—"placelessly perish[ing] without a grave"—are by virtue of that fact to be refused resurrections. Instead, the serenity with which Queequeg approaches his "endless end," the beauty of the "last revelation" which encroaching death affords him—these make Queequeg's dying, not a termination, but rather a climax of immense dignity and significance. In one of the major resolutions of *Moby-Dick*, Ishmael waxes poetic concerning Queequeg's special Polynesian thanatopsis. The prospect of being buried at sea in one of the "dark canoes" or coffins which he had seen in Nantucket pleases Queequeg, "for it was not unlike the custom of his own race, who, after embalming a dead warrior, stretched him out in his canoe, and so left him to be floated away to the starry archipelagoes; for not only do they believe that the stars are isles, but that far beyond all visible horizons, their own mild, uncontinented seas, interflow with the blue heavens; and so form the white breakers of the milky way" (110: *396*).

Such language on such a topic signals unequivocally Ishmael's return to health and sanity. Thanks to Queequeg, and to the prelusive insights of the Arsacidean bower, death for Ishmael has lost its sting. Nothing could be more therapeutic for the young man who paused before coffin warehouses and brought up the rear of every funeral procession, than to watch the manner in which Queequeg greets his own particular coffin:

> Leaning over in his hammock, Queequeg long regarded the coffin with an attentive eye. He then called for his harpoon, had the wooden stock drawn from it, and then had the iron part placed in the coffin along with one of the paddles of his boat. All by his own request, also, biscuits were then ranged round the sides within: a flask of fresh water was placed at the head, and a small bag of woody earth scraped up in the hold at the foot; and a piece of sail-cloth being rolled up for a pillow, Queequeg now entreated to be lifted into his final bed, that he might make trial of its comforts, if any it had. He lay without moving a few minutes, then told one to go to his bag and bring out his little god, Yojo. Then crossing his arms on his breast with Yojo between, he called for the coffin lid . . . to be placed over him. The head part turned over with a leather hinge, and there lay Queequeg in his coffin with little but his composed countenance in view. "Rarmai" (it will do; it is easy), he murmured at last, and signed to be replaced in his hammock. (110: 397)

The unidentified "one" of this passage, whom Queequeg asks to bring him Yojo, is most certainly the same unidentified "one" whom Queequeg calls "in the grey morning watch" to request that a Nantucket coffin be built—and both are certainly Ishmael, forced through his love for the savage to engage in the things of death and the ministrations of dying. Like the man who plunges into water to overcome his fear of water, Ishmael is plunged by Queequeg into death, so that he may be psychologically reborn.

The melioration of Ishmael's death-hypo having thus been achieved, Queequeg goes on to demonstrate his metanaturalistic control by deciding that his death will have to be postponed:

> But now that he had apparently made every preparation for death . . . Queequeg suddenly rallied; . . . and thereupon, when some expressed their delighted surprise, he . . . said, that the cause of his sudden convalescence was this;—at a critical moment, he had just recalled a little duty ashore, which he was leaving undone; and therefore had changed his mind about dying: he could not die yet, he averred. They asked him, then, whether to live or die was a matter of his own sovereign will and pleasure. He answered, certainly. In

a word, it was Queequeg's conceit, that if a man made up his mind to live, mere sickness could not kill him: nothing but a whale, or a gale, or some violent, ungovernable, unintelligent destroyer of that sort. (110: *398*)

Ishmael continues to speak by indirections. Just as Queequeg's request for a coffin, and later for Yojo, were both delivered to an unnamed "one," so here "delighted surprise" at the savage's sudden convalescence is expressed by a vague "some," an oddly unspecified "they." All are obviously Ishmael, in an agony of anxious hope, making queries of his bosom friend so crucial to his own well-being and psychological survival that he dare not admit he is making them. Nothing could be more eloquent than this sustained indirection, this touchingly transparent covertness. Both testify to the fact that Queequeg's crisis is Ishmael's crisis. The cannibal, coming back of his own volition from the grave's edge, brings an astonished and redeemed Ishmael with him.

This is the ultimate meaning of noble Queequeg: as a figure of death, he is a source of life. He is therefore the alpha and omega of *Moby-Dick*, linking birth and death, and making them one. Repeatedly, Queequeg gives life rather than taking it away. First, when the green bumpkin who had been mimicking him on the *Moss* is knocked overboard, it is Queequeg who springs "from the side with a long living arc of a leap," and retrieves the greenhorn from the freezing foam. "From that hour," Ishmael tells us, "I clove to Queequeg like a barnacle; yea, till poor Queequeg took his last long dive" (13: *60–61*). Second, when the *Pequod's* tackles part and the sperm whale's head begins its plunge to the bottom with Tashtego trapped inside, it is again "my brave Queequeg" who dives to the rescue, with obstetrical dexterity accomplishing "the deliverance, or rather, delivery of Tashtego" (78: *289–90*). Finally, it is Queequeg who keeps Ishmael afloat "for almost one whole day and night" after the *Pequod* is sunk by Moby Dick ("Epilogue": *470*). For what appears to be a coffin is really Queequeg transmogrified. One recalls that when it became apparent that he would not need the carpenter's coffin, Queequeg spent "Many spare hours ... in carving the lid with all manner of grotesque figures and drawings; and it seemed that hereby he was striving, in his rude way, to copy parts of the twisted tattooing on his body" (110: *399*). Thus does the image of Queequeg, "rising with great force," emerge from the ocean's depths to rescue Ishmael, and thus does Queequeg's death become Ishmael's life.[5]

It takes Ishmael some time, however, to extend to the natural world and natural process the reconciliation which Queequeg represents. The cannibal's return from the grave's edge occurs in Chapter 110; it is his last substantive scene in *Moby-Dick*. And yet only four chapters later, in "The Gilder," we find Ishmael obsessively returning to what he called, fifty chapters earlier, the "universal cannibalism of the sea" (58: *235*). The *Pequod*, now on the Japanese fishing grounds, encounters a sustained period of "mild, pleasant weather." "At such times," Ishmael tells us, "under an abated sun; afloat all day upon smooth, slow heaving swells; . . . these are the times of dreamy quietude, when beholding the tranquil beauty and brilliancy of the ocean's skin, one forgets the tiger heart that pants beneath it; and would not willingly remember, that this velvet paw but conceals a remorseless fang" (114: *405*). Five chapters later Ishmael returns again to the predatory vitality which lies hidden beneath the bland surface of an apparently benign world. "Warmest climes but nurse the cruellest fangs," he asserts just before the typhoon strikes, "the tiger of Bengal crouches in spiced groves of ceaseless verdure" (119: *413*). Such are the terms of Ishmael's final problem. He is reconciled to Queequeg-in-man. He is not yet reconciled to Queequeg-in-nature. But come to terms he does, in the last chapter of *Moby-Dick* except for the three devoted to the chase of the White Whale. This final chapter is called "The Symphony," a title which suggests a terminal harmony, a climactic integration of elements as yet unreconciled. These elements turn out to be the two terms of nature's most fundamental and puzzling dualism: the Queequeg-mixture of the benign and the predatory, the gentle and the brutal, the minatory and the mild. This dualism is rendered macrocosmically in "The Symphony," as the two natural "firmaments" of the *Pequod's* primordial world—the *air* and the *sea*:

> It was a clear steel-blue day. The firmaments of air and sea were hardly separable in that all-pervading azure; only, the pensive air was transparently pure and soft, with a woman's look, and the robust and

man-like sea heaved with long, strong, lingering swells, as Samson's chest in his sleep.

Hither, and thither, on high, glided the snow-white wings of small, unspeckled birds; these were the gentle thoughts of the feminine air; but to and fro in the deeps, far down in the bottomless blue, rushed mighty leviathans, sword-fish, and sharks; and these were the strong, troubled, murderous thinkings of the masculine sea. (132: *442*)

Ishmael here dovetails two distinct metaphors. The most obvious one is sexual: the air is feminine, the sea is masculine. To each of these domains are assigned qualities which, like the pyramidism and leviathanism of other chapters, are cosmically constitutive. The masculine sea is "murderous." The feminine air is "gentle." The second metaphor is less conventional. Ishmael renders the various animals of the *Pequod's* sea-world as *thoughts*. The "unspeckled birds" are feminine thoughts; the "leviathans, sword-fish, and sharks" are masculine thoughts. In "The Symphony," all external reality is subsumed under a dualized metaphor of mind.

Of these two interlocked metaphors, one sexual and the other psychological, it is the latter—the world as mind—which is most freighted with philosophical significance. The idea of an equivalence between the physical and mental worlds is not new in *Moby-Dick*. "O Nature, and O soul of man!" exclaims Ahab, "how far beyond all utterance are your linked analogies! not the smallest atom stirs or lives in matter, but has its cunning duplicate in mind" (70: *264*). Ahab is saying, consistently with his "input" epistemology, that it is mind which duplicates the world. In Chapter 132 Ishmael turns this equivalence around. By filling the natural "firmaments" of air and sea with "gentle" and "murderous" thoughts, he is asserting that it is the world which duplicates mind. Thus, "The Symphony" represents the last and definitive statement in *Moby-Dick* of the metaphor of the illuminating lamp-mind. It signals a final novelistic resolution, Ishmael's projection of a restructured and reintegrated system of intellectual and affective imperatives out upon external reality. In this almost-final chapter, in one decisive thrust of the creative imagination, Ishmael executes a moral reconstruction of his world.

Since that restructured world duplicates mind, it may be taken as an index to the final state of Ishmael's inner being. The fundamental metaphor, of gentle bird-thoughts and predatory fish-thoughts, is far-fetched; Ishmael is straining for a meaning. But that flaw in the art of the passage should not prevent us from seeing that Ishmael is trying to apprise us, now that the voyage is almost done, of where he stands in relation to himself. Nothing in *Moby-Dick*, not the squid nor the shark nor Leviathan, has terrified Ishmael more than his *own mind*. Whatever sharkishness he has perceived in the external world could hardly match the conceptual and imaginative sharkishness which perpetually darkens the clear stream of thought. "For we are all killers, on land and on sea," he asserts, "Bonapartes and Sharks included" (32: *125*). In thought, in intention, in desire, in impulse, in image, all men are capable of horrors for which no words are adequate and no symbols sufficient. It is this fear of the mind—his own mind—which is the final measure of Ishmael's illness. By the same token, it will be through reconciliation with the terrible facts of mind that Ishmael's recovery can best be measured.

The locus of such a rapprochement of the self with itself will have to lie not so much with the "feminine" thoughts of the gentle air—which present no problems—as with the "troubled, murderous thinkings" of the masculine sea, the "mighty leviathans, swordfish, and sharks" of the mind. Throughout *Moby-Dick*, it has been the predatory dynamism which such sea-creatures represent, especially when conceived as psychological correlates, which has brought Ishmael to the verge of devil-worship. The problem of *mental* sharkishness has appeared insoluble. But in "The Symphony" a solution—or at least a mode of reconciliation—is found. In a major analogical extension, the predatory elements of natural and psychological process are reconceptualized as a specifically *masculine* dynamism. The significance of this shift is clear. Within the sexual metaphor of "The Symphony," masculinity stands as one term of a dynamic principle which is *constructive and life-generating rather than destructive and life-obliterating*. Busy reshaping his world, Ishmael is in the process, in these penultimate pages, of converting the destructive elements of *Moby-Dick* into constructive elements. He accomplishes this by expanding the sexual metaphor into a marriage metaphor:

> Aloft, like a royal czar and king, the sun seemed giving this gentle air to this bold and rolling sea; even as bride to groom. And at the

girdling line of the horizon, a soft and tremulous motion . . . denoted
the fond, throbbing trust, the loving alarms, with which the poor
bride gave her bosom away. (132: *442*)

Since the external mind-world of "The Symphony" is a cunning
duplicate of the internal mind-world, this marriage of feminine air
and masculine sea can be taken as reflecting a final synthesis in Ishmael's mind and heart. He now sees that the brutal, the ensanguined,
the predatory in natural process, while they stand forever beyond
the reach of the "government" which is man's special province, are
nevertheless part of an on-going, immanent, virtually immortal act
of creation and renewal. The processes of the cosmos are counter-
entropic, constructive rather than destructive. The appearances of
the demonic and malign in nature are just that: appearances. The
world, though terrible, is good. The cosmos, though frightful, is
benign. There are many things in the natural world that ought to be
avoided. There is nothing in the natural world that ought to be
feared. Man's peace of mind is threatened only when the world is
misunderstood. *Moby-Dick* is the story of such a misunderstanding—
and of Ishmael's gradual attainment, through pain and terror and
travail, of a true apprehension of the nature of things. The result
is a symphony, a final harmony between Ishmael and his world.

NOUMENAL EPIPHANY
The Three Days' Chase

ONE OF THE SIMPLICITIES underlying *Moby-Dick* which should not escape observation is that Melville really wrote two novels in a single creative act. One is the dramatic *Moby-Dick*. The other is the ideational *Moby-Dick*. The dramatic novel deals with the chase of the White Whale; the ideational novel deals with the ideas this chase engenders. The distinction is important because, while the dramatic novel ends (obviously) as the *Pequod* sinks beneath the waves, the ideational novel actually ends some twenty-five pages earlier with Chapter 132, "The Symphony." Through the marriage of the "gentle" air and the "murderous" sea, Ishmael synthesizes the dichotomies which, as he thinks, sunder both life and reality. (Whether Melville or the reader finds this synthesis satisfactory is, as I have indicated, another question.)

But although Ishmael has achieved a spiritual rebirth, a series of insights which tend toward the resolution of his hypos, these shifts in the texture of his perceptions still require some sort of external validation. The idiom in which such validation might be cast is suggested in an earlier passage where Ishmael tries to formulate the ultimate "meaning" of the forehead—the brow—in humans, in cattle, even in whales. "Human or animal," he asserts, "the mystical brow is as that great golden seal affixed by the German emperors to their decrees. It signifies—'God: done this day by my hand' " (79: *292*).*
It is in this authenticative sense that Ishmael's reconstituted perceptions need a seal set upon them. The natural world must, however cryptically or obscurely, indicate that Ishmael's version of the world—and of Leviathan—is true, and that Ahab's is false. It is in these terms that the appearance of Moby Dick must be understood.

But the word *appearance* hardly covers what actually occurs. Moby Dick does not simply appear. Rather, he *manifests* himself. When he is sighted from the mainmast by Ahab, Stubb observes that they find him in his natural, undisturbed state. "He is heading straight to leeward, sir," the second mate reports, "right away from us; cannot have seen the ship yet" (133: *447*). Ishmael will in the succeeding chapter recollect the majestic tranquillity of this unaware whale, speaking of the "calm and indolent spoutings . . . [and] the peaceable gush of that mystic fountain in his head" which characterize Moby Dick's first appearance (134: *455*). The boats are lowered, the eager hunters rowing in careful silence:

> Like noiseless nautilus shells, their light prows sped through the sea; but only slowly they neared the foe. As they neared him, the ocean grew still more smooth; seemed drawing a carpet over its waves; seemed a noon-meadow, so serenely it spread. At length the breathless hunter came so nigh his seemingly unsuspecting prey, that his entire dazzling hump was distinctly visible, sliding along the sea as if an isolated thing, and continually set in a revolving ring of

* The number before the colon in all parenthetical references in the text indicates chapter, which will be the same for most American editions of *Moby-Dick*; the italicized numbers after the colon indicate page in the Norton Critical Edition of *Moby-Dick*, edited by Harrison Hayford and Hershel Parker (New York: W. W. Norton & Company, 1967).

finest, fleecy, greenish foam. He saw the vast, involved wrinkles of the slightly projecting head beyond. Before it, far out on the soft Turkish-rugged waters, went the glistening white shadow from his broad, milky forehead, a musical rippling playfully accompanying the shade; and behind, the blue waters interchangeably flowed over into the moving valley of his steady wake; and on either hand bright bubbles arose and danced by his side. But these were broken again by the light toes of hundreds of gay fowl softly feathering the sea, alternate with their fitful flight; and like to some flag-staff rising from the painted hull of an argosy, the tall but shattered pole of a recent lance projected from the white whale's back; and at intervals one of the cloud of soft-toed fowls hovering, and to and fro skimming like a canopy over the fish, silently perched and rocked on this pole, the long tail feathers streaming like pennons. (133: *447*)

Evidently, this is more than a simple appearance. It is rather an *epiphany*, analogous to the epiphany—the wordless manifestation of natural meaning—which occurs in *Pierre* at a moment of high crisis. Almost destroyed by the shattering revelations which Isabel has made to him, Pierre, having fled to the woods, is lying prostrate with despair directly under the "Terror Stone," a vast mass of rock poised on a stony knife-edge. Suddenly nature epiphanizes itself: "A down-darting bird, all song, swiftly lighted on the unmoved and eternally immovable balancings of the Terror Stone, and cheerfully chirped to Pierre. The tree-boughs bent and waved to the rushes of a sudden, balmy wind; and slowly Pierre crawled forth, and stood haughtily upon his feet, . . . and went his moody way."[1]

The epiphanal message which nature vouchsafes to Pierre is susceptible to explication, and so is Ishmael's. On the one hand, the great White Whale, not so much albino as albescent, is the last of those primal forms, those etiolate noumenal shapes, which are intuitively apprehended throughout *Moby-Dick* in all their unwarped anteperceptual simplicity: the cenotaph, the squid, the spirit-spout, the snowy albatross. As such, Moby Dick is not only Leviathan but Leviathan*ism*, a qualitative as well as a substantive entity, the ultimate, cosmically comprehensive noumenon. On the other hand, the "noon-meadow" waters through which Moby Dick swims, the "greenish foam" which precedes him and the "blue waters" which follow him, the "bright bubbles" which arise from the "musical

rippling" of his steady progress, and the "gay fowl" which canopy
him—all these elements, rendered with a baroque, almost oriental
sensuousness, give analogical expression to the phenomenal realm of
tingent gorgeousness which Ahab has dismissed as mere "pasteboard," and which Ishmael, when still in the grip of the Ahabian
thesis, saw as nothing more than "harlot" colors "laid on from without" (36: *144*; 42: *170*). It is no accident that Ishmael describes the
ocean through which Moby Dick swims as a "carpet," a serene expanse of "soft Turkish-rugged waters." The phrasing immediately
recalls the "freshet-rushing carpet" of King Tranquo's Arsacidean
weaver-god (102: *374*), the definitive cyclic image for the phenomenal derma which, as Ishmael thinks, conceals reality.

But this is exactly the point of Ishmael's epiphanal vision. He suddenly sees, and we are intended to see, that phenomena do not
"conceal" reality. Rather, they *are* reality. This is to say that the
appearance of Moby Dick is an epistemological *event*. I have suggested that the philosophical substrate of *Moby-Dick* proposes the
discontinuous nature of reality—a discontinuity which finds protometaphorical formulation in the schemata of *color: interface: non-
color*. What Ishmael witnesses is the obliteration of the discontinuity which has haunted him. The epistemologically chromatic
elements of the epiphany cannot be separated from the achromatic:
Moby Dick and the lovely world through which he swims are not
two things, but one thing. This ontological coalescence sets the
whale-as-noumenon apart from most of the other primal forms
which Ishmael cites. St. John's vision of the Heavenly Choirs, with
the redeemed in white robes before a white throne on which a Holy
One sits "white like wool" is utterly bereft of color; the polar bear
moves through a world as "ghastly white" as himself; the "unspotted
whiteness" of Ishmael's first albatross is encountered in snowy "Ant-
arctic seas"; the "marble pallor" of the dead is reinforced rather
than minimized by the "hue of the shroud in which we wrap them";
ghosts are never seen against a chromatic background, but rather
rise in a "milk-white fog"; pale Death rides an equally pale horse;
and the horror of Lima, the city that has "taken the white veil,"
consists in the total absence of color, even "the cheerful greenness
of complete decay" (42: *163–68*).

In contrast, Moby Dick is fused with the color-world. As early as Chapter 41, *before* Ishmael's long meditation on "The Whiteness of the Whale," he speaks of Moby Dick's "vivid aspect, when seen gliding at high noon through a dark blue sea, leaving a milky-way wake of creamy foam, all spangled with golden gleamings" (41: *159*). Similarly, when he appears to the sullen crew of the *Town-Ho*, Ishmael describes the way the White Whale was "lit up by a horizontal spangling sun," so that he "shifted and glistened like a living opal in the blue morning sea" (54: *221*). It is this unity, not only aesthetic but ontological, of the White Whale with the color-world which is adumbrated at the outset of the Three Days' Chase. Not only is Moby Dick surrounded by green foam and blue water and irridescent bubble; he blends with these elements, and indeed seems to generate them. In front of Moby Dick's "dazzling hump," Ishmael remarks, "far out on the soft Turkish-rugged waters, went the glistening white shadow from his broad, milky forehead, a musical rippling playfully accompanying the shade." So pervasive is the effect of fusion that the White Whale himself seems no longer white. Ishmael observes the "tall but shattered pole of a recent lance project[ing] from the white whale's back." It appears to him to be similar to the "flag-staff" rising from a ship. The analogy suggests that Moby Dick himself is that ship, carrying that flag-staff—but for Ishmael he is no pallid vessel, but rather the *"painted hull of an argosy"* (italics mine). Like the generic whale of an earlier passage, whose spout was irradiated by a rainbow (85: *314*), Moby Dick is here endowed with philosophical chromaticity. The interface between noumenon and phenomenon collapses entirely: Ishmael's world is at last truly and totally one.

Through the course of the epiphany, Ishmael stresses the tranquil mildness of Moby Dick; there is little in the undisturbed whale to suggest the "murderous monster" (41: *155*) of the early "Moby Dick" chapter:

> A gentle joyousness—a mighty mildness of repose in swiftness, invested the gliding whale. Not the white bull Jupiter swimming away with ravished Europa clinging to his graceful horns; his lovely, leering eyes sideways intent upon the maid; with smooth bewitching fleetness, rippling straight for the nuptial bower in Crete; not Jove, not that great majesty Supreme! did surpass the glorified White Whale as he so divinely swam. (133: *447*)

The metaphor here is one of visionary sexual transport, an essentially erotic ecstasy coupled with a not-entirely submerged allusion to the literally physical yet hieratic, sexual yet sacerdotal, union of the human and the animal. Ishmael is recasting the ontological and perceptual coalescence of the preceding paragraph in terms of a naturalistically mythopoeic theology, the categories of which are affective rather than discursive. The epiphany that he sees he also feels, testimony to the healing wholeness which is Leviathan's gift to any man who has the courage, as Ishmael has, to be truly "social" with a "horror" (1: *16*). For the horror—or at least the terror—coexists with the mildness of Moby Dick, just as it coexists with the mildness of Queequeg:

> And thus, through the serene tranquillities of the tropical sea, among waves whose hand-clappings were suspended by exceeding rapture, Moby Dick moved on, still withholding from sight the full terrors of his submerged trunk, entirely hiding the wrenched hideousness of his jaw. But soon the fore part of him slowly rose from the water; for an instant his whole marbleized body formed a high arch, like Virginia's Natural Bridge, and warningly waving his bannered flukes in the air, the grand god revealed himself, sounded, and went out of sight. (133: *448*)

This characteristic blending of the mild and the minatory is best exemplified by Moby Dick's "deformed lower jaw" (41: *159*), here rendered as a concealed "hideousness." So dramatic a deformity must be set in context; certainly its hideousness is meliorated when one recalls Ishmael's account of how Sperm Whales acquire such dislocations. The bulls of the species, he has told us, "sometimes come to deadly battle, and all for love. They fence with their long lower jaws, sometimes locking them together." The result is not infrequently "furrowed heads, broken teeth, scolloped fins; and in some instances, wrenched and dislocated mouths" (88: *329*). Moby Dick's misaligned mandible may possibly prove him a monster; it certainly proves him a lover.[2] The ambivalence—or better, the coalescence—of meaning is precisely parallel to the dual significations of Queequeg's tomahawk-pipe.

Before Moby Dick dives and the battle begins, however, Ishmael, in a particularly vivid instance of the shrouded idiom of the novel, gives us—if we are willing to read closely enough—the veritable cause, the actual reason for, the history of juggernaut violence which has made Moby Dick a legend in the fisheries. Ishmael comes, in fact, as close as one can reasonably expect to *assigning blame* for the bloody and destructive reputation which is the anomalous concomitant of the White Whale's divine serenity:

> On each soft side—coincident with the parted swell, that but once laving him, then flowed so wide away—on each bright side, the whale shed off enticings. No wonder there had been some among the hunters who *namelessly transported and allured by all that serenity, had ventured to assail it*; but had fatally found that quietude but the vesture of tornadoes. Yet calm, enticing calm, oh, whale! thou glidest on, to all who for the first time eye thee, no matter how many in that same way thou may'st have bejuggled and destroyed before. (133: *447–48*; italics mine)

The first thing to be said is that this passage does *not* have to do with the ontological, epistemological, or affective significations which are the concern of the three paragraphs already examined. Rather, Ishmael is here examining the moral effect—the effect in the realm of action and consequence—of the "glorified" White Whale upon those who are granted a glimpse of him. What Moby Dick does, in an extension of both the overt and covert sexual metaphors of the preceding paragraph, is *entice*. Because of the religio-aesthetic thrust of the surrounding context, a superficial reading is certain to leave one with the impression that Ishmael is still dealing with the *beauty* of Moby Dick. But this is not what the paragraph says. What actually entices the hunter is Moby Dick's "mildness of repose," his "quietude," the "serene tranquillities of the tropical sea" which adorn his progress. I have italicized the key phrase: some of those who have seen Moby Dick have been *"namelessly transported and allured by all that serenity,"* and as a consequence *"had ventured to assail it"*—assail, that is, if the paragraph means what it says, not so much the White Whale himself, but rather the deific *serenity* he exhibits.

Such a reading throws a new and final light on Captain Ahab's motivations. He has himself used the word *allure* in connection with Moby Dick. Captain Boomer of the *Samuel Enderby* asked Ahab if he did not think Moby Dick was best let alone. "He is," the *Pequod's* Captain brusquely responded. "But he will still be hunted, for all that. What is best let alone, that accursed thing is not always what least *allures*. He's all a magnet!" (100: *368*; italics mine). Ishmael has already suggested that hate-filled Ahab is *driven toward* a Moby Dick who "heaped" him; Ahab's magnet-metaphor suggests instead that he has been *drawn to* a Moby Dick who "allured" him. If this is the case, then neither the loss of his leg nor the subsequent groin-injury is, after all, the primary cause of Ahab's monomaniacal quest. Before Ahab was dismembered by *violent* Moby Dick, he must have been seduced by *serene* Moby Dick. Natural serenity, not natural power, is therefore the bedrock issue of the entire novel. Such a reading clarifies the rather puzzling symbolism of the beckoning spirit-spout which, for weeks on end, is glimpsed on moonlit nights floating in the silver distances beyond the *Pequod's* prow. Ishmael speculates that this "flitting attendance of the one still and solitary jet [may have] gradually worked upon Ahab," so that "he was now prepared to connect the ideas of mildness and repose with the first sight of the particular whale he pursued" (59: *236–37*)—a prediction confirmed by the event. Ahab, though Ishmael does not say so, is obviously among the unspecified "some" who have been "namelessly transported and allured" by the great White Whale's overawing serenity—a serenity for which the spirit-spout is visible correlate.

The consequence of such a line of argument is an unexpected in-version of the fundamental dynamic of *Moby-Dick*. Ahab claims that in attacking the White Whale he is attacking the malign. But in assailing the serenity of Moby Dick he is really attacking the *benign*, since it is impossible to conceive of the natural tranquillity and god-like quietude which the whale exhibits in these epiphanal paragraphs as other than good. A malign tranquillity is a contradic-tion in terms.[3] Thus we come to the final puzzle of the novel: why does Ahab disturb the benign, violate the peaceable, strike out at the good? Ishmael gives us no answer. His phrasing simply establishes the causal connection between benignity and assault. Melville, of course, returned to the problem in *Billy Budd*. Claggart, too, is "namelessly transported and allured"—in this instance, by Billy's goodness. His unprovoked attack on serene Billy is as intensely per-sonal as Ahab's first, jack-knife assault on Moby Dick. Melville suggests that Claggart's viciousness is the consequence of "natural depravity," but this is simply to name the phenomenon, not to explain it. An explanation, however, may be at hand. To be human is to be aware, and to be aware is to lack serenity. The serenity of nature thus becomes an affront to our condition, the quietude of the world a mockery of our estate. In this situation, the overwhelming impulse is to reach out and mark nature with our pain, impress on the vastness of the natural world the sign of our suffering. Technological man possesses the means to do this—and *Moby-Dick*, with its emphasis on rigging and sail and block and tackle, its attention to the physical manipulation of vast masses of material, its concentration on processing and manufacture, is a pervasively technological book. But one need not go to technology to study the "nameless" impulse which moves both Claggart and Ahab. All of us have, if only occasionally, contemplated nature in its quietude. We have, perhaps, come upon a serene alpine lake in that dusky and windless hour just after sunset, gazing for a moment at the way shoreline and mountain and evening cloud are reflected in the water's placidly flawless surface. And we know our first, our immediate impulse. It is to stoop, pick up a pebble, and idly toss it into the center of "all that serenity." It is that universal impulse, probably forever nameless, which lies at the heart of Captain Ahab, and of *Moby-Dick*.

Before Moby Dick becomes aware of our presence and the Three Days' Chase begins, we can profitably use these moments of epiphanal stasis to make some essential distinctions. Most explanations of the meaning of the White Whale have been debilitated by the erection of false alternatives. Moby Dick, the critics suggest, is evil, *or* Moby Dick is good. But it does great injustice to the subtlety of Melville's creative imagination to cast the terminal issues of the novel in such a reductionist idiom. A more suggestive approach is to examine the battle with Moby Dick in terms of the categories which inform Ahab's quarter-deck speech, which finally separate Ishmael from Ahab, and which shape the epistemological mainstream of the book—the distinction between *object* and *event*. The last three chapters present the White Whale in two simultaneous guises. On the one hand, Moby Dick is the whale-as-noumenon. On the other hand, Moby Dick is the whale-as-process. Since he is both things at once, he represents the coalescence of the ontologically dichotomized: Moby Dick is a sort of Behaving Pyramid.

Because of the immense power of Melville's narrative gift, of the two aspects of Moby Dick it is the pyramidism which has generally been neglected. Understandably, we find what Moby Dick does much more compelling than what he is. But the pyramidism is there, and must be attended to: Moby Dick has a "high, pyramidical white hump" (41: *159*)—and we have already examined Melville's persistent connection of the Sperm Whale's hump with the pyramid-figure (56: *230–31*; 65: *255*; 79: *292*), as well as the constellation of meanings associated with the pyramid in Stubb's "Queen Mab" dream (31: *115–16*) and in the extracetological evidence. In Stubb's dream the pyramid suggested artifactuality. In the White Whale himself the pyramid suggests the presence of intelligence, perhaps of intention, the possibility of a teleological substrate. But careful discriminations are necessary. The astonishing geometricity of the snow-flake crystal, the aerodynamic elegance of the hawk's wing, hint at purpose without themselves being purposeful. Snow-flakes do not intend, and neither do wings. So with Moby Dick: the hint of purpose which his pyramidism gives us must not incautiously be converted into purposefulness. The Teleological Whale is not *necessarily* an Intending Whale. Moreover, the arguments which apply to the whale-as-object apply also to the whale-as-event. Events in nature—including behavioral events—may exhibit the same teleological substrate, the same apparent thrust toward a final cause. But if nature is able to *be* intelligently without being intelligent, she is also able to *act* intelligently without being intelligent—a pair of propositions which, while forever beyond the ken of outraged Ahab, have achieved the force of the self-evident in the age of molecular biology and the Double Helix. This, then, is the purpose of the reiterative pyramidism of *Moby-Dick* in general and of the White Whale in particular: it is intended to prevent a facile resolution of the issues of the Three Days' Chase in simplistically anthropomorphic and mentalistic terms.

Such discriminations are necessary because one must distinguish between Presumptive Moby Dick and Veritable Moby Dick, between the pre-epiphanal "murderous monster" and the post-epiphan-

al "grand god." Presumptive Moby Dick is developed most exten-
sively in Chapter 45, appropriately entitled "The Affidavit." Ishmael
is, he tells us, deeply concerned with "establishing in all respects the
reasonableness of the whole story of the White Whale, more especially the catastrophe" (45: *177*). What he wishes the reader to
accept as "reasonable" at this—be it noted—*early* point in *Moby-Dick*
is the historical possibility of a Presumptive White Whale of the
Richard III variety, anthropomorphic and mentalistic, exhibiting
cool intelligence and prepensive malice. The skeptical reader must
be brought to believe that the Sperm Whale—any Sperm Whale—
"is in some cases sufficiently powerful, knowing, and judiciously
malicious, as with direct aforethought to stave in, utterly destroy,
and sink a large ship; and what is more, the Sperm Whale *has* done
it" (45: *178*). It is the element of *calculation* in these attacks which
sets the behavior of *Physeter catodon* apart from the impulsive
charge of the lion or the reflexive lurch of the shark: ". . . it is very
often observed that, if the sperm whale, once struck, is allowed time
to rally, he then acts, not so often with blind rage, as with *wilful,
deliberate designs of destruction*" (45: *181*; italics mine). Ishmael
stresses that the Sperm Whale does not merely respond to immediate
assault; he is quite capable of prosecuting an intelligently sustained
offensive of his own which turns pursuers into pursued. "In more
than one instance, he has been known, not only to chase the assailing
boats back to their ships, but to pursue the ship itself, and long withstand all the lances hurled at him from its decks" (45: *181*). Indeed,
the Presumptive Leviathan of "The Affidavit" exhibits that behavior
most terrifying in any wild beast, the capacity and the inclination to
initiate hostilities. Ishmael repeats the story of one Commodore
"J——" who was stopped while sailing from Oahu to Valparaiso
"by a portly sperm whale, that begged a few moments' confidential
business with him. That business consisted in fetching the Commodore's craft such a thwack, that with all his pumps going he made
straight for the nearest port to heave down and repair" (45: *179*).
Captain Boomer of the *Samuel Enderby* has observed the same
capacity for calculated initiative in Moby Dick himself. When his
crew gave chase to a pod of "four or five" whales and succeeded in
fastening to one, Moby Dick intervened even though he himself was
not under attack. "Presently up breaches from the bottom of the

sea a bouncing great whale, with a milky-white head and hump, all crows' feet and wrinkles. ... Well, this old great-grandfather ... runs all afoam into the pod, and goes to snapping furiously at my fast-line" (100: *365*). It is this presumptive version of Moby Dick, Leviathan conceived of as "some unknown but still reasoning thing" (36: *144*), which makes it possible for "some" of the *Pequod's* crew—including, obviously, Ishmael—to fear that the spirit-spout encountered on the Carrol Ground is really Moby Dick's, calculatedly leading the *Pequod* on "in order that the monster might turn round upon us, and rend us at last in the remotest and most savage seas" (51: *201*).

The important point about Presumptive Leviathan, the evidently intelligent and apparently calculating whale of "The Affidavit," is that he is *not* a "story-book" or "made-up" whale, is *not* the purely literary and imaginative product of mythopoeic artifice in the sense that Beowulf's Grendel is. Quite the opposite. He is fact, not fiction. For his Presumptive Whale Melville went, not to his imagination, but to history. At just about the time that the young ex-schoolmaster began his brief and sporadic whaling career, shipping successively as common seaman aboard the *Acushnet*, the *Lucy Ann*, and the *Charles and Henry* (1841–43), a real whale, a true albino and a genuine rogue, achieved sufficient notoriety in the Pacific fisheries so that Jeremiah N. Reynolds wrote him up under the title, "Mocha Dick: or the White Whale of the Pacific," and published the article in the May, 1839, issue of *Knickerbocker Magazine*. It is not certain that Melville ever saw this article. But it is as certain as such things can ever be that Melville could not spend the better part of three years aboard various whalers during the peak of Mocha Dick's fame and not hear enough about him to germinate half-a-dozen *Moby-Dicks*.[4]

If the historical Mocha Dick provided the seed, another—and unnamed—historical whale provided the seed-ground. On 20 November, 1820, the Nantucket whaling-ship *Essex*, Captain George Pollard, was twice struck by a large Sperm Whale and sunk. The first mate, Owen Chase, in 1821 published the *Narrative of the Most Extraordinary and Distressing Shipwreck of the Whale-Ship Essex*, *of Nantucket; Which Was Attacked and Finally Destroyed by a Large Spermaceti-Whale.*[5] Melville did not acquire his own copy of Chase's story until April of 1851 when his father-in-law, Lemuel Shaw, gave him a copy which he had picked up during a visit to Nantucket. But Melville did not need a copy to write *Moby-Dick.* In 1841, aboard the *Acushnet*, the crew had told him the story, and when the *Acushnet* spoke a whaler with Chase's son on board, Melville talked with him, and briefly borrowed his copy of his father's narrative.

As a consequence, the original *Narrative* is only important in *Moby-Dick* for an extended footnote, probably added when the manuscript was almost finished, appended to "The Affidavit" and reproducing four quotations from Owen Chase:

> The following [says Ishmael] are extracts from Chase's narrative: "Every fact seemed to warrant me in concluding that it was anything but chance which directed [the whale's] operations; he made two several attacks upon the ship, at a short interval between them, both of which, according to their direction, were calculated to do us the most injury, by being made ahead, and thereby combining the speed of the two objects for the shock; to effect which, the exact manœuvres which he made were necessary. His aspect was most horrible, and such as indicated resentment and fury. He came directly from the shoal which we had just before entered, and in which we had struck three of his companions, as if fired with revenge for their sufferings." Again: "At all events, the whole circumstances taken together, all happening before my own eyes, and producing, at the time, impressions in my mind of decided, calculating mischief, on the part of the whale (many of which impressions I cannot now recall), induce me to be satisfied that I am correct in my opinion."
>
> Here [continues Ishmael] are his reflections some time after quitting the ship, during a black night in an open boat, when almost despairing of reaching any hospitable shore. "The dark ocean and swelling waters were nothing; the fears of being swallowed up by some dreadful tempest...seemed scarcely entitled to a moment's thought; the dismal looking wreck, and *the horrid aspect and revenge of the whale*, wholly engrossed my reflections, until day again made its appearance."
>
> In another place...he speaks of *"the mysterious and mortal attack of the animal."* (45: *179n*)

It seems reasonable to assume that the four quotations which Ishmael here reproduces represent those points which arrested Melville's attention in the sailor yarns which he heard on the *Acushnet*, which caught his eye in his probably hasty reading of Chase's son's copy of the *Narrative*, and which lodged in his mind through the succeeding decade. If this is the case, then the footnote in "The Affidavit" is important because it throws light on the meaning of *Moby-Dick* in just the way that Holinshed's *Chronicles* help one to arrive at an estimate of what Shakespeare was about in his history plays. Melville is unmistakably intent—*at this point in Moby-Dick*—upon gathering every shred of evidence he can for a Presumptive Whale which is unequivocally an "unknown but still reasoning thing." He wants to push to the very limits of credibility the hypothesis that Leviathan is calculatingly and prepensively malign. He wants, in short, to document and authenticate the Ahabian whale. In this he succeeds, even though the authentication is couched in the ambiguous, endlessly qualified idiom habitual to Ishmael. Chase's whale is all that Ahab could desire as justification for his rage and vengeance. The whale that sunk the *Essex* was indubitably a "murderous monster."[6]

The literal historicity of the Ahabian whale is important because it placed Melville—by the time that *Moby-Dick* was one-third written—in that creative posture which he found most congenial: where he had historical sources on which to draw for inspiration and validation. Lewis Mumford has remarked that "Like DeFoe, Melville was closely chained to the document, the fact, the experience," an aspect of his creative sensibility which irritated at least one contemporary reviewer: *Moby-Dick*, he complained, was largely a business of "barefaced pillage and extract."[7] Howard P. Vincent has documented the extent of the pillage and the scope of the extraction in *The Trying-Out of Moby-Dick* and in the Explanatory Notes to the Hendricks House edition of the novel.[8] The young schoolmaster who claimed that he had swum through libraries was speaking for an author who had in fact imperturbably fed Thomas Beale's *The Natural History of the Sperm Whale*, Frederick Bennett's *Narrative of a Whaling Voyage*, J. Ross Browne's *Etchings of a Whaling Cruise*, Henry T. Cheever's *The Whale and His Captors*, and William Scoresby's *An Account of the Arctic Regions*[9] into the try-works of his creative imagination, shamelessly appropriating as his own whatever fritters of fact promised to be of use. *Moby-Dick*, it is safe to assert, would never have been written if Melville had not had such non-fictional sources on his desk or in his memory. He did not simply use such documents. Rather, he tended to follow their factual substrate, if not slavishly, then the next thing to it. The superb story, *Benito Cereno*, is based almost literally, except for tonal heightening and dramatic reformulation, on Captain Amasa Delano's *Narrative of Voyages and Travels in the Northern and Southern Hemispheres* (Boston, 1817). Similarly, while constructing the portrait of the Indian-hater, Colonel Moredock, in *The Confidence-Man: His Masquerade*, Melville drew in the most detailed and literal way upon James Hall's *Sketches of History, Life, and Manners, in the West* (Philadelphia, 1835).[10] Such considerations establish a single point which is crucial for an understanding of the Three Days' Chase in *Moby-Dick*. The normal procedure was for Melville to hew tightly to the salient topography and essential features of his historical sources. This was his habitual method of work. Substantive alterations are the exception rather than the rule. It follows that we should expect the White Whale to conform in nearly all significant respects to the Presumptive Leviathan, based on Mocha Dick and the *Essex* whale, which Ishmael is at pains to develop in the first third of the novel. If Moby Dick is in any way *not* Chase's whale and Reynolds' whale, then Ishmael's departures from the available sources must be accounted for. The meaning of the Three Days' Chase, in short, may lie not so much in what Melville puts in, but rather in what he *leaves out*.

If one strips away the dramatic and rhetorical incrustations, reducing the Three Days' Chase to essential *action*, one is immediately struck with the minimal and in many respects equivocal nature of the White Whale's actual behavior. On the first day, as the three boats noiselessly approach, Moby Dick, at last detecting their presence, dives into the depths only immediately to rise again with "wonderful celerity." Peering over the side, Ahab sees him first as a "white living spot no bigger than a white weasel," a spot which grows until the "glittering mouth" of the great White Whale yawns directly beneath him. He adroitly whirls the boat about to escape but, "with that malicious intelligence ascribed to him," Moby Dick instantly alters his underwater posture and takes the entire bow of the boat in his jaws, shaking "the slight cedar as a mildly cruel cat her mouse." For several moments the whale "dallie[s] with the doomed craft in this devilish way," and then bites the boat in two, throwing Ahab "flat-faced upon the sea." Then, so that he can see all about him, Moby Dick "pitch-poles," rising from the water in a vertical position and slowly revolving like a spindle. Apparently maddened by the sight of the splintered halves of the boat, he executes a "planetarily swift" and rapidly contracting circle whose center gradually becomes Ahab's bobbing head. But at the penultimate moment the *Pequod* comes between Ahab and the whale, and contact is broken (133: *448–50*). It is this rather meager handful of evolutions which comprises the entirety of the first day's encounter. When the chapter is reduced to action, it is apparent that none of Moby Dick's actual behaviors is sufficiently decisive to suggest real intelligence. Despite Ishmael's anthropomorphic stress on the "devilish" and "crafty" movements of the whale, everything he does is well within the response-capacity of any highly-developed animal. All that the first battle establishes is that Moby Dick is not stupid—but no animal, and certainly no wild animal, is stupid.

If Moby Dick's behavior on the first day lacks sustained focus and resolutely prosecuted direction, these elements are even less apparent in the second day's encounter. After a night of "pertinacious pursuit," at daybreak and less than a mile ahead, Moby Dick announces his presence by "breaching." "Rising with his utmost velocity from the furthest depths, the Sperm Whale thus booms his entire bulk into the pure element of air, and piling up a mountain of dazzling foam, shows his place to the distance of seven miles and more." In some cases, Ishmael asserts, breaching may be taken as the whale's "act of defiance" (134: *455*). This is a perfectly acceptable proposition, just so long as we do not unthinkingly convert an act of defiance into an act of intelligence. Many animals are capable of defiance, but we do not usually regard such behavior as intelligent, and neither should we do so, without more warrant than Ishmael chooses to supply, in the case of Moby Dick. In any case, having so breached, Moby Dick then becomes, on this second day, the "first assailant, . . . rushing among the boats with open jaws, and a lashing tail, offer[ing] appalling battle on every side; and heedless of the irons darted at him from every boat, seemed only intent on annihilating each separate plank of which those boats were made." If Melville—or Ishmael—were intent upon demonstrating intelligence or malignity in the White Whale, this handling of the event-continuum represents another missed opportunity. Moby Dick does not *choose* a single boat, does not *decide* upon an adversary, does not *follow* any apparent plan of action. Rather, he engages, like the veritable animal he is, in unfocused "appalling battle" randomly prosecuted "on every side." So undirected are his maneuvers, so "untraceable" his evolutions, that when three irons are planted in him, the lines become immediately "crossed and recrossed, and in a thousand ways entangled." As a consequence, two of the boats are destroyed in an unmistakably accidental and random way: "That instant, the White Whale made a sudden rush . . . ; by so doing, irresistibly dragged the more involved boats of Stubb and Flask towards his flukes; dashed them together like two rolling husks on a surf-beaten beach, and then, diving down into the sea, disappeared." But only for a moment. Rising again with great speed, Moby Dick shoots perpendicularly under the remaining boat— Ahab's—and "dash[ing] his broad forehead against its bottom, . . . sent it, turning over and over, into the air; till it fell again—gunwale downwards—and Ahab and his men struggled out from under it, like seals from a sea-side cave" (134: *456–57*). The destruction of Ahab's boat is clearly different from the destruction of Stubb's and Flask's. The White Whale—to phrase the idea anthropomorphically —"intends" it. But the capacity to injure an enemy, and to execute the stark maneuvers requisite to such a goal, is not an argument for intelligence—else the squid and the shark are intelligent. Moby Dick's lunge at Ahab's boat is no more intelligent—and no less—than the bovine lunge of an exasperated bull.

Such an analysis of the first and second day's battle with the White Whale suggests that the intending and prepensive whale of the first third of the book, the Presumptive Leviathan of "The Affidavit," has now been abandoned by both Melville and Ishmael. The White

Whale of the first two days is an animal and only an animal, indistinguishable in his essential vulnerability and his circumscribed capacity for response from all the other whales which Ishmael has encountered in the textual continuum subsequent to his postulation of Presumptive Leviathan. Such a reading is reinforced by the only element of Moby Dick's behavior which *is* consistent, sustained, and focused—his steady progress, over the course of three days and two nights, in a leeward direction. When, on the first day, the *Pequod* sails between Moby Dick and the swimming Ahab, the whale makes no slightest effort to circumvent this ineffectual stratagem. Rather, he abruptly and immediately resumes the leeward course which he was pursuing when first sighted. His behavior suggests that the encounter with the *Pequod* was, from his cachalotic point of view, not a confrontation or a battle, but only an unwelcome *interruption* of some secret and compellingly urgent Leviathanic business that he already had in hand. So swift is his progress to leeward that even with double-banked oars he cannot again be approached. "But the added power of the boat did not equal the added power of the whale, for he seemed to have treble-banked his every fin; swimming with a velocity which plainly showed, that . . . the chase would prove an indefinitely prolonged, if not a hopeless one." Only the *Pequod* herself, "stacking her canvas high up, and sideways out-stretching it with stun-sails, like the double-jointed wings of an albatross" (133: *451*), is able to keep up with Moby Dick's swift and undeviating progress downwind. If the whale had chosen to swim to windward, neither the *Pequod* nor her boats would ever have come near him again.

This stress on Moby Dick's tenacious prosecution of his leeward journey might be taken as a mere element of verisimilitude were it not for the fact that Ishmael introduces the second day's chase by discussing the phenomenon at length—and by ending the discussion with a typically shrouded sentence of hinting significance:

> Here be it said, that this pertinacious pursuit of one particular whale, continued through day into night, and through night into day, is a thing by no means unprecedented in the South sea fishery. For such is the wonderful skill, prescience of experience, and invincible confidence acquired by some . . . Nantucket commanders;

that from the simple observation of a whale when last descried, they will, under certain given circumstances, pretty accurately foretell both the direction in which he will continue to swim for a time, while out of sight, as well as his probable rate of progression during that period.... So that to this hunter's wondrous skill, the proverbial evanescence of a thing writ in water, a wake, is to all desired purposes well nigh as reliable as the steadfast land. And as the mighty iron Leviathan of the modern railway is so familiarly known in its every pace, that, with watches in their hands, men time his rate as doctors that of a baby's pulse; ... even so, almost, there are occasions when these Nantucketers time that other Leviathan of the deep, according to the observed humor of his speed; and say to themselves, so many hours hence this whale will have gone two hundred miles, will have about reached this or that degree of latitude or longitude.... *Inferable from these statements, are many collateral subtle matters touching the chase of whales.* (134: *453–54*; italics mine)

The tantalizing opacity of the closing sentence of this otherwise crystalline specimen of Ishmael's expository skill is yet another instance of the taste he shares with cryptic Elijah for "ambiguous, half-hinting, half-revealing, shrouded ... talk" (19: *88*). In the very first chapter of *Moby-Dick*, while discussing man's eternal fascination with water, Ishmael concluded that "Surely all this is not without meaning" (1: *14*)—and then failed to specify what "meaning" he had in mind. Similarly, in his contemplation of the cenotaphs of the Whaleman's Chapel, and while cataloguing the myths and proverbs with which men have surrounded the fact of death, he again assured us that "All these things are not without their meanings" (7: *41*)—and again refused to supply the "meanings" he himself had postulated. In both cases Ishmael is telling the reader in the most unequivocal way that his story *does mean*, and that the meanings are accessible—but the reader must in some important instances discover them for himself. The oblique sentence I have italicized performs the same function, and at an especially crucial point in the narrative. When Ishmael off-handedly asserts that "inferable" from the locomotive predictability of migrating Leviathan are "many collateral subtle matters touching the chase of whales," he is covertly telling us that the leeward progress of Moby Dick is not a mere inexplicable quirk of cetacean behavior, but an important fact, the significance of which the reader may—or may not—unearth for himself.

This meaning, one may suggest, lies in the gradual shift from the Presumptive Whale of the first third of *Moby-Dick* to the Necessitarian Whale of the last third. It was in Chapter 85, "The Fountain," while describing Leviathan's inexorable need to remain on the surface of the water until his blood is fully oxygenated—the physiological imperative termed *"having his spoutings out"*—that Ishmael asserted that the great whale, like all else in nature, was subject to "the great necessities" (85: *311*). Moby Dick's migration, which the best efforts of Ahab cannot interrupt, stands as manifestation of such ineluctable necessity. The White Whale may be a "grand god," but he is also a necessitarian god, bound to the infinitely complex web of natural process. Ishmael anticipates these meanings when, in Chapter 44, "The Chart," he explains that while "it might seem an absurdly hopeless task [for Ahab] thus to seek out one solitary creature in the unhooped oceans of this planet," such an objective is actually well within the realm of possibility. For whales, "when making a passage from one feeding-ground to another," swim "with such undeviating exactitude, that no ship ever sailed her course, by any chart, with one tithe of such marvellous precision." So true is this that Ishmael is able to postulate a collation of all the logs of the entire whaling fleet during a single season which would prove beyond question that "the migrations of the sperm whale . . . correspond in invariability to those of the herring-shoals or the flights of swallows" (44: *171–72*). In short, Leviathan is impelled by inexorable primal impulse, and moves as he moves because he must.

Thus, for the last time in *Moby-Dick*, and in an ultimately definitive way, cetological fact becomes philosophical fact. To the extent that Moby Dick becomes Necessitarian Leviathan, to precisely that extent he ceases to be the Presumptive Leviathan of "The Affidavit." That which is instinctual cannot be malicious. That which is compulsive cannot be prepensive. One must view Moby Dick's progress, deifically magnificent though it is, as one views the movement of herring-shoals and the flights of swallows. Such vibrations of the unalterable warp of the natural world[11] are neither evil, nor are they good. They are, baldly, events. They are, simply, beautiful. They are, inescapably, process. Moby Dick's leeward journey is therefore a final, epiphanal manifestation of that which Ishmael earlier called "the general stolidity discernible in the whole visible world; which while pauselessly active in uncounted modes, still eternally holds its peace, and ignores you, though you dig foundations for cathedrals" (107: *388*). For three successive days the White Whale displays this stolidity, steadily attempting to hold his peace, to maintain his course, to pursue the inscrutable leviathanic processes which define his being. "So, so," exclaims Ahab at the end of the first day's fight,"I see him! there! there! going to leeward still; what a leaping spout!" As night falls, he queries the mast-head: "How heading when last seen?" Comes the reply from aloft: "As before, sir,—straight to leeward" (133: *451, 452*). The same stress on overriding process characterizes the termination of the second day's battle: "But soon, as if satisfied that his work for that time was done, [Moby Dick] pushed his pleated forehead through the ocean, and trailing after him the intertangled lines, continued his leeward way at a traveller's methodic pace" (134: *457*).

It is, however, his behavior on the third day, *before* the final catastrophe, which suggests most strongly that the events which Ahab egotistically and anthropomorphically regards as "battles" with an "enemy" are in fact mere causal *interpositions* in the inexorable activity of pyramidically unaware process. As on the second day, Moby Dick makes a randomly rushing, reflexive attack on all three boats, damaging the two which the mates command, but leaving Ahab's virtually intact (135: *464*). The traditional locutions which Ishmael employs to describe this encounter may make it seem a battle, but it is not. It is essentially a collision, a transitory causal concatenation. Like the first two encounters, it falls far short of the sustained, focused, and sequential attack which might, however equivocally, suggest intelligence or malice. Moreover, Ishmael makes it clear that from Moby Dick's cetacean point of view the "attack" is no more than a momentary irritant, a minute blemish in the otherwise flawless continuum of imperturbable causation and necessitarian imperative. The collision past, the random rush exhausted, the great whale's migration is instantly resumed:

... for ... as if the particular place of the last encounter had been *but a stage* in his leeward voyage, Moby Dick was now again steadily swimming forward. ... He seemed swimming with his utmost velocity, and now only intent upon pursuing his own straight path in the sea. (135: *465*; italics mine)

Starbuck provides the terminal commentary on this steady leewarding, employing the anthropomorphic locutions one would expect from a forthright sailor. "Oh! Ahab," he cries, "not too late is it, even now, the third day, to desist. See! Moby Dick seeks thee not. It is thou, thou, that madly seekest him!" Newton Arvin has extended Starbuck's point while retaining Starbuck's simplistic conceptual bases: "Moby Dick appears never to have sought these encounters himself," Arvin remarks, "and to have dealt out ruin only when provoked by his pursuers. Demoniac as he can be when hunted and harpooned, he himself seems rather to evade than to seek these meetings."[12] The point is right, but the paradigm is wrong. To suggest that Moby Dick is capable of deliberate "evasion," prepensive "seeking," or "demoniac" attack is to obscure the meaning of the White Whale's leeward voyage, to ignore the ontological pyramidism of which he is the central symbol, and to propose as the final truth of *Moby-Dick* an only slightly modified version of the Ahabian whale and the Presumptive Leviathan of "The Affidavit."

This analysis, however, closes out the alternatives at a point in the narrative continuum where Ishmael chooses to keep them open. As Moby Dick swims rapidly away, the two staved boats are hoisted to the side of the *Pequod*, and Ahab, hoisting sail in his own boat and passing close to the ship, orders Starbuck to turn it about and follow at a careful distance. Borne to leeward by both sail and oar, Ahab rapidly approaches the whale, which appears to falter for the first time. Ishmael offers alternative explanations for this development, keeping alive to the penultimate moment, as it were, both Necessitarian Leviathan and Presumptive Leviathan. On the one hand, Moby Dick may simply be "fagged by the three days' running chase, and the resistance to his swimming in the knotted hamper he bore." On the other hand, the abatement of the whale's speed might be due to "some latent deceitfulness and malice in him" (135: *465*). The reader is thus still confronted with a choice, and with a problem of interpretation. It does not, however, accord well with the Ahabian version of the White Whale that Moby Dick seems "strangely oblivious . . . as the whale sometimes will" to the advance of Ahab's boat. It is this odd oblivion to obvious danger which permits Ahab to get "fairly within the smoky mountain mist" of the fish's spout where, "with body arched back, and both arms lengthwise high-lifted to the poise, he darted his fierce iron, and his far fiercer curse into the hated whale." Moby Dick's convulsive reaction to this assault throws Ishmael from the boat but, "afloat and swimming," he is able to see the remainder of Ahab's crew desperately dragging the boat, by means of the line, once again up alongside the whale. It is at this moment that the line parts, and Moby Dick begins that famous maneuver toward which the whole novel has tended:

> Hearing the tremendous rush of the sea-crashing boat, the whale wheeled round to present his blank forehead at bay; but in that evolution, catching sight of the nearing black hull of the ship; seemingly seeing in it the source of all his persecutions; bethinking it—it may be—a larger and nobler foe; of a sudden, he bore down upon its advancing prow, smiting his jaws amid fiery showers of foam. (135: 466–67)

Two points need to be made. First, Ishmael here continues to employ the equivocal idiom of such chapters as "The Affidavit," "Moby Dick," and "The Whiteness of the Whale." Moby Dick *seemingly* sees the *Pequod* as the source of his persecutions; he *may* think it a larger and nobler antagonist. The elimination of these qualifications would constitute a validation of the reality of Presumptive Leviathan—but Ishmael refuses to resolve the novel in this way. To the very end, he continues to offer the reader a possible way of understanding his story, and then in the same sentence he all but withdraws that possibility.

Second, the final maneuver of the White Whale displays that same reflexive character which has defined the "battles" of all three days of the chase. Wheeling about to present his forehead to the pursuing boat, Moby Dick accidentally *catches sight* of the approaching *Pequod*; he *suddenly* turns from boat to ship. Moreover, although his attack on the *Pequod* represents the supreme example of those "living acts" and "undoubted deeds" in the processes of the natural world which persuade Ahab that there is "some unknown but still reasoning thing" behind the mask of appearances (36: *144*), this final opportunity to demonstrate the presence of such inscrutable and malicious intelligence goes unexploited. The attack, the maneuver itself, is bereft of dramatic or imaginative development, exhibiting that raw linearity which one associates with the abrupt out-thrusting of a fist. The "attack" on the *Pequod* is little more than a causal translation from Point A to Point B, devoid of any suggestion of what Ishmael calls "direct aforethought" (45: *178*). It is true that the whale's behavior is not quite the instance of almost geometrical reflexiveness that I have suggested here. Starbuck engages in evasive maneuvers, twice altering course with the command to "up helm!"—and Moby Dick responds to these stratagems. "Nay, nay!" Starbuck exclaims in despair, "... He turns to meet us!" (135: *467*). But this dramatically minimal trace of calculating responsiveness in the White Whale only emphasizes the fact that Melville is *not* concerned with establishing the verity of either Presumptive Leviathan or the Ahabian whale.

One might argue, of course, that Melville's central problem in this closing scene is one of credibility, and that to have endowed the White Whale's behavior with a greater degree of intelligent calculation would have been to convert subtle hints into bald facts, destroying the reader's suspension of disbelief at the most crucial point. But such an argument overlooks the fact that Melville had ample historical precedent for making Moby Dick a creature of unmistakable intelligence and malign intent. That precedent, of course, is the behavior of the *Essex* whale. The excerpts from Chase's *Narrative* which Ishmael reproduces provide all the warrant necessary for the authentication of Presumptive Leviathan:

> Every fact [says Chase] seemed to warrant me in concluding that it was anything but chance which directed [the *Essex* whale's] operations; he made two several attacks upon the ship, at a short interval between them, both of which, according to their direction, were calculated to do us the most injury, by being made ahead, and thereby combining the speed of the two objects for the shock; to effect which, the exact manœuvres which he made were necessary. (45: *179n*)

Moby Dick does *not* act in this way. He makes only one attack on the *Pequod*, even though Melville must have been aware that the repetition of such behavior would do more than anything else to convert the possibly accidental into the certainly intentional. Neither does he engage in any of the elaborate evolutions which characterized the behavior of Chase's whale. In order to strike the *Essex* twice from a head-on position, Chase's whale would have had to get ahead of the ship, come at it, swing about after the first blow, swim rapidly ahead a second time, swing about once again and—all the while integrating his course and speed with the ship's course and speed—*do a second time exactly what he did the first*. That the *Essex* whale did just this is confirmed by Chase's stress on the "calculated" nature of his "two several attacks," and the "exact" character of the maneuvers made to accomplish them. Melville's refusal to exploit the dramatic potential of these facts must therefore be understood as an unequivocal rejection of the Ahabian whale and the Ahabian thesis concerning the external world. Ahab's "unknown but still reasoning thing" *fails to appear* in the epiphanally final pages of *Moby-Dick*.

The picture is, however, not quite as tidy as my analysis suggests. Residual dramatic details drawn from Ahabian Leviathan—and perhaps from Chase's overwrought imagination—surface here and there. The clearest instance is Moby Dick's *appearance* as he rushes down upon the *Pequod*. Chase had reported that the "aspect" of the *Essex* whale "was most horrible, and such as indicated resentment and fury," a fact which he found so terrible that it blotted out any subsequent sense of the precariousness of his own situation in a tiny boat on the dark ocean: ". . . the dismal looking wreck, and the *horrid aspect and revenge of the whale*, wholly engrossed my reflections, until day again made its appearance" (45: *179n*). These details reappear in Ishmael's description of Moby Dick attacking with "Retribution, swift vengeance, eternal malice . . . in his whole aspect" (135: *468*). This is unmistakably the Ahabian whale, a prepensive Leviathan both aware and intending. But we may take this dramatic detail as nothing more than vestigial phrasing from a now-rejected conception of the whale. We are, indeed, at liberty *not to believe* that Moby Dick—or the *Essex* whale for that matter—could possibly have displayed an "aspect" suggesting either rage or vengeance. For Ishmael has repeatedly made a point, both factual and philosophical, of the *blankness*, the expressionlessness, which is perhaps the most arresting element of the Sperm Whale's appearance:

> But in the great Sperm Whale, this high and mighty god-like dignity inherent in the brow is so immensely amplified, that gazing on it, in that full front view, you feel the Deity and the dread powers more forcibly than in beholding any other object in living nature. For you see no one point precisely; not one distinct feature is revealed; no nose, eyes, ears, or mouth; no face; he has none, proper; nothing but that one broad firmament of a forehead, pleated with riddles; dumbly lowering with the doom of boats, and ships, and men. (79: *292*)

Moby Dick's "aspect," in short, conveys a pyramidical sense of the deity and power of the natural world—and that, even in battle, is all it *can* convey.

But if the White Whale's attack on the *Pequod* is not intentional in the Ahabian sense, what then is it? The answer may lie buried in Chapter 74, "The Sperm Whale's Head—Contrasted View," which contains another—and for our purposes final—instance of Ishmael's taste for underground sentences of easily-missed significance. He remarks that the Sperm Whale's vision is radically split: his eyes are at each side of the massive battering-ram, low down and yards back from the front, and thus "effectually divided . . . by many cubic feet of solid head." The consequence is an absolute frontal vulnerability which Ishmael asks us to try to imagine occurring in man: "If your bitterest foe were walking straight towards you, with dagger uplifted in broad day, you would not be able to see him." It is this, Ishmael thinks, which accounts for "the extraordinary vacillations of movement displayed by some whales when beset by three or four boats; . . . timidity and liability to queer frights . . . [are] common to such whales." And then the sentence of covert signification: "This peculiarity of the whale's eyes is a thing always to be borne in mind in the fishery; *and to be remembered by the reader in some subsequent scenes*" (74: *278–80*; italics mine). Ishmael did not write this sentence merely to fill out a paragraph; surely he had something specific in mind. The matter must probably stand forever beyond formal proof, but one is compelled to the conclusion that Ishmael wishes us to keep the whale's split vision in mind in those "subsequent scenes" devoted to the chase of Moby Dick. Afflicted with frontal blindness, the White Whale, as he turned to confront Ahab's pursuing boat, may well have gotten himself into a position where *he could not see Ahab but could see Ahab's ship*. If this is the case, then his sinking of the *Pequod* may be the product, not of inscrutable intelligence and malign intent, but simply of blind "timidity" and a tragic susceptibility to "queer frights." Surgeon Bunger of the *Samuel Enderby* suggests as much: ". . . what you take for the White Whale's malice," he tells Ahab, "is only his awkwardness. For he never means to swallow a single limb; he only thinks to terrify by feints" (100: *368*). If Bunger is right, then what Starbuck says about the loss of Ahab's leg may apply equally to the attack on the *Pequod*: Moby Dick, he told Ahab, was only a "dumb brute" that "smote thee from blindest instinct" (36: *144*). Tragic vulnerability and helpless blindness, rather than prepensive malice and intending vision, may thus be the definitive elements in the denouement of the novel.

Such a reading of the Three Days' Chase makes it clear that to ask whether the White Whale is "good" or "evil" is to ask an imprecise, essentially meaningless question. Ceaselessly active in uncounted modes, the whale—and the world that he represents—is morally neutral. But to say that the world is neither good nor evil is not to say that the world cannot be, in specific instances, good *for man*, or evil *for man*. One must simply use the terms "good" and "evil" with the caution of the man who habitually refers to certain animals as "predators" while being ironically conscious that a "predator" is nothing more than a creature who wants something that human beings also want. Taken in this subtly qualified way, one may legitimately employ the terms "good" and "evil" in connection with Leviathan. We may, for example, perceive that the whale suffers as we suffer, is bound to necessity as we are bound— with a consequent increase in our sense of identity with that inscrutable *other* which is the world. This is good for us. We may humanize vast Leviathan, perceiving that his heart beats as ours beats, that he needs warmth as we need it, that he lives in the air as we also live, so that he becomes, alien though he is, Brother Whale —and such an imaginative shaping of external fact may precipitate a sense of brotherhood with things far more mysterious and terrible than *Physeter catodon*. This, too, is good for us. Conversely, we may contemplate those aspects of Leviathan which are evil for us: his juggernaut power, his insensate ponderosity, his incredible size, the blind, indifferent urgency of his processes—though it might be argued that to perceive and, through Leviathan, imaginatively apprehend and articulate these evils is itself good.

In all these instances we are, of course, using the mind as a lamp to illuminate and give moral coloration to the cosmic house in which we live. There is nothing wrong or misleading in this creative process, and for the best of all reasons: we can do nothing else and still be human. All that is necessary is that we never forget that our perceptions are, to an undefined degree, projections of ourselves. This is the tragedy of Ahab. He forgot, or never understood, that the image he saw in the world was in part an image of himself. But Ishmael knows the meaning of Narcissus, and never forgets it. Consequently, Ishmael never—despite his Christian background and Ahab's temporary influence—really sees either the whale or the world as *antagonist*. He is part of the world, at one with it, and so cannot conceive of it as adversary. Here, perhaps, we touch on that meaning of *Moby-Dick* of most relevance to technological man in the latter half of the twentieth century. If we have debauched our air and polluted our streams it has been because, like Ahab, we have seen the world as a thing to be attacked and conquered. Like Ahab, Western Man has been tragically seduced by "all that serenity." Thanks almost entirely to Queequeg, Ishmael is able to offer us an alternative way of seeing things, is able to elevate a mere sailor's yarn to the level of what N. Scott Momaday has called a "vision quest," which he defines as a "quest after vision itself." *Moby-Dick*, at the deepest level, *is* a vision—a way of seeing things— and this may be its ultimate significance for a technological world now sick unto death.

NOTES

ALL CITATIONS to *Typee, Omoo, Mardi, Redburn, White-Jacket,* and *Pierre* are from *The Writings of Herman Melville,* ed. Harrison Hayford, Hershel Parker, and G. Thomas Tanselle (15 vols. projected: Evanston and Chicago: Northwestern Univ. Press and The Newberry Library, 1968, 1969, 1970, or 1971)—hereafter cited as "Northwestern-Newberry." All citations to *The Confidence-Man, Clarel,* and *Collected Poems* are from the variously edited volumes of the incomplete Hendricks House Edition (New York or Chicago: 1954, 1960, and 1947 respectively)—hereafter cited as "Hendricks House." Most other citations are from the "Constable Edition" of *The Works of Herman Melville,* ed. Raymond M. Weaver (16 vols.; London: 1922–24), reissued in facsimile (New York: Russell & Russell, Inc., 1963)—hereafter cited as "Constable-Russell." Finally, all citations to *Moby-Dick* are from the widely available Norton Critical Edition of the novel, ed. Harrison Hayford and Hershel Parker (New York: W. W. Norton & Co., 1967), the text of which is based essentially on the forthcoming and definitive Northwestern-Newberry edition.

CHAPTER I

1. *Herman Melville* (New York: William Sloane, 1950; Norton, 1957), p. 154.

2. Although Melville spoke in a letter to Richard Bentley (5 June 1849) of "the metaphysical ingredients (for want of a better term)" of *Moby-Dick* (Jay Leyda, ed., *The Melville Log* [New York: Harcourt, 1951], I, 306), most students have found it somewhat difficult to take these "ingredients" with entire seriousness. Charles Anderson contemptuously dismissed the "sailor metaphysics" of *Moby-Dick* in his early study (*Melville in the South Seas* [New York: Columbia Univ. Press, 1939], p. 4), Richard Chase asserts that "As a thinker, Melville was an inspired amateur" (*The American Novel and Its Tradition* [New York: Doubleday, 1957], p. 90), and more recently Luther S. Mansfield has pointed out that "Melville was not an original or systematic philosopher, and lacked the trained habits of thought for that profession. As a man of feeling and an artist, he never accepted the demands for consistency a general formulation would entail..." ("Some Patterns from Melville's 'Loom of Time,'" in Sydney J. Krause, ed., *Essays on Determinism in American Literature* [Kent, Ohio: Kent State Univ. Press, 1964], p. 20). Merrell R. Davis and Merton Sealts have both remarked on the problems of philosophical sources and influences: Sealts points out that "to distinguish the relative importance of various influences on Melville—Plato, Neoplatonism, Gnosticism, Milton, Spinoza, and Goethe, to mention several—is impossible on the basis of the available evidence" (Sealts quoted and discussed in Davis, *Melville's Mardi: A Chartless Voyage* [New Haven: Yale Univ. Press, 1952], p. 181n).

Certainly the eclectic, derivative, tatterdemalion quality of Melville's philosophical speculations is unmistakable; a search for consistency will be bootless. But this does not mean in the case of a specific work such as *Moby-Dick*, that we cannot seek for an *aesthetically* consistent rendering of certain salient philosophical ideas which may or may not, among themselves, be philosophically *in*consistent. If we further confine ourselves insofar as is possible to Ishmael and Ahab rather than Melville, the task will be greatly simplified. Most helpful, whatever line of attack one takes, is Chapter I of William Braswell's *Melville's Religious Thought* (Durham, N. C.: Duke Univ. Press, 1943), esp. pp. 14–15.

3. Northwestern-Newberry *Pierre: Or, the Ambiguities*, p. 289.

4. Ahab's fifty-foot giant, eyeless, but with a skylight in his head, of-

fers a suggestive parallel to Locke's concept, following the analogy of the *camera obscura*, of the mind as a "dark room" for which the senses are "windows." Such a concept, as M. H. Abrams points out, follows the eighteenth-century view that "the mind in perception [is] a passive receiver for images presented ready-formed from without." Abrams quotes Locke: "For, methinks, the understanding is not much unlike a closet wholly shut from light, with only some little openings left, to let in external visible resemblances, or ideas of things without: would the pictures coming into such a dark room but stay there, and lie so orderly as to be found upon occasion, it would very much resemble the understanding of a man, in reference to all objects of sight, and the ideas of them." See *The Mirror and the Lamp: Romantic Theory and the Critical Tradition* (New York: Oxford Univ. Press, 1953; Norton, 1958), p. 57.

5. Ishmael's skepticism can be found in other of Melville's characters. The narrator of *Pierre* dismisses Plato, Spinoza, and Goethe as a "guild of self-impostors," while the author-hero of the book which Pierre himself writes speaks of Spinoza and Plato as "chattering apes," and Goethe as an "inconceivable coxcomb" (pp. 208, 302). These are, however, all full-blown "idealists" and "compensationists" advancing the thesis, as Vivia has it, that "night was day, and pain only a tickle."

6. Useful here are Howard P. Vincent's "Laplandish speculations" on the meaning of the passage (*The Trying-Out of Moby-Dick* [Boston: Houghton, 1949], p. 251), as well as the notes of Vincent and Luther S. Mansfield in the Hendricks House edition of *Moby-Dick* (New York, 1952), pp. 765–66. See also the attack on the "Apostles," followers of the transcendental school, in *Pierre* (p. 267). Their ineffectuality is developed in terms of "Kant," meaning "can't" (or possibly "cant"); as Vincent and Mansfield point out, there is little reason to take this satiric passage as an attack on Kant himself. For a summary of the possibilities of Kantian influence, see Henry A. Pochmann, *German Culture in America: 1600–1900* (Madison: Univ. of Wisconsin Press, 1957), pp. 436–40, and also Paul Brodtkorb, Jr., *Ishmael's White World: A Phenomenological Reading of Moby-Dick* (New Haven and London: Yale Univ. Press, 1965), pp. 11–12, 153.

7. For an antipodal interpretation which stresses the *in*substantiality rather than the substantiality of *Moby-Dick*, see "Ishmael as Teller" in Edgar A. Dryden, *Melville's Thematics of Form: The Great Art of Telling the Truth* (Baltimore: Johns Hopkins Press, 1968), pp. 83–113.

270   *The Salt-Sea Mastodon*

For Mr. Dryden, the world of *Moby-Dick* is "obviously literary" and Ishmael's identity "purely verbal"; it follows that Ishmael's "primary concern" is not whales or his own hypos, but rather "the act of writing"; in this attenuated world, Ishmael "retreat[s] from the realm of objects to a verbal realm," removing "himself from both nature and society" to "a fanciful world of his own creation."

8. William Ellery Sedgwick appears to accept Ahab's analysis when he asserts that in perception "the object is indifferent, the subject is all that is needed because the subject always sees himself." Pip's summation is a statement, Sedgwick asserts, of the "solipsism of consciousness" (*Herman Melville: The Tragedy of Mind* [Cambridge: Harvard Univ. Press, 1945], pp. 111–12). This solipsism is rendered as a "gulf" by Merlin Bowen; Pip, he suggests, "seems to guess how impassable is the gulf between the mind and its object" (*The Long Encounter: Self and Experience in the Writings of Herman Melville* [Chicago: Univ. of Chicago Press, 1960], p. 122). R. W. Watters, too, sees the object of perception as essentially indifferent, a "blank existence upon which form or meaning is projected by the observer" so that for any object perceived there will be "innumerable meanings" ("The Meanings of the White Whale," *University of Toronto Quarterly*, 20 [1951], 163). Milton R. Stern, finally, by insisting on more than an indifferent blank "out there," by affirming Melville's belief in an "independent actuality," "the matter of experience," meliorates the solipsism of earlier readings, but he nonetheless sees a "steady relativism" implicit in the "multiple view" technique of the "Doubloon" chapter ("Some Techniques of Melville's Perception," *PMLA*, 73 [1958], 255–56). It is true that the seven perceivers of the doubloon derive seven different meanings, but if Stern is right about an independent actuality which is the matter of experience, one ought to be able to argue the possibility of a true, final, or ultimate meaning. Whether any of the seven perceivers reaches it would of course be another question.

9. *The Mirror and the Lamp*, p. 31.

CHAPTER II

1. *American Renaissance* (New York: Oxford Univ. Press, 1941), p. xiv. Walker Cowen points out that "The problem of whether perception and the sources of the imagination lay in the external object or in the mind was made more difficult in America where writers were determined to be original and to draw upon the materials of their native

environment." Melville participated in this exploration: "His library of art books and his notes reveal that he was eager to learn how plastic artists could, for example, impart a sense of movement to still forms with the play of color or light and darkness." See *Melville's Marginalia* (1965), in Hershel Parker, ed., *The Recognition of Herman Melville* (Ann Arbor: Univ. of Michigan Press, 1967), p. 343. For a general survey of sight-as-perception metaphors, see R. Dilworth Rust, "Vision in *Moby-Dick*," *Emerson Society Quarterly*, No. 33 (1963), pp. 73–75.

2. *The Letters of Herman Melville*, ed. Merrell R. Davis and William H. Gilman (New Haven: Yale Univ. Press, 1960), p. 146.

3. Hendricks House *The Confidence-Man: His Masquerade*, ed. Elizabeth S. Foster, p. 271.

4. Hendricks House *Collected Poems of Herman Melville*, ed. Howard P. Vincent, p. 6.

5. Northwestern-Newberry *Pierre: Or, the Ambiguities*, p. 165.

6. Northwestern-Newberry *Mardi: And a Voyage Thither*, p. 249.

7. Constable-Russell *Works*, XIII, 144–50, 167. I think it possible to accept my "straight" reading of the epistemological implications of Melville's short story, and yet at the same time acknowledge with qualifications the thesis of Egbert S. Oliver in " 'Cock-A-Doodle-Doo!' and Transcendental Hocus Pocus," *New England Quarterly*, 21 (1948), 204–16, that the story is a satirical attack on that optimistic extreme of transcendentalism which suggests that one can make his own world. Conceivably Melville could eclectically absorb a Kantian epistemology without also accepting the radical transcendentalism which is one possible consequence of that epistemology. In any case, a valuable corrective to overwrought interpretation is Hershel Parker, "Melville's Satire of Emerson and Thoreau: An Evaluation of the Evidence," *American Transcendental Quarterly*, No. 7, Part 2 (Summer, 1970), pp. 61–66.

8. *The Mirror and the Lamp* (New York: Oxford Univ. Press, 1953; Norton, 1958), pp. vi, 54, 58, 66–67, 52. In both Wordsworth and Coleridge, Abrams points out, the mind is frequently pictured "as active rather than inertly receptive, and as contributing to the world in the very process of perceiving the world" (p. 58). Coleridge manifests a constant concern with "how the poetic mind acts to modify or transform the materials of sense" (p. 55), a concern which Wordsworth reflects in his 1816 assertion that "Throughout, objects . . . derive their influence not from what they are actually in themselves, but from such

as are bestowed upon them by the minds of those who are conversant with or affected by those objects" (p. 54). In *The Prelude* Wordsworth asserts that "A plastic power Abode with me, a forming hand," which he also describes as "An auxiliar light / Came from my mind which on the setting sun / Bestow'd new splendor." Coleridge, after reading *The Prelude*, himself spoke of Wordsworth as a projector: "When power streamed from thee." Abrams also cites Christopher North asserting that "we create nine-tenths at least of what appears to exist externally," so that those who ponder "the living Book of Nature ... behold in full the beauty and the sublimity, which their own immortal spirits create." A final example is Abrams' citation of David Hume describing the way the faculty of "taste" functions, "gilding or staining all natural objects with the colours, borrowed from internal sentiment, [raising], in a manner, a new creation" (pp. 60–64). It is interesting to note that Mr. Abrams begins his third chapter, "Romantic Analogues of Art and Mind," with a headnote taken from *Moby-Dick*, the passage on the Kantian and Lockean whale-heads (p. 47).

9. *Herman Melville* (New York: William Sloane, 1950; Norton, 1957), p. 188.

10. "The Two Temples," in Constable-Russell *Works*, XIII, 173–76. For variant discussions see Richard H. Fogle, *Melville's Shorter Tales* (Norman: Univ. of Oklahoma Press, 1960), pp. 38, 85; also James Baird, *Ishmael* (Baltimore: Johns Hopkins Press, 1956), p. 94.

CHAPTER III

1. Jay Leyda, *The Melville Log: A Documentary Life of Herman Melville* (New York: Harcourt, 1951), I, 291, 287; II, 649; Howard C. Horsford, "The Design of the Argument in *Moby-Dick*," *Modern Fiction Studies*, 8 (1962), 237–38; William Braswell, "Melville as a Critic of Emerson," *American Literature*, 9 (1937), 319, 331; also see the Hendricks House edition of *Moby-Dick* (New York, 1952), ed. Luther S. Mansfield and Howard P. Vincent, pp. 798–99.

2. *The Spirit Above the Dust: A Study of Herman Melville* (London: John Lehmann, 1951), p. 133. The problem of whether *whiteness* in *Moby-Dick* means something or nothing is hardly minor. Assertions such as that of Paul Brodtkorb, Jr., that "the emotion that constitutes white makes vibrantly visible as a presence the nothingness with which all existence is secretly sickened" (*Ishmael's White World: A Phenomenological Reading of Moby-Dick* [New Haven: Yale Univ. Press,

1965], p. 119), have the effect of cutting the entire novel loose from any controlling or normative reality outside of Ishmael's mental processes (and Mr. Brodtkorb finds even these "not wholly trustworthy" [p. 125]), making an essentially solipsistic, raptly tentative reading inevitable. Under such a critical rubric *Moby-Dick* becomes little more than a random series of obscurely sourced Ishmaelian "moods" (pp. 13–17). (For a suggestive discussion of the mythological and psychological ramifications of whiteness, see Chapter VIII of James Baird, *Ishmael* [Baltimore: Johns Hopkins Press, 1956], pp. 256–77).

3. Hendricks House *Collected Poems of Herman Melville*, ed. Howard P. Vincent, pp. 203–04.

4. Northwestern-Newberry *Pierre: Or, the Ambiguities*, p. 295.

5. *Herman Melville* (New York: Harcourt, 1929), p. 246.

6. Hendricks House *Clarel: A Poem and Pilgrimage in the Holy Land*, ed. Walter E. Bezanson, pp. 62, 70.

7. Leyda, *The Melville Log*, I, 410.

8. *Ibid.*, II, 623.

9. *The Letters of Herman Melville*, ed. Merrell R. Davis and William H. Gilman (New Haven: Yale Univ. Press, 1960), pp. 292–93.

10. Hendricks House *Collected Poems*, pp. 374–76.

11. Northwestern-Newberry *Mardi: And a Voyage Thither*, p. 437.

12. Northwestern-Newberry *Pierre*, p. 342.

13. Northwestern-Newberry *White-Jacket: or The World in a Man-of-War*, pp. 320–21.

14. Intro. to Riverside edition of *Moby-Dick* (Boston: Houghton, 1956), p. vii.

15. *The American Novel and Its Tradition* (New York: Doubleday, 1957), p. 108.

16. Ishmael's use of Narcissus here places the mirror *outside* the mind, as an analogue for reality. Compare to F. O. Matthiessen's treatment of "The Imagination as Mirror," *American Renaissance* (New York: Oxford Univ. Press, 1941), pp. 253–64.

17. *In Defense of Reason* (Denver: Alan Swallow, 1943), p. 200.

18. *The Machine in the Garden: Technology and the Pastoral Ideal in America* (New York: Oxford Univ. Press, 1964), pp. 277–319.

19. Hendricks House *Collected Poems*, p. 205.

20. *Journal of a Visit to Europe and the Levant, October 11, 1856 —May 6, 1857, by Herman Melville*, ed. Howard C. Horsford (New Haven: Princeton Univ. Press, 1955), p. 263.

21. Northwestern-Newberry *Omoo: A Narrative of Adventures in the South Seas*, pp. 114, 65.

22. Northwestern-Newberry *Mardi*, p. 492.

23. "Some Techniques of Melville's Perception," *PMLA*, 73 (1958), 256.

24. *Letters*, p. 79.

CHAPTER IV

1. See the notes to the Hendricks House edition of *Moby-Dick*, ed. Luther S. Mansfield and Howard P. Vincent (New York, 1952), p. 689.

2. *Melville's Quarrel With God* (Princeton: Princeton Univ. Press, 1952), pp. 10–11. Even if Melville quarreled with God, there is very little evidence to suggest that *Ishmael* ever did. After Father Mapple's sermon, the Christian Jehovah never again figures in any significant way in Ishmael's on-going consciousness except for some suspiciously conventional and possibly satiric references to the Deity such as the panegyric to the "Spirit of Equality," the "great democratic god," which concludes Chapter 26 (*105*). Once at sea, the *Pequod* sails deeper and deeper into a metanaturalistic cosmos where the conventional God simply does not exist—a fact which would account for Ishmael's failure to quarrel with Him. Ahab, of course, is another matter.

3. Nathalia Wright points out that Melville's treatment of the Jonah story is highly selective: "There is nothing in [Father Mapple's] sermon about Jehovah's compassion for the repentent city, his pardon, and his gentle remonstrance with his harsh prophet" (*Melville's Use of the Bible* [New York: Octagon, 1969], p. 83). This selectivity is apparently the consequence of an "outraged conclusion" which Howard C. Horsford sees Melville, Ahab, and Ishmael all making: "The creation, we have the highest assurance, manifests the Creator; but his creation

is notorious for its suffering, its indifferent injustice, its ruthless energy and merciless, predatory nature; therefore, such must be its Creator" ("The Design of the Argument in *Moby-Dick*," *Modern Fiction Studies* [Autumn, 1962], p. 240). I do not think such "outrage" accurately describes Ishmael, for whom the Christian God simply ceases to exist, but it is nevertheless evident in those crew-members who *do* retain to the end at least a residually Christian world-view. Stubb tells open-mouthed Flask how the Devil once sauntered into the "old flagship" and demanded a hapless mortal upon whom he had cast his evil eye. "I want John," says the Devil. "Take him," says the "old governor." Thus casually does the Christian God turn over us mortals to the powers of evil. Stubb hints that the Devil has such freedom because the "old governor" actually fears him. "Who's afraid of him, except the old governor who daresn't catch him and put him in double-darbies, as he deserves, but lets him go about kidnapping people; aye, and signed a bond with him, that all the people the devil kidnapped, he'd roast for him?" And then, with vast irony: "There's a governor!" (73: 276–77).

4. See T. Walter Herbert, Jr., "Calvinism and Cosmic Evil in *Moby-Dick*," *PMLA*, 84 (1969), 1613–19: "Since man's nature is contaminated by original sin, and since God is absolutely righteous, a man must reject his own nature totally before he can be reconciled to God" (p. 1614). The Calvinistic ideas which Mr. Herbert persuasively applies to Father Mapple's sermon are less persuasively applied to the White Whale. If Moby Dick is taken Calvinistically, then all the naturalistic meanings which attach to him go by the board.

5. *Melville's Early Life and Redburn* (New York: New York Univ. Press, 1951), p. 235.

6. Northwestern-Newberry *Redburn: His First Voyage*, p. 293.

7. *Herman Melville* (New York: Twayne, 1963), p. 55.

8. For a full discussion of the various sources from which Melville may have derived his knowledge of the Pequod Indians' tragic history, see the Hendricks House edition of *Moby-Dick*, ed. Luther S. Mansfield and Howard P. Vincent (New York, 1952), pp. 631–33, and also Kenneth W. Cameron's "Etymological Significance of Melville's *Pequod*," *Emerson Society Quarterly*, No. 29 (1962), pp. 3–4. Mansfield and Vincent, in attempting to relate the Pequod War to the Book of Job miss, it seems to me, the essential meaning of the ship's name for all of *Moby-Dick*.

9. Northwestern-Newberry *Typee: A Peep at Polynesian Life*, pp. 177–79. There also is some evidence that Melville intended Yojo to carry phallic overtones. In Chapter 95, ironically entitled "The Cassock," Ishmael describes what he delicately calls the "grandissimus" of the male Sperm Whale, "that unaccountable cone,—longer than a Kentuckian is tall, nigh a foot in diameter at the base, and jet-black as Yojo, the ebony idol of Queequeg." The "pelt" is removed from this prodigy, stretched and shaped, and donned like a cassock by the mincer as he slices the "horse-pieces" of blubber into "bible leaves" for the try-pots (95: *351*). The phallicism, if it is there, would be in consonance with Yojo's meaning as a naturalistic life-relation, as fertile as the transcendental Jehovah-relation is sterile.

CHAPTER V

1. *Herman Melville* (New York: Twayne, 1963), p. 96; *Melville and the Comic Spirit* (Cambridge: Harvard Univ. Press, 1955), p. 97.

2. Northwestern-Newberry *Pierre: Or, the Ambiguities*, p. 205.

3. Northwestern-Newberry *Typee: A Peep at Polynesian Life*, p. 155.

4. Northwestern-Newberry *Mardi: And a Voyage Thither*, pp. 497, 228.

5. Constable-Russell *Works*, XIII, 276–311; esp. pp. 281, 306, 283, 295, and 287.

6. *Journal of a Visit to Europe and the Levant, October 11, 1856– May 6, 1857, by Herman Melville*, ed. Howard C. Horsford (New Haven: Princeton Univ. Press, 1955), pp. 33, 273–76; 117–19; 123. See Melville's poem, "The Great Pyramid," for a generalized statement of the symbolism of this figure, in Hendricks House *Collected Poems of Herman Melville*, ed. Howard P. Vincent, pp. 254–55. For a detailed discussion of pyramid symbolism in Melville, with a different emphasis than I have used here, see Dorothee M. Finkelstein, *Melville's Orienda* (New Haven: Yale Univ. Press, 1961), esp. pp. 130–44.

7. The pyramid-figure also carries a clear psychological meaning. Walter E. Bezanson points out that "The pyramids for Melville were a primal image of the unknown self—immense, mysterious, penetrable only here and there by dark shafts" (Intro. to Hendricks House *Clarel: A Poem and Pilgrimage in the Holy Land*, p. xvii). Melville himself

makes the point best in *Pierre*: "Appalling is the soul of a man! Better might one be pushed off into the material spaces beyond the uttermost orbit of our sun, than once feel himself fairly afloat in himself! ...By vast pains we mine into the pyramid; by horrible gropings we come to the central room; with joy we espy the sarcophagus; but we lift the lid— and no body is there!—appallingly vacant as vast is the soul of a man!" (pp. 284–85).

CHAPTER VI

1. *Herman Melville* (New York: William Sloane, 1950; Norton, 1957), pp. 176–77. For an analysis of Ahab as cheap Gothic see Martin Green, *Re-appraisals: Some Commonsense Readings of American Literature* (London: Hugh Evelyn, 1963), pp. 87–112. The best discussion of Ahab's mechanism is Leo Marx, *The Machine in the Garden: Technology and the Pastoral Ideal in America* (New York: Oxford Univ. Press, 1964), pp. 297–300.

2. *The Letters of Herman Melville*, ed. Merrell R. Davis and William H. Gilman (New Haven: Yale Univ. Press, 1960), p. 79.

3. Cf. Henry Murray's remark that "*this* god-defier is no Prometheus, since all thought of benefitting humanity is foreign to him," in *Moby-Dick Centennial Essays*, ed. Tyrus Hillway and Luther S. Mansfield (Dallas: Southern Methodist Univ. Press, 1953), p. 18.

4. Matthew 13, *14*; Mark 4, *12*; Luke 8, *10*; John 12, *40*; Acts 28, *26*; and Romans 11, *8*.

5. Since, perversely, I find Ahab compelling in spite of everything I have said here, I am especially grateful for Alan Lebowitz's humane and judiciously sympathetic analysis of the *Pequod's* Captain which, on alternate days, I find as persuasive as my own. See *Progress Into Silence: A Study of Melville's Heroes* (Bloomington: Indiana Univ. Press, 1970), pp. 3–19, 137, 144–45.

CHAPTER VII

1. *The Letters of Herman Melville*, ed. Merrell R. Davis and William H. Gilman (New Haven: Yale Univ. Press, 1960), p. 96.

2. *Man's Changing Mask: Modes and Methods of Characterization in Fiction* (Minneapolis: Univ. of Minnesota Press, 1966), p. 108. The ambiguity and shrouding of Ishmael's language has provided fertile

ground for misunderstanding concerning the status of truth in *Moby-Dick*. Joseph Conrad dismissed the novel with the assertion that it had "not a single sincere line in the 3 vols of it" (January 1907 letter to Humphery Milford, in *Moby-Dick as Doubloon: Essays and Extracts 1851–1970*, ed. Hershel Parker and Harrison Hayford [New York: Norton, 1970], pp. 122–23). This alleged "insincerity" of the Ishmaelian idiom is institutionalized as an aesthetic of negative artifice by James Guetti in *The Limits of Metaphor: A Study of Melville, Conrad, and Faulkner* (Ithaca: Cornell Univ. Press, 1967). For Mr. Guetti, Ishmael's "special languages"—taxonomic, historical, eulogistic, epic, legal, naturalistic, bibliographical, geologic, cosmologic, phallic, etc., are all "essentially artificial ways of talking about whales." As a consequence, "the special vocabularies of *Moby-Dick* communicate in a primarily negative manner," and Ishmael becomes a narrator "whose language functions to display its insufficiency," and who moves through the novel "destroy[ing] as he must the value of verbal forms as perceptions of reality" (pp. 15–16, 41, 28).

3. Melville used the idea of the voyage-as-death as early as *Omoo*, in the anecdote of the sailor named Ropey who, when his wife deserted him, "meditated suicide—an intention carried out; for the next day he shipped as landsman aboard the Julia, South Seaman" (Northwestern-Newberry *Omoo: A Narrative of Adventures in the South Seas*, p. 54).

4. *Letters*, p. 132.

5. Northwestern-Newberry *Redburn: His First Voyage*, p. 62.

6. *The Trying-Out of Moby-Dick* (Boston: Houghton, 1949), p. 105; "The Image of Society in *Moby-Dick*," in *Moby-Dick Centennial Essays*, ed. Tyrus Hillway and Luther S. Mansfield (Dallas: Southern Methodist Univ. Press, 1953), p. 74.

7. "Hawthorne and His Mosses," in Constable-Russell *Works*, XIII, 136.

8. *Billy Budd, Sailor*, ed. Harrison Hayford and Merton M. Sealts, Jr. (Chicago: Univ. of Chicago Press, 1962), p. 186.

9. Northwestern-Newberry *Redburn*, p. 252.

10. Hendricks House *Clarel: A Poem and Pilgrimage in the Holy Land*, ed. Walter E. Bezanson, p. 104.

11. *Journal of a Visit to London and the Continent by Herman Mel-*

ville, ed. Eleanor Melville Metcalf (Cambridge: Harvard Univ. Press, 1948), p. 5.

12. Jay Leyda, *The Melville Log: A Documentary Life of Herman Melville: 1819–1891* (New York: Harcourt, 1951), II, 651.

13. Northwestern-Newberry *Mardi: And a Voyage Thither*, p. 237.

14. "The Happy Failure," in Constable-Russell *Works*, XIII, 210–19.

15. Northwestern-Newberry *Pierre: Or, the Ambiguities*, pp. 284–85.

16. *Ibid.*, p. 139.

17. *Letters*, p. 125.

18. Northwestern-Newberry *Pierre*, p. 204. While it does not deal with the vortex, the empty coffin, the hollow pyramid, the shark's maw, or other specific articulations of the void in *Moby-Dick*, Robert Martin Adams' is a finely nuanced and witty discussion of Ishmael's (and Melville's) handling of nullity. See *Nil: Episodes in the Literary Conquest of the Void During the Nineteenth Century* (New York: Oxford Univ. Press, 1966), pp. 141–48.

19. Northwestern-Newberry *Mardi*, p. 441.

20. *Ibid.*, pp. 288–89.

21. *Letters*, p. 241.

CHAPTER VIII

1. For a Biblical approach to the "two-whale" problem in *Moby-Dick*, see Nathalia Wright, "Moby Dick: Jonah's or Job's Whale?" *American Literature*, 37 (1965), 190–95; reprinted in Nathalia Wright, *Melville's Use of the Bible* (New York: Octagon, 1969), pp. 189–94.

2. Intro. to Riverside edition of *Moby-Dick* (Boston: Houghton, 1956), p. xiii.

3. Northwestern-Newberry *Mardi: And a Voyage Thither*, p. 597. Richard Chase, in *The American Novel and Its Tradition* (New York: Doubleday, 1957), has pointed out (p. 91) that the major truth which Melville finally derived from his life's experience was that "Man lives in an insoluably dualistic world." Various students have noted the way in which this ultimate conclusion is reflected in Melville's cetology. Newton Arvin and Donald Weeks have called attention to the "dual

nature" of Melville's whale, and the "multivalence" of the whale as symbol (Arvin, *Herman Melville* [New York: Sloane, 1950; Norton, 1957], p. 191; Weeks, "The Two Uses of *Moby-Dick*," *American Quarterly*, 2 [1950], 157). Finally, Millicent Bell, in "Pierre Bayle and *Moby-Dick*," *PMLA*, 66 (1951), 641–48, has correlated Melville's thought, as well as Ishmael's narrative handling of the whale, with the persistently dualistic tendencies in the speculations of Pierre Bayle. (Miss Bell resists more successfully than I the temptation to categorize the Leviathan of *Moby-Dick* as Bayle's *Whale*.)

CHAPTER IX

1. In Edmund Wilson, *The Shock of Recognition* (Garden City, N. Y.: Doubleday, 1943), p. 1044.

2. Northwestern-Newberry *Mardi: And a Voyage Thither*, p. 376.

3. Intro. to Riverside edition of *Moby-Dick* (Boston: Houghton, 1956), p. vi; *The Example of Melville* (Princeton: Princeton Univ. Press, 1962), p. 104.

4. Northwestern-Newberry *White-Jacket: or The World in a Man-of-War*, p. 208. John Seelye was perhaps the first to suggest the presence of counter-epic elements in *Moby-Dick*. See *Melville: The Ironic Diagram* (Evanston, Ill.: Northwestern Univ. Press, 1970), p. 64.

5. There is a certain irony in the fact that a very early reviewer of *Moby-Dick* detected and stressed the humanizing of the whale to a greater degree than any critic since. *Moby-Dick*, asserted this anonymous reviewer, "is all whale. Leviathan is here in full amplitude. Not one of your museum affairs, but the real, living whale, a bona-fide, warm-blooded creature, ransacking the waters from pole to pole. His enormous bulk, his terribly destructive energies, his habits, his food, are all before us. Nay, even his lighter moods are exhibited. We are permitted to see the whale as a lover, a husband, and the head of a family. So to speak, we are made guests at his fire-side; we set our mental legs beneath his mahogany, and become members of his interesting social circle." From the New York *Spirit of the Times*, 6 December 1851; reprinted in *Moby-Dick as Doubloon: Essays and Extracts (1851–1970)*, ed. Hershel Parker and Harrison Hayford (New York: Norton, 1970), p. 63.

6. A ton is a good guess. "An average sperm whale calf," asserts Victor B. Scheffer, "at birth is fourteen feet long and weighs a ton; a mother

whale is thirty-eight feet long and weighs sixteen tons." Scheffer's data also confirm Ishmael's impression of the precocious friskiness of these youngsters. "The Little Calf on the Tropic of Cancer is far more advanced in body development than any newborn human child. He is wide-eyed, alert, and fully able to swim. Every whale of every kind is in fact precocious at birth; it has to be, for within brief moments it finds itself awash in a grown-up world—no nest, no den, no shelter except the dark shadow of the mother floating beside it." See *The Year of the Whale* (New York: Scribner's, 1969), p. 13.

7. Sixteen months of gestation, not nine, is apparently correct. "The four-year cycles of reproduction seem to be most common. A female [sperm whale] in the Northern Hemisphere conceives in May of year I, gives birth in September of year II after a gestation period of sixteen months, nurses her calf for two years, or until September of year IV, rests for eight months, and is reimpregnated in May of year V. Some females, though, are apparently on a two-year cycle and they are reimpregnated in May of year III while they are still nursing. The months mentioned are the peak or popular months for breeding activity, but the breeding time is not sharply defined; the pairing season may in fact extend for eight months and the birth season a corresponding length of time." Despite Ishmael's suggestion, whale's milk might be a trifle heavy for strawberries: "[The calf] follows his mother like a shadow and grows rapidly on his diet of thick milk, over one-third of it pure fat. (The blue dairy milk delivered to my doorstep each morning contains only four percent fat.) ... He will grow steadily throughout the long suckling period, gaining an average of seven pounds a day." See *The Year of the Whale*, pp. 7, 17.

8. Victor B. Scheffer makes the same point. "Though whales are the strangest of all mammals—the farthest out from the mainstream of mammal life—the most highly modified—they have no structures fundamentally *new* but only familiar ones reworked. They have the same familiar parts as dogs and cats and cows and other mammals of the land." See *The Year of the Whale*, p. 61.

9. My reading of the specifically cetological material should be supplemented by J. A. Ward's. He suggests that Melville uses cetology in an attempt to "balance the extraordinary with the ordinary" through an "intense literalness" which not only gives *Moby-Dick* a "steady foundation," but also provides a perdurable physical basis for Ishmael's metaphysical flights. See "The Function of the Cetological Chapters in *Moby-Dick*," *American Literature*, 28 (1956), 164–83. Equally useful

is Edward Rosenberry's analysis of a "comic leitmotif" in *Moby-Dick* arising from a "basic whale-man metaphor"; the consequence is a handling of the cetological data which is "primarily humorous and richly figurative." See *Melville and the Comic Spirit* (Cambridge: Harvard Univ. Press, 1955), pp. 107–08.

10. Hendricks House *Clarel: A Poem and Pilgrimage in the Holy Land*, ed. Walter E. Bezanson, p. 176; italics mine.

CHAPTER X

1. *A Reading of Moby-Dick* (Chicago: U. of Chicago Press, 1950), p. 18.

2. The complexities of the corpusant scene, and Ahab's address to the fire, have received considerable attention. Useful for background is C. C. Walcutt's "The Fire-Symbolism in *Moby-Dick*," *Modern Language Notes*, 59 (1944), 304–10, as well as Paul W. Miller's "Sun and Fire in Melville's *Moby-Dick*," *Nineteenth-Century Fiction*, 8 (1958), 139–44. Thomas Vargish's "Gnostic Mythos in *Moby-Dick*," *PMLA*, 81 (1966), 272–77, is a tightly reasoned discussion of Melville's (and Ishmael's) possible knowledge of the doctrine that the God of Matter, the Demiurge or Creator, was the inferior of a Supreme Being who ruled the spiritual worlds. Ahab's query concerning his "sweet mother" is seen by Vargish as a reference to "the Gnostic myth of the fallen mother [Sophia]—she who fell from overweening love of the Supreme Being." Finally, William Braswell, in *Melville's Religious Thought* (Durham: Duke Univ. Press, 1943), suggests that Melville became familiar with the Paulicians, the Manichees, and the Gnostics through cross reference reading in Bayle. "Here Melville may have become acquainted with the Gnostic theory that the Creator of the Universe is an inferior Deity." This, Braswell argues, could be the source of Ahab's defiance. "In primitive Christian times the Gnostics urged rebellion against the Creator of the Universe. They taught that He is an emanation from a higher power, that He is ignorant of His genealogy, and that He tyrannically governs the world in the belief that He is the Supreme God" (pp. 52, 62). In any case, whatever the sources of the "Candles" chapter, Melville was capable of conceiving of a God both less than ultimate and less than omnicompetent. "We incline to think that God cannot explain His own secrets," he remarked in an 1851 letter to Hawthorne, "and that He would like a little information upon certain points

Himself." See *The Letters of Herman Melville*, ed. Merrell R. Davis and William H. Gilman (New Haven: Yale Univ. Press, 1960), p. 125.

3. A valuable counterpoint to my discussion of Ahab's entropism and Ishmael's cyclicism is John Seelye's "diagrammatic" analysis, in which the *line* is associated with Ahab because of the linear and absolutist structure of his unifocal quest, while the *circle* is associated with Ishmael because of the relativistic, reiterative, and polyfocal nature of the Ishmaelian sensibility. See *Melville: The Ironic Diagram* (Evanston: Northwestern Univ. Press, 1970), pp. 6–7 and Ch. V, "*Moby-Dick*: Line and Circle," pp. 60–73.

4. Descartes, starting from the theories of Copernicus and Galileo, developed the idea that all motion was circular, and that the cosmic material tended to form vortices—a pre-Newtonian attempt to account for the spherical shape of all major celestial bodies, their rotational motion, and their circular orbits. James Baird suggests that in Melville the vortex represents "descent into water, the emblematic essence of God," an interpretation which does not quite meet the implications of the void at the center of all vortexical activity. See *Ishmael* (Baltimore: Johns Hopkins Univ. Press, 1956), pp. 266–73. For a suggestive discussion of the vortex in Hindu thought, see H. B. Kulkarni, *Moby-Dick: A Hindu Avatar* (Logan, Utah: Utah State Univ. Press, 1970), esp. pp. 48–49.

5. Northwestern-Newberry *Pierre: Or, the Ambiguities*, p. 267.

6. Ishmael's meditation on the Loom of Time is interrupted by Tashtego's cry of "There she blows!" Leaping to his feet, Ishmael tells us, "the ball of free will dropped from my hand" (47: *186*). I cannot attach any definitive significance to this incident. To suggest that Ishmael here loses volitional control is to vitiate the meaning of the immediately preceding fifty lines in favor of this single line. The whole thrust of "The Mat-Maker" suggests that one may, in the literal world, drop the ball of yarn which has *symbolized* free will, but one can hardly "drop" free will itself, or be accidentally deprived of it (Ahab's loss of free will is, of course, intentional). The existence of free will, under the mat-maker paradigm, would in fact seem to be as necessary as necessity itself.

7. For an antipodal interpretation of the theism-atheism question in *Moby-Dick*—as well as a logically terminal specimen of the sibylline-incantatory school of Melville criticism—see Martin Leonard Pops,

The Melville Archetype (Kent, Ohio: Kent State Univ. Press, 1970). This Jungian-Freudian reading proposes a pervasively religious novel in which Ishmael "intuits the divine presence" (p. x), variously designated as "Sacred Reality," "Absolute Reality," and the "Beyond." Mr. Pops, I think, correctly perceives Ishmael's transcendental tendencies, but not their concomitant metanaturalistic truncation. Consequently he is prevented from seeing that Ishmael's redemption and survival depend precisely on his gradual realization that there is no "divine presence," much less a "Beyond" for It to inhabit. Since, in the world of *Moby-Dick*, any transcendentally conceived "divine presence" is bound to turn out to be a shark-proliferating "dam Ingin," the steady erosion of belief in Ishmael represents a genuine liberation and escape from horror.

8. Northwestern-Newberry *Pierre*, p. 9. The image of the whale skeleton overgrown with vines occurs also in *Mardi*, when the narrator, trying to win the confidence of Yillah, asks her to recall the time "when we ran up and down in our arbor, where the green vines grew over the great ribs of the stranded whale." See Northwestern-Newberry *Mardi: And a Voyage Thither*, p. 143. For a technological reading of "A Bower in the Arsacides," see Leo Marx, *The Machine in the Garden: Technology and the Pastoral Ideal in America* (New York: Oxford Univ. Press, 1964), pp. 295, 310–12. Daniel G. Hoffman's more general reading is in *"Moby-Dick*: Jonah's Whale or Job's?" *Sewanee Review*, 69 (1961), 221–22.

9. Melville's sense of the Pacific as the primordial sea, to which the Atlantic and Indian oceans are subsidiary, is astonishingly prescient. Current geological theory postulates the existence of two primal landmasses, Laurasia above the equator and Gondwanaland below, the rest of the surface of the earth being but a vastly expanded Pacific Ocean. See J. Tuzo Wilson, "Continental Drift," *Scientific American*, 208 (1963), 86–100; and Patrick M. Hurley, "The Confirmation of Continental Drift," *ibid.*, 218 (1968), 53–64. Speculation on continental drift began at least as early as Francis Bacon (1620), and a study based on fossil evidence, Antonio Snider's *La Création et ses Mystères Dévoilés*, was published just seven years after *Moby-Dick* (1858).

10. Hendricks House *Collected Poems of Herman Melville*, ed. Howard P. Vincent, pp. 394–97. Lewis Mumford, in *Herman Melville* (New York: Harcourt, 1929), was the first to point out the importance of the reconciliation with cosmic dynamism which "Pontoosuce" represents,

although he did not attempt to develop the underlying cyclicism of Melville's conception (pp. 244–45).

11. Hendricks House *Clarel: A Poem and Pilgrimage in the Holy Land*, ed. Walter E. Bezanson, pp. 333, 156–57. For a useful explication of the ideas of "Pontoosuce" in other poems, see Chapter VIII, "Cyclical Time," in William Bysshe Stein, *The Poetry of Melville's Late Years* (Albany: SUNY Press, 1970). "All of [Melville's] symbols of flowers, birds, animals, and insects," Mr. Stein points out, "mirror the inseparable marriage of life and death in the universe, and all of them unite to urge belief in the myth of the eternal return—time ceaselessly renewing itself" (p. 178).

12. Northwestern-Newberry *Mardi*, pp. 9–10.

13. *Ibid.*, p. 210.

14. Ishmael's images of weaving, of death, and of the green of life appear in an especially condensed form in *Clarel*: "And where the vine / And olive in the darkling hours / Inweave green sepulchers of bowers . . ." (Hendricks House *Clarel*, p. 96).

CHAPTER XI

1. *The American Adam: Innocence, Tragedy and Tradition in the Nineteenth Century* (Chicago: Univ. of Chicago Press, 1955), p. 146.

2. *The Example of Melville* (Princeton: Princeton Univ. Press, 1962), pp. 106, 178.

3. The ontological equivalence of sharks and angels is suggested in *Mardi* where, after describing Jarl's obsessive hatred of sharks, the narrator remarks: "Yet this is all wrong. As well hate a seraph, as a shark. Both were made by the same hand." See Northwestern-Newberry *Mardi: And a Voyage Thither*, p. 40.

4. For an examination of the historical and transcultural implications of Queequeg's pipe, see Hennig Cohen, "Melville's Tomahawk Pipe: Artifact and Symbol," *Studies in the Novel*, 1 (1969), 397–400.

5. For an explication of the coffin symbolism, see Louis Leiter's "Queequeg's Coffin," *Nineteenth-Century Fiction*, 13 (1958), 249–54. For Queequeg to be taken as a Christ-figure was only a question of the fullness of time. See Carl F. Strauch, "Ishmael: Time and Personality in *Moby-Dick*," *Studies in the Novel*, 1 (1969), 480. But surely Queequeg's

immense power as a redemptive figure—certainly for Ishmael and probably for the reader—resides precisely in the fact that he exhibits *no* Christian or Christomorphic characteristics.

CHAPTER XII

1. Northwestern-Newberry *Pierre: Or, the Ambiguities*, p. 135.

2. Indeed, a phrenological analysis suggests that Moby Dick, far from being a monster, is a perfect *love* of a whale whose dominant quality is the "Animal Propensity" termed "Amativeness." See Harold Aspiz, "Phrenologizing the Whale," *Nineteenth-Century Fiction*, 23 (1968), 25.

3. Unless, of course, one's critical posture is based on the assumption that everything *must* be other than it appears. For Bruce H. Franklin, the epiphany of Moby Dick is "a revelation of horror, the revelation of fearfully potent malice masked by graceful beauty." The White Whale evinces, according to Franklin, "as much as a mute animal can, the intelligent malignity ascribed to him.... His malice and intelligence become unquestionable." See *The Wake of the Gods: Melville's Mythology* (Stanford: Stanford Univ. Press, 1963), pp. 64–65.

4. See the Hendricks House edition of *Moby-Dick*, ed. Luther S. Mansfield and Howard P. Vincent (New York, 1952), pp. 691–95. The original Reynolds article was published in the *Knickerbocker Magazine*, 13 (May 1839), 377–93, but Mansfield and Vincent think it more likely that Melville may have seen a brief discussion of Mocha Dick carried in the "Editor's Table" of the same magazine, July, 1846. A third possibility is about 100 words on Mocha Dick in the March, 1849, issue; see Cecil D. Eby, Jr., "Another Breaching of 'Mocha Dick'," *English Language Notes*, 4 (1967), 277–79. Some idea of the rumors Melville may have heard while aboard the *Acushnet* can be gained from "The Career of Mocha Dick," an anonymous article in the Detroit *Free Press* of 3 April, 1892. On 5 July, 1840, for example, the English whaling brig *Desmond* lowered two boats in pursuit of Mocha Dick, whereupon the whale suddenly turned about, chewed one boat to pieces, and taking the other in his mouth, lifted it thirty feet out of the water. Seventeen months later Mocha Dick breached again on the east coast of Japan near a coasting vessel. "It was passed over as a trifling incident, but ten or fifteen minutes later the leviathan was discovered rushing [for no apparent reason] down in the wake of the craft with all the steam he

could put on. . . . He struck the craft in her stern and wrecked her in an instant." See Jay Leyda, ed., *The Melville Log* (New York: Harcourt, 1951), I, 106–07, 154–55.

5. New York: W. B. Gilley, 1821. Reprinted with an introduction by B. R. McElderry, Jr., as *Shipwreck of the Whaleship Essex* (New York: Corinth, 1963). This edition also contains the brief deposition of Captain George Pollard, as well as that of the second mate, Thomas Chapple. When Melville finally acquired his own copy of the *Narrative*, he added eighteen pages of commentary at the back of the volume. These addenda are also included in the McElderry edition, but they are disappointing. Melville discusses the attack and its consequences, but says nothing at all about the manner of the assault, and refrains from speculating on either the possibility of intention in the whale or Chase's subjective conviction that the fish was in a vast and focused rage. For a summary of the historical complexities, see Henry F. Pommer, "Herman Melville and the Wake of the *Essex*," *American Literature*, 20 (1948), 290–304.

6. Victor B. Scheffer confirms that the rogue Sperm Whale is more than merely a product of Ahab's imagination. "He is always a large bull, a solitary, surly aggressive chap who cannot fit into any group." Ethological research also offers an explanation for his often unprovoked attacks on ships. "Probably the answer lies in his strong territorial instinct, basically sexual. The sperm-whale bull is the only large whale that attacks ships. He is also the only one known to guard a harem and to battle with rival bulls for possession of females. When the 'ship animal' invades his territory, it disrupts the dominance order; he rushes to the attack." See *The Year of the Whale* (New York: Scribner's, 1969), pp. 111–12. For a fascinating summary of such historically verified attacks, see J. David Truby, "The Turbulent Wars That Whales Have Fought Against Man," *Smithsonian*, 3 (May, 1972), 58–65. Nor is *Physeter catodon* contemplating a cessation of hostilities: on 20 October, 1970 the 200-ton Swedish ship *Vastanvind* was sunk by a "huge whale" off the Canary Islands. See the New York *Times* for 21 October, 1970.

7. *Herman Melville* (New York: Harcourt, 1929), p. 44; London *Literary Gazette and Journal of Science and Art*, 6 December, 1851, reprinted in *Moby-Dick as Doubloon: Essays and Extracts (1851–1970)*, ed. Hershel Parker and Harrison Hayford (New York: Norton, 1970), p. 60.

8. Boston: Houghton, 1949; New York: 1952.

9. Respectively, London, 1839; London, 1840; New York, 1846; New York, 1850; and Edinburgh, 1820.

10. See Harold H. Scudder, "Melville's *Benito Cereno* and Captain Delano's *Voyages*," *PMLA*, 43 (1928), 502–32. Egbert S. Oliver also reproduces relevant portions of Delano's *Voyages* in the Hendricks House edition of *The Piazza Tales* (New York: Farrar, 1948), pp. 230–34. The chapter from Hall which Melville used is entitled "Indian hating.—Some of the sources of this animosity.—Brief account of Col. Moredock," in *Sketches*, II, 74–82; Elizabeth S. Foster reproduces the pertinent material in the Hendricks House edition of *The Confidence-Man* (New York, 1954), pp. 334–38.

11. William Glasser, in "Moby Dick," *Sewanee Review*, 77 (1969), 483, has suggested that Moby Dick's leeward migration is related to the necessitarian imperatives developed in Chapter 47, "The Mat-Maker."

12. *Herman Melville* (New York: William Sloane, 1950; Norton, 1957), p. 187.